Lecture Notes of the Institute for Computer Sciences, Social Informatics and Telecommunications Engineering 426

More information about this series at https://link.springer.com/bookseries/8197

Ana Lúcia Martins · Joao C Ferreira ·
Alexander Kocian (Eds.)

Intelligent Transport Systems

5th EAI International Conference, INTSYS 2021
Virtual Event, November 24–26, 2021
Proceedings

 Springer

Editors
Ana Lúcia Martins ⓘ
Lisbon University Institute
Lisbon, Portugal

Joao C Ferreira ⓘ
Lisbon University Institute
Lisbon, Portugal

Alexander Kocian ⓘ
University of Pisa
Pisa, Italy

ISSN 1867-8211 ISSN 1867-822X (electronic)
Lecture Notes of the Institute for Computer Sciences, Social Informatics
and Telecommunications Engineering
ISBN 978-3-030-97602-6 ISBN 978-3-030-97603-3 (eBook)
https://doi.org/10.1007/978-3-030-97603-3

This Springer imprint is published by the registered company Springer Nature Switzerland AG
The registered company address is: Gewerbestrasse 11, 6330 Cham, Switzerland

Preface

We are delighted to introduce the proceedings of the fifth edition of the International Conference on Intelligent Transport Systems (INTSYS 2021) from the European Alliance for Innovation (EAI). This conference brought together researchers, developers, and practitioners from around the world who are leveraging and developing Intelligent Transportation Systems (ITS) to increase efficiency, safety, and mobility, and tackle Europe's growing emission and congestion problems.

INTSYS 2021 covered the following topics: disruptive technology for intelligent transportation systems; intelligent transportation systems in epidemic areas; data science for cooperative intelligent transportation systems; AI innovation in intelligent transportation systems; diversity in transportation systems for people and goods; public transit planning and operation in the era of automation, electrification, and personalization; edge intelligence for the Internet of Vehicles; blockchain and big data-enabled intelligent vehicular communication; and intent-based networking for 5G-envisioned Internet of Connected Vehicles. This edition received 31 submissions from which the technical program of INTSYS 2021 was developed, consisting of 15 full papers. All papers were subjected to a double-blind peer-review process with a minimum of three reviews per paper.

Concerning the committees, it was a great pleasure to work with the excellent organizing team of the EAI, which was essential for the success of the INTSYS 2021 conference. In particular, we would like to express our gratitude to Conference Manager Elena Davydova for all the support she provided in all areas. We would like also to express our gratitude to all the members of the Technical Program Committee, who helped in the peer-review process for the technical papers, and thus ensured a high-quality technical program. We would like to thank the extensive list of external reviewers from several areas of expertise and from numerous countries around the world. A special acknowledgement must be addressed to all the authors for their effort producing such good quality papers and also for the extremely rich and positive feedback shared at the conference.

We strongly believe that the INTSYS conference provides a good forum for all researchers, developers, and practitioners to discuss all science and technology aspects that are relevant to ITS. It is becoming a privileged space for knowledge sharing and networking. We also expect that the future INTSYS conferences will be as successful and stimulating as this year's, as indicated by the contributions presented in this volume.

December 2021

Ana Lúcia Martins
Joao C Ferreira
Alexander Kocian

Organization

Steering Committee

Imrich Chlamtac   University of Trento, Italy
Oscar Mayora   Fondazione Bruno Kessler, Italy
Venet Osmani   Fondazione Bruno Kessler, Italy

Organizing Committee

General Chairs

Joao C Ferreira   Iscte-Instituto Universitário de Lisboa, Portugal
Ana Lúcia Martins   Iscte-Instituto Universitário de Lisboa, Portugal

Technical Program Committee Chair

Alexander Kocian   University of Pisa, Italy

Sponsorship and Exhibit Chair

Helgheim Berit Irene   Molde University, Norway

Local Chair

Teresa Galvão   FEUP and INESCTEC, Portugal

Workshops Chair

Ulpan Tokkozhina   Iscte-Instituto Universitário de Lisboa, Portugal

Publicity and Social Media Chair

Maria C. Pereira   Iscte-Instituto Universitário de Lisboa, Portugal

Publications Chair

Vera Costa   FEUP, Portugal

Web Chair

Bruno Mataloto   Iscte-Instituto Universitário de Lisboa, Portugal

Posters and PhD Track Chair

Rosaldo Rosseti   FEUP, Portugal

Panels Chair

Luis Elvas   Inov and Iscte-Instituto Universitário de Lisboa,
                                   Portugal

Demos Chair

Frederica Gonçalves   University of Madeira and ITI/LARSyS, Portugal

Tutorials Chair

Ana Madureira   ISEP, Portugal

Technical Program Committee

Adreano Lino	Federal University of Western of Pará, Brazil
Ana Lucia Martins	Iscte-Instituto Universitário de Lisboa, Portugal
Ana Madureira	ISEP, Portugal
Atilla Altintas	Chalmers University of Technology, Sweden
Bruno Mataloto	Iscte-Instituto Universitário de Lisboa, Portugal
Carlos M. P. Sousa	Molde University College, Norway
Cheng Yin	Queen's University Belfast, UK
Dagmar Caganova	Slovak University of Technology in Bratislava, Slovakia
Diana Mendes	Iscte-Instituto Universitário de Lisboa, Portugal
Federico Costantini	Università degli Studi di Udine, Italy
Frederica Gonçalves	University of Madeira, Portugal
Gabriel Pestana	Inov, Portugal
Ghadir Pourhashem	Slovak University of Technology in Bratislava, Slovakia
Giuseppe Lugano	University of Žilina, Slovakia
Isabel Almeida	Iscte-Instituto Universitário de Lisboa, Portugal
Isabell Storsjö	Hanken School of Economics, Finland
Joao C Ferreira	Iscte-Instituto Universitário de Lisboa, Portugal
Lia Oliveira	Universidade de Aveiro and ESCE, Portugal
Lorna Uden	Staffordshire University, UK
Lubos Buzna	University of Žilina, Slovakia
Luis Elvas	Inov, Portugal
Marek Kvet	University of Žilina, Slovakia
Maria C. Pereira	Iscte-Instituto Universitário de Lisboa, Portugal
Michal Kohani	University of Žilina, Slovakia

Contents

Data Analytics

Mobility

The Day-Ahead Forecasting of the Passenger Occupancy in Public Transportation by Using Machine Learning

Atilla Altıntaş[1]([✉])(iD), Lars Davidson[1](iD), Giannis Kostaras[2], and Maycel Isaac[2]

[1] Division of Fluid Dynamics, Department of Mechanics and Maritime Sciences, Chalmers University of Technology, SE-412 96, Gothenburg, Sweden
altintas@chalmers.se
[2] Synteda AB, Skånegatan 29, 412 52 Göteborg, Sweden

Abstract. Public transport is one of the main infrastructures of a sustainable city. For this reason, there are many studies on public transportation which mostly answer the question of "when my next bus will arrive?". However now when the public is under the restrictions of the Covid-19 pandemic and learning to live with new social rules such as "social distance" a new yet crucial question arise on public transportation: "how crowded my next bus will be?" To prevent the crowdedness in public transportation the traffic regulators need to forecast the number of passengers the day ahead. In this study, in cooperation with Synteda, we suggest a machine learning algorithm that forecasts the occupancy in a bus or tram the day ahead for each stop for a route. The input data is past passenger travel data provided by the Västtrafik AB which is the public transportation company in Gothenburg, Sweden. The hourly data for the precipitation and temperature also has been added to the forecasting method; the database of precipitation and temperature is obtained by the SMHI, Swedish Meteorological and Hydrological Institute.

Keywords: Artifical intelligence · SVR · Machine learning · Forecasting · Public transport

1 Introduction

The reliability of the public transport system, especially in terms of travel time and space availability, greatly affects the quality of life of travelers [12]. However many researchers have proposed to predict bus arrival times such as [8,18], only a few previous studies have focused on predicting space availability. References [10, 13,17] tried to develop an effective solution to solve these type of difficulties with the introduction of AI and ML. A research team from the University of Pittsburgh has studied forecasting bus passenger capacity in the whole urban bus transit system by using a random forest machine learning algorithm and obtained good approximations [4].

© ICST Institute for Computer Sciences, Social Informatics and Telecommunications Engineering 2022
Published by Springer Nature Switzerland AG 2022. All Rights Reserved
A. L. Martins et al. (Eds.): INTSYS 2021, LNICST 426, pp. 3–12, 2022.
https://doi.org/10.1007/978-3-030-97603-3_1

The day-ahead forecasting of the occupancy of the public transport recently become an important area of study. The Covid-19 pandemic made this problem much more difficult to solve for the traffic regulators. Jenelius and Cobecauer [9] studied the Covid-19 related passenger occupancy differences in the three most populated regions of Sweden, namely, Stockholm, Västra Götaland and Skåne. The results show a large amount of decrease in 2020, which is changing in between 40% to 60% depending on the regions.

For forecasting purposes, a number of strategies have recently been built, which can be split into two categories: traditional mathematical statistics and machine learning methods. Regression analysis [2] and time series analysis [7] are employed. Lu et al. [11] applied a deep learning algorithm and they suggested that a sample selection algorithm might improve the prediction accuracy. Novikov et al. [14] selected a number of criteria that effect the number of passengers and suggested a multicriteria optimization problem to design a transport infrastructure. A review and comparison of the methods are given in Ref [16], where ten different state-of-the-art forecasting methods are applied to predict the traffic flow. They used two real-world datasets, first dataset describes the traffic flow in the city center of Lyon (France), while the second is from Marseille that describes the traffic in the city outskirts. As a result, they suggest that the Lasso and Support Vector Regressions (SVR) methods are superior to the other approaches that they have used.

In this study, we forecast the occupancy of the tram or bus route by using the SVR. The present method has also been used for forecasting accuracy of highway tollgates traveling time [3]. The results show that SVR can successfully forecast the day-ahead occupancy for a route for each stop for each trip.

The paper is organized as follows. First, the method is given followed by the application of the method to database. The results are summarized and addressed in the following section, and some concluding remarks are given in the final section.

2   SVR Method

The Support Vector Regression (SVR) is an algorithm for machine learning, which is a variant of Support Vector Machine (SVM) [6,15]. SVR has widely been applied to forecasting problems. Consider a time-series data,

$$D = (X_i, y_i), 1 \leq i \leq N,$$

where X_i represents the ith element and y_i corresponds the target output data. The SVR function, f, is a linear function which is issued to formulate the nonlinear relation between input and output data as: $f(X_i) = \omega^T \phi(X_i) + b$, where ω, b and $\phi(X_i)$ are the weight vector, bias and function that maps the input vector X into a higher dimensional feature space, respectively. ω and b are obtained by solving the optimization problem:

$$min \frac{1}{2}\|\omega\|^2 + C \sum_{i=1}^{N}(\xi_i + \xi_i^*) \tag{1}$$

subject to:

$$y_i - \omega^T(\psi(x)) - b \le \epsilon + \xi_i$$
$$\omega^T(\psi(x)) + b - y_i \le \epsilon + \xi_i \tag{2}$$
$$\xi_i, \xi_i^* \ge 0.$$

The first term of Eq. 1 measures the flatness of the function. The parameter C balances the trade-off between the complexity of the model and its generalization ability. The cost of error is measured by the variables, ξ_i and ξ_i^*.

The final SVR function is obtained as:

$$y_i = f(X_i) = \sum_{i=1}^{N}((\alpha_i - \alpha_i^*)K(X_i, X_j)) + b \tag{3}$$

where $K(X_i, X_j)$ is the Kernel function [15] and α_i and α_i^* are the Lagrange multipliers.

2.1 Application to Västtrafik database

The data are provided by Västtrafik AB [1] which is the company responsible for public transport services involving buses, ferries, trains, and the Gothenburg tram network in the Västra Götaland region, Sweden.

Table 1. Dictionary for the Vasttrafik data.

Operating Day Date	Departure Date Actual
- The start of an operating day is usually around 5 AM and can end as late as 3AM of the next day.	- Actual date change at midnight.
	Departure Time Actual
Stop Area Name	- Its the time in HHMM when the tram left the first stop.
- Name of the stop area.	Stop Area Name
	- Name of the stop area.
Sequence Number	- Identifies the route.
- The order in which the stops comes for the specific trip.	Boarding
Departure Load	- Number of travelers getting on.
- Number of travelers when departing from the stop.	Alighting
Arrival Load	- Number of travelers getting off.
- Number of travelers when arriving at the stop.	Seating Capacity
Stop Route Variant ID	- Number of seats.
- Route that the tram is taking.	Total Capacity
Comfort Capacity	- Maximum number of people allowed onboard.
- Estimation of the number of people that can comfortably get on the train, seated and standing.	

The data consist of a list of records of actual passenger counting data in Gothenburg area (Table 1). Number of trips measured varies by the route. It varies by 15%–100% depending on the line. The data include *OperatingDay-Date*, which is the start of an operating day. *DepartureDateActual*, is the actual date change at midnight. *DepartureTimeActual*, is the time when the tram leaves the first stop. However, if the time starts with a zero it's not included. *StopAreaNumber*, is the identifier for a stop (i.e. station) name. *StopAreaName*, is the name of the stop. *TechnicalLineNumber*, identifies the route. In this database all trams in Gothenburg start with 50 followed by the actual number of the tram.

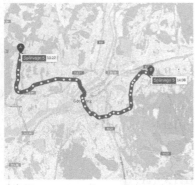

(a) Route map for tram number 5.

(b) Route map for tram number 2.

Fig. 1. Maps for the routes that have been studied in this work. The figures are taken from the Västtrafik website.

Example: 5005 is tram number 5. *SequenceNumber*, denotes the order of the stops for the specific trip. *Boarding*, number of travellers getting on and *Alighting*, number of travellers getting off. *DepartureLoad*, number of travellers when departing from the stop and *ArrivalLoad*, number of travellers when arriving at the stop. *StopRouteVariantId*, informs which route the tram is taking. A route can vary depending on time, day and season. *SeatingCapacity*, is the number of seats of the vehicle. *TotalCapacity*, is the maximum number of people allowed on the tram and *ComfortCapacity*, estimation of the number of people that can comfortably get on the tram, seated and standing.

The travel time data of the vehicles are divided into two hours of time-windows from 08 : 00 in the morning to 18 : 00 in the evening. That means, for example, trip that starts after 08 : 00 and finishes before 10 : 00 will be in the 08:00–10:00 time-window. Therefore five time-windows have been used for each day. There are missing records which means that the variant of the route was not operating in that time-window.

Table 2. The data points used in the forecasting.

1—Number of stops	Tram no: 5		Tram no: 2	
	36		27	
	Number of data points for training	Number of data points for forecasting	Number of data points for training	Number of data points for test
08.00–10:00	1440	36	1620	81
10:00–12:00	1692	72	2430	81
12:00–14:00	1820	72	2322	81
14:.00–16:00	1656	72	2403	54
16:00–18:00	2340	72	2997	81

The prediction is performed for tram line 5 (see Fig. 1(a)) and for the tram line 2 (see Fig. 1(b)) for the hours (08:00–18:00). For the tram number 5 and 2, the route variant that we have used in this study has 36 and 27 stops, respectively. The prediction is for every 2 h time-window between 08:00–18:00 and therefore there are five time-windows to forecast. The *StopAreaNumber* and *SequenceNumber* have been taken from Västtrafik database. Together with these data, an hourly database for precipitation and temperature has been downloaded and included to the forecasting process. The database has been obtained via the SMHI, the Swedish Meteorological and Hydrological Institute, website. The *DayType* is coded as 1,2,3,4,5,6 and 7 for the days of the week starting with the monday. If it is a national holiday then that day is coded as zero. The data predicted are *ArrivalLoad*.

The data are split into two data sets as training for the period of 01-01-2020 (day-month-year) to 22-02-2020 and test for the last day, 23-02-2020 (see Table 2). The aim here is to study the next day forecasting ability of the SVR method by using the aforementioned features.

The data scaled are applied by min-max scaling method to an interval of $[-1, 1]$ before the SVR process. The radial basis function (RBF) is chosen as the kernel function, which is written as:

$$K(X_i, X_j) = exp(-\gamma \|X_i - X_j\|^2), \tag{4}$$

where the parameter γ, intuitively defines the degree to which the effect of a single example of training reaches. In this study $\gamma = 0.96$. We have obtained the best predicitons for $C = 4.3$ and $\epsilon = 0.2$ and kept same for all predictions. The values here agree with the study of Ref. [5].

3   Results and Discussion

54 days have been used in the study which start at 1st of January to 23rd of February 2020. The 23rd of February has been randomly chosen. The trips of last day (23-02-2020) are predicted by using the trips of the previous days. We would like to clarify that all the parameters in SVR are kept the same for all predictions.

A total of five two-hour time-window predictions for the hours, 08:00–18:00, for the day 23-02-2020 are given in Figs. 2 and 3, and the mean square (MSE) and root mean square error (RMSE) are given in Tables 3 and 4, for the tram line 5 and 2, respectively. In the tables the best approximation is given in a separate column and also highlighted in red.

For tram number 5, there are two trips for the time-windows, 10:00–12:00, 12:00–14:00, 14:00–16:00, 16:00–18:00 for 23rd of February 2020, whereas there was only one trip in the time-window 08:00–10:00 (see Fig. 2). For tram number 2, there are three trips for the time-windows, 08:00–10:00, 12:00–14:00, 14:00–16:00, 16:00–18:00 for 23rd of February 2020, there was only two trips in the time-window 08:00–10:00 (see Fig. 3).

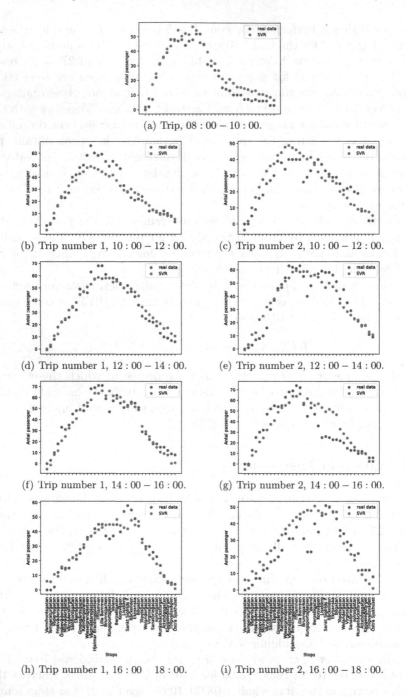

(a) Trip, 08 : 00 − 10 : 00.

(b) Trip number 1, 10 : 00 − 12 : 00.

(c) Trip number 2, 10 : 00 − 12 : 00.

(d) Trip number 1, 12 : 00 − 14 : 00.

(e) Trip number 2, 12 : 00 − 14 : 00.

(f) Trip number 1, 14 : 00 − 16 : 00.

(g) Trip number 2, 14 : 00 − 16 : 00.

(h) Trip number 1, 16 : 00   18 : 00.

(i) Trip number 2, 16 : 00 − 18 : 00.

Fig. 2. The passenger occupancy predictions for tram number 5 for the time-windows, 08:00–10:00 to 16:00–18:00, each trip and for each 36 stops. The data are for the date 23-02-2020. The number of the figures for each time-window is the number of the trips for that time interval.

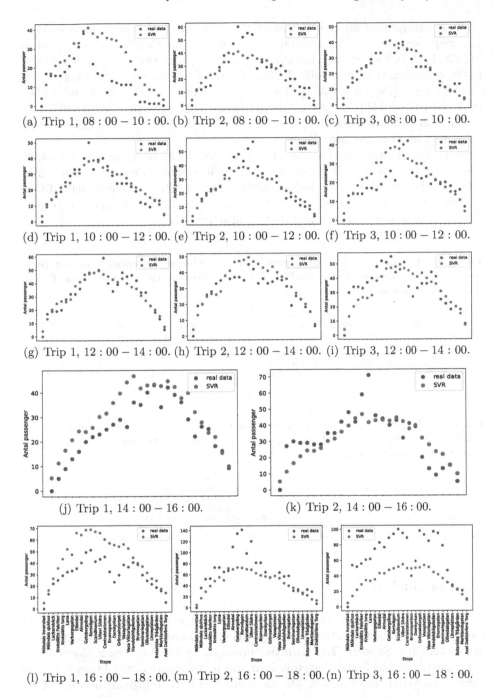

(a) Trip 1, 08 : 00 − 10 : 00. (b) Trip 2, 08 : 00 − 10 : 00. (c) Trip 3, 08 : 00 − 10 : 00.

(d) Trip 1, 10 : 00 − 12 : 00. (e) Trip 2, 10 : 00 − 12 : 00. (f) Trip 3, 10 : 00 − 12 : 00.

(g) Trip 1, 12 : 00 − 14 : 00. (h) Trip 2, 12 : 00 − 14 : 00. (i) Trip 3, 12 : 00 − 14 : 00.

(j) Trip 1, 14 : 00 − 16 : 00.   (k) Trip 2, 14 : 00 − 16 : 00.

(l) Trip 1, 16 : 00 − 18 : 00. (m) Trip 2, 16 : 00 − 18 : 00. (n) Trip 3, 16 : 00 − 18 : 00.

Fig. 3. The passenger occupancy predictions for tram number 2 for the time-windows, 08:00–10:00 to 16:00–18:00, each trip and for each 27 stops. The data are for the date 23-02-2020. The number of the figures for each time-window is the number of the trips for that time interval.

The features that are used as input data in the forecasting are, *StopAreaNumber*, *SequenceNumber*, *Temperature*, *Precipitation* and *DayType* abbreviated as S1, S2, T, P, D, respectively. For the tram number 5, for the time-window 08:00–10:00, a combination of S1+S2+T (Fig. 2(a)), for the time window 10:00–12:00, S1+S2+T+P (Figs. 2(b), 2(c)), for the time-window 12:00–14:00 and 14:00–16:00, S1+S2+T+D (Figs. 2(d), 2(e) and Figs. 2(f), 2(g), respectively) and finally for the time window 16:00–18:00, S1+S2+T+P+D (Figs. 2(h), 2(i)) gives a better approximation (see also Table 3).

For tram number 2, for the time-windows 08:00–10:00 and 12:00–14:00, a combination of S1+S2 (Figs. 3(a), 3(b), 3(c)) and (Figs. 3(g), 3(h), 3(i), respectively), for the time windows 10:00–12:00, 14:00–16:00 and 16:00–18:00, S1+S2+D, (Figs. 3(d), 3(e), 3(f)), (Figs. 3(j), 3k and Figs. 3l, 3m, 3n, respectively) gives a better approximation (see also Table 4).

Table 3. The passenger occupancy prediction errors for tram number 5, for five time-windows between, 08:00–18:00 (see Figs. 3(a)–3(n)). MSE = mean square error, RMSE = root mean square error.

Tram no: 5	S1+S2		S1	S2	T	S1+S2+P		S1+S2+D		S1+S2+T+P		S1+S2+T+D		S1+S2+P+D		S1+S2+T+P+D		Best approximation
	MSE	RMSE	MSE	RMSE	MSE	RMSE	MSE	RMSE	MSE	RMSE	MSE	RMSE	MSE	RMSE	MSE	RMSE	
08.00–10:00	0.0688	0.2623	0.1333	0.3652	0.0599	0.2448	0.0847	0.2910	0.0998	0.3160	0.1423	0.3773	0.0625	0.2501	0.1233	0.3512	S1+S2+P
10:00–12:00	0.1268	0.3561	0.1239	0.3520	0.1224	0.3498	0.1681	0.4100	0.2655	0.5153	0.1657	0.4071	0.1239	0.3520	0.1768	0.4205	S1+S2+T+P
12:00–14:00	0.0896	0.2993	0.1077	0.3282	0.0943	0.3071	0.0851	0.2917	0.098	0.3137	0.0759	0.2755	0.0911	0.3018	0.1301	0.3608	S1+S2+T+D
14:.00–16:00	0.3431	0.5857	0.2610	0.5109	0.3410	0.5839	0.1617	0.4021	0.2654	0.5152	0.1371	0.3703	0.1555	0.3943	0.1414	0.3761	S1+S2+T+D
16:00–18:00	0.3723	0.6102	0.2213	0.4704	0.4187	0.6471	0.0504	0.2246	0.2473	0.4973	0.0595	0.2440	0.0546	0.2338	0.0489	0.2211	S1+S2+T+P+D

Table 4. The passenger occupancy prediction errors for tram number 2, for five time-windows between, 08:00–18:00 (see Figs. 3(a)–3(n)). MSE = mean square error, RMSE = root mean square error.

Tram no: 2	S1+S2		S1+S2+T		S1+S2+P		S1+S2+D		S1+S2+T+P		S1+S2+T+D		S1+S2+P+D		S1+S2+T+P+D		Best approximation
	MSE	RMSE	MSE	RMSE	MSE	RMSE	MSE	RMSE	MSE	RMSE	MSE	RMSE	MSE	RMSE	MSE	RMSE	
08.00–10:00	0.2063	0.4542	0.2111	0.4594	0.3458	0.5880	0.3458	0.5880	0.2117	0.4601	0.4389	0.6625	0.3303	0.5747	0.4468	0.6684	S1+S2
10:00–12:00	0.2227	0.4720	0.1761	0.4197	0.2725	0.5220	0.1297	0.3602	0.1902	0.4361	0.1690	0.4111	0.1615	0.4018	0.1788	0.4229	S1+S2+D
12:00–14:00	0.1065	0.3264	0.1269	0.3563	0.1108	0.3329	0.2616	0.5115	0.1284	0.3583	0.1325	0.3641	0.1444	0.3801	0.1359	0.3687	S1+S2
14:.00–16:00	0.2184	0.4673	0.1482	0.3850	0.2150	0.4637	0.1058	0.3253	0.1561	0.3951	0.1072	0.3274	0.1186	0.3444	0.1169	0.3419	S1+S2+D
16:00–18:00	0.7865	0.8868	1.2030	1.0968	0.8834	0.9399	0.5428	0.7367	1.3768	1.1733	1.1572	1.0757	0.6284	0.7927	0.9229	0.9606	S1+S2+D

4 Conclusion

In this study, a Support Vector Regression based machine learning algorithm has been applied to the actual passenger occupancy data for two different routes in Gothenburg, Sweden. The database provided by the Västtrafik Gothenburg is supported by the hourly precipitation and temperature data obtained by the website of SMHI, the Swedish Meteorological and Hydrological Institute. Furthermore, day type features are also added to the forecasting. The prediction results are compared for the combination of all the features, two features always kept in the forecasting, *StopAreaNumber*, *SequenceNumber*. The Västtrafik data have been used for the hours 08:00–18:00. The data set has been split into five, two-hours time windows. All the parameters are kept for all predictions.

The results shows that by using the previous two months passenger occupancy data, it is possible to predict the next day's occupancy at each stop a tram route. The day that the passenger occupancy is forecasted has been chosen randomly, which is the 23rd of February 2020. The previous data, starting with the 1st of January 2020 has been used in training the forecasting method. The data set used here is relatively small number. However, the approximations follows the real data very close, an exception is the 16:00–18:00 time interval of tram number 2. When we analyze the data we saw that in the 23rd of February 2020, in that time interval, the occupancy was extremly high which did not occur in any previous days.

As an overall result, with the method we have used here the next day's passenger occupancy has been predicted as close as a 5% of mean-square error (MSE) error. For tram number 5, for the day 23-02-2020, we have achieved an approximation to the real data with less than an MSE error of 8% for the three time-windows out of five. For the other two time-windows the errors are 13% and 27%. For tram number 2, for three out of five time-windows, real data have been predicted with less than an MSE error of 13%. The other two are 20% and an extreme occupancy time-window has been estimated with an error of 54%. Therefore we claim that the machine learning algorithm used in this study could be beneficial in public transportation regulators and also forecasting studies to obtain better approximations on next day passenger occupancy in public transportation.

Acknowledgement. We would like to thank to Västtrafik for the data provided. The precipitation and the temperature data downloaded from the SMHI, Swedish Meteorological and Hydrological Institute website. First author thanks to Jonatan Petterson from Västtrafik for the contribution on the dictionary of Västtrafik data.

References

1. Västtrafik.   https://www.vasttrafik.se/en/about-vasttrafik/vasttrafik-ab/. Accessed 15 Sept 2021
2. Alam, I., Farid, D.M., Rossetti, R.J.F.: The prediction of traffic flow with regression analysis. In: Abraham, A., Dutta, P., Mandal, J.K., Bhattacharya, A., Dutta, S. (eds.) Emerging Technologies in Data Mining and Information Security, pp. 661–671. Springer, Singapore (2019)
3. Altıntaş, A., Davidson, L.: EMD-SVR: a hybrid machine learning method to improve the forecasting accuracy of highway tollgates traveling time to improve the road safety. In: Martins, A.L., Ferreira, J.C., Kocian, A., Costa, V. (eds.) Intelligent Transport Systems, From Research and Development to the Market Uptake, pp. 241–251. Springer, Cham (2021)
4. Arabghalizi, T., Labrinidis, A.: How full will my next bus be? A framework to predict bus crowding levels (2019). https://doi.org/10.13140/RG.2.2.12969.75368
5. Dahl, M., Brun, A., Kirsebom, O.S., Andresen, G.B.: Improving short-term heat load forecasts with calendar and holiday data. Energies **11**(7), 1678 (2018)

6. Faraj, M.I., Bigun, J.: Synergy of lip-motion and acoustic features in biometric speech and speaker recognition. IEEE Trans. Comput. **56**(9), 1169–1175 (2007)
7. Ghosh, B., Basu, B., O'Mahony, M.: Multivariate short-term traffic flow forecasting using time-series analysis. IEEE Trans. Intell. Transp. Syst. **10**(2), 246–254 (2009)
8. Hong, W.C., Dong, Y., Zheng, F., Lai, C.Y.: Forecasting urban traffic flow by SVR with continuous ACO. Appl. Math. Model. **35**(3), 1282–1291 (2011)
9. Jenelius, E., Cebecauer, M.: Impacts of Covid-19 on public transport ridership in Sweden: analysis of ticket validations, sales and passenger counts. Transp. Res. Interdisciplinary Perspect. **8**, 100242 (2020)
10. Liu, L., Chen, R.C.: A novel passenger flow prediction model using deep learning methods. Transp. Res. Part C Emerg. Technol. **84**, 74–91 (2017)
11. Lu, W., Ma, C., Li, P.: Research on sample selection of urban rail transit passenger flow forecasting based on SCBP algorithm. IEEE Access **8**, 89425–89438 (2020)
12. Lunke, E.B.: Commuters' satisfaction with public transport. J. Transp. Health **16**, 100842 (2020)
13. Ma, Z., Xing, J., Mesbah, M., Ferreira, L.: Predicting short-term bus passenger demand using a pattern hybrid approach. Transp. Res. Part C Emerg. Technol. **39**, 148–163 (2014)
14. Novikov, A., Eremin, S., Kulev, A.: Methodology of passenger public transport organization within the context of long-term territorial development of a city. In: MATEC Web of Conferences, vol. 341, p. 00064. EDP Sciences (2021)
15. Qiu, X., Suganthan, P.N., Amaratunga, G.A.: Short-term electricity price forecasting with empirical mode decomposition based ensemble kernel machines. Procedia Comput. Sci. **108**, 1308–1317 (2017)
16. Salotti, J., Fenet, S., Billot, R., El Faouzi, N.E., Solnon, C.: Comparison of traffic forecasting methods in urban and suburban context. In: 2018 IEEE 30th International Conference on Tools with Artificial Intelligence (ICTAI), pp. 846–853. IEEE (2018)
17. Samaras, P., Fachantidis, A., Tsoumakas, G., Vlahavas, I.: A prediction model of passenger demand using avl and apc data from a bus fleet. In: Proceedings of the 19th Panhellenic Conference on Informatics, PCI 2015, pp. 129–134. Association for Computing Machinery, New York, NY, USA (2015)
18. Yu, B., Lam, W.H., Tam, M.L.: Bus arrival time prediction at bus stop with multiple routes. Transp. Res. Part C Emerg. Technol. **19**(6), 1157–1170 (2011)

Real-Time Traffic Monitoring and Status Detection with a Multi-vehicle Tracking System

Lu Wang$^{(\boxtimes)}$, Chan Tong Lam, K. L. Eddie Law, Benjamin Ng, Wei Ke, and Marcus Im

School of Applied Sciences, Macao Polytechnic Institute, Macao, China
{lu.wang,ctlam,eddielaw,bng,wke,marcusim}@ipm.edu.mo
https://www.ipm.edu.mo/esca/en/index.php

Abstract. With live street videos posted online, the Macao Government provides means to the general public to assess the latest road traffic conditions. After reviewing over these videos, a person may decide to change the travel route from the one he or she initially plans to take. To let road users make decisions better and faster, it would be desirable to design an automated software, being a component of an Intelligent Transport System, which offers proper suggestions to the users instantly upon analyzing all available live videos. In this paper, we propose to create a real-time road traffic condition estimation system. Its design is based on a combination of deep learning algorithms: the YOLOv5, DeepSORT, and the Non-Maximum Suppression algorithms. Putting together the YOLOv5 with our proposed two-stage NMS strategy, the improvement on the efficiency of object detection on live videos is noticeable. Our two-stage strategy removes the requirement to manually tune the NMS parameters continuously. With DeepSORT, we are able to track moving vehicles, and create motion trajectories, which we can use filtering strategy to assess the latest road traffic conditions. Since different lanes on a road may have different traffic situations, we separate the lanes based on angles and propose to use a lane status score independently for each lane. Through the experimental results, our system design could estimate the traffic status in real-time without requiring any manual parametric adjustments.

Keywords: Traffic transport systems · Multi-vehicle tracking · Road traffic status · Deep learning algorithms

1 Introduction

From an individual perspective, traffic congestion might affect a person's expected arrival time at a destination. It could lead to a consequential event such as missing a scheduled appointment, a gathering, or a musical show etc.

The work was supported by The Science and Technology Development Fund, Macao SAR (File no. 0001/2018/AFJ).

A. L. Martins et al. (Eds.): INTSYS 2021, LNICST 426, pp. 13–25, 2022.
https://doi.org/10.1007/978-3-030-97603-3_2

But collectively, from the financial perspective, the aggregate impact could affect the economy of a city [1], and it may be equivalent to virtually up to multi-billion dollars loss for a metropolitan city on estimation. Therefore, it is important to relieve or reduce the rate of occurrences of the traffic jams, especially it is beneficial to those who pay attentions to current road traffic conditions and scrutinize their own travel plans.

In order to subside the impacts on social, economic and touristic developments of a city, the Macao Government Transport Policy [1] attempting to optimize the road traffic conditions. The Macao Transport Bureau (DSAT) provides numerous live videos online [2], and people can go through them before making any travel plans. Browsing traffic video from multiple cameras is time consuming. It would be convenient if users could access traffic information digitally rather than on video.

In this paper, a novel vehicular monitoring system is proposed to identify the road traffic status in real-time. Our goal is to allow users to use our proposed system to dynamically and instantly determine if there is a traffic congestion at an intersection. With the rapid development of artificial intelligent technologies [3] and using the live video streams as inputs, we propose a road traffic monitoring system by applying deep learning algorithms on these input videos, we may be able to identify the road traffic status instantly, and generate helpful recommendations to users, if being asked. This system hence removes the needs of going through each online video sequentially by a human being in order to make the decision on the travel path afterwards.

Until today, there were a few traffic status detection systems proposed for Macao [4–6]. In [4], an economical real-time traffic congestion detection system was proposed. Its design was based on the low frame-rate online video provided by the Macao Government, but it used Haar-like features to detect vehicles. Then in [5], a real-time traffic analysis system was proposed to perform the correlation analysis, using the online traffic maps and the real-time information of available parking spaces from a government website. In another paper [6], an improved system was designed with neural network-based YOLOv3 [7] for vehicular detection and an mIOU (mean Intersection-Over-Union) method was proposed to estimate the current traffic state, but input images were from the low frame rate web cameras.

Recently, many street monitoring web cameras in Macao [1] have been upgraded from one frame every five seconds to about thirty frames per second. The frame resolutions are also improved. In other words, the input sources have been enhanced from still images to video streams. This permits us to examine more sophisticated deep learning algorithms regarding vehicular tracking [8], and traffic condition identifications through video analysis [9]. Indeed, deep learning-based algorithms are popular and essential for object detections. However, the resources required to track a large number of cameras simultaneously can be costly.

Frontier research works on both object detection [3,10] and tracking are crucial in making the multi-object tracking (MOT) operations successful. This will be our research focus in this paper to carrying out MOT on road traffic through videos in order to determine whether the roads being monitored are congested or not.

2   System Architecture

Management of road traffic is always complicated. Drivers may react differently under the same traffic congestion scenarios. Some may try to switch lanes often, some may just stay put unchanged, some may decide to change routes completely, or some may go back where they start the journeys. In this section, we focus on designing a real-time multiple vehicles tracking system on streets with web cameras. The system operational model is shown in Fig. 1 below. In the system, the videos from web cameras are and will be cached in memory. The vehicle detection, identification and path tracking will be carried out in our proposed system. In fact, upon using the online videos from Macao Government, we can easily achieve one of our primary design goals, i.e., a low cost system in nature.

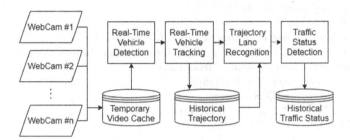

Fig. 1. System model and components.

The traffic monitoring system consists of two components [6]. One is to identify and track the motions of the vehicles. Another is to interpret the number of lanes, and their respective traffic status, such as the moving directions and status of traffic congestion.

Multi-lane roads are the main scenario we consider. A fixed lane mask is an intuitive solution that allows the system to consider one lane at a time. However, this requires marking each lane and cannot be adapted to lane changes. We therefore use recent historical vehicle trajectories to identify lanes, which can be adapted to different situations without the need for manual labelling.

Regarding the object detection mechanisms, the accuracy in general is not high if there are limited computational resources. The small-scale computation models may restrict the efficiency and degrade the overall system performance. The Non-Maximum Suppression (NMS) is the standard choice on finding the bounding boxes for object detections. However, the NMS parameters usually need to be manually adjusted for the actual situation. These manual adjustment requirements are due to different factors (for example, the lighting effect, etc.), and make NMS less effective on overall system performance.

The YOLOv5 (You Only Look Once) [11] is a PyTorch-based implementation of a set of pre-trained neural network models for fast object detections. In our proposed design, we integrate a YOLOv5 model with our recommended two-stage NMS strategy for rapid recognizing moving vehicles. The DeepSORT [12] is executed for vehicular trajectory tracking, and then we apply our filtering strategy in Sect. 3 to obtain the high-quality trajectories. The full algorithm is described in Algorithm 1.

Algorithm 1: Multi-vehicle Detection and Tracking System

Require: Video data $\mathcal{V}$
     Loose NMS parameters p_{nms}
     Min detection box size L_{box}
     Min confidence threshold C_{min}
     DeepSORT algorithm $F_{DeepSORT}$
     Trajectory length threshold L_{traj}
     Trajectory detected frame ratio threshold r
     Trajectory jump threshold γ
1: **while** True **do**
2:    Update lane separate threshold set t_i from history
3:    Update traffic time set t_{min}, t_{max} for every lane from history
4:    Get next video segment $\mathcal{V}$ from cache
5:    Detection boxes $\mathcal{D} = \texttt{YOLOv5}(\mathcal{V})$
     // Two-stage NMS strategy
6:    $\mathcal{D} = NMS(\mathcal{D}, p_{nms})$ with loose parameters
7:    Filter detection, $\mathcal{D} = category\_filter(\mathcal{D})$
8:    $\mathcal{D} = box\_size\_filter(\mathcal{D}, L_{box})$
9:    $\mathcal{D} = confidence\_filter(\mathcal{D}, C_{min})$
10:   Trajectory $\mathcal{T} = F_{DeepSORT}(\mathcal{V}, \mathcal{D})$
     // Trajectory filter strategy
11:   Filter the trajectory $\mathcal{T} = traj\_len\_filter(\mathcal{T}, L_{traj})$
12:   $\mathcal{T} = frame\_ratio\_filter(\mathcal{T}, r)$
13:   $\mathcal{T} = jump\_traj\_filter(\mathcal{T}, \gamma)$
14:   For every lane, calculate the median passing times $\{t_{lane}\}$
15:   For every lane, current traffic score $\mathcal{S}_{lane} = (t_{lane} - t_{min})/(t_{max} - t_{min})$
16: **end while**

Through successful multi-vehicle tracking operations, we can differentiate different lanes on roads with the moving directions of the vehicles. Each lane must be handled separately. We should define indicators with less erroneous results caused by the camera shakes. The indicators being used are the interval transit time and the number of vehicles passing through in an interval. Since the online videos from web cameras are not annotated, we have to manually annotate some videos in order to evaluate the performance of our system. The evaluation result shows that our system has good performance.

The operation details of our proposed system are outlined in Algorithm 1. And in summary, the flow of different operations are as followed. Since some cameras update video frames every 5 s, data from multiple cameras are first temporarily cached. Then the multi-GPU vehicle detection service processes the cached video in real-time. The YOLOv5l model we use can process up to 177 frames per second per GPU. With our two-stage NMS strategy, we obtain acceptable detection results without requiring manual optimization of the NMS parameters from multiple cameras. Then the DeepSORT algorithm is used to track the trajectory of all vehicles in real time, and its appearance model is also provided by a multi-GPU service to support multiple cameras. To avoid low quality trajectories affecting traffic status detection, we filter using our trajectory quality assessment score. By counting recent historical trajectories, we identify different lanes to evaluate traffic status individually. Our traffic status scores are determined by comparing historical traffic speeds with short-term average travel speeds.

3   Multi-vehicle Tracking Mechanisms

3.1   Real-Time Vehicle Detection with Multiple Cameras

The YOLO is a family of neural network models for object detections. It is well known due to its speed and accuracy [11]. Shortly after the release of YOLOv4 [10], the YOLOv5 [3] implementation is based on the PyTorch framework. Its pre-trained models are easy to use, and are friendly to different engineering applications.

Among the YOLO sub-models, the YOLOv5s model can reach 500 fps on V100 GPU [3]. This allows us to perform real-time object detection on multiple videos on a single GPU. Considering the speed and accuracy, we select the YOLOv5l model, and use a pre-trained model due to the fact that the online videos from Macao Government are not labeled.

In general, object detection model gives a higher number of detected object than the actual number. This leads to select the Non-Maximum Suppression (NMS) algorithm which can find the best detection box among all possible choices.

3.2   Two-Stage NMS Strategy

As aforementioned, the NMS algorithm parameters usually need to be optimised manually. In a single fixed dataset, it is inexpensive to adjust the parameters. But with multiple cameras in the real world, different scenes require different NMS parameters, and the optimal parameters also vary with the lighting. Therefore it is costly to manually adjust the NMS parameters in our system.

Some algorithms try to adjust the parameters automatically. The adaptive NMS [13] use a neural network to estimate the density scores, which was used to adjust the threshold dynamically. This performed well in high density tracking. The disadvantage of this approach was that new models needed to be trained, which increased the computational power requirement for real-time detection and thus increasing cost.

Fig. 2. Issues due to different NMS parameters, Left: false detections with loose threshold; Right: missed detection with tighter threshold.

In this section, we propose a two-stage NMS strategy to solve the parametric setting issue. This strategy is to run NMS with loosely set parameters, and then executes a heuristic filtering.

Usually, as shown in Fig. 2, NMS parameters can lead to missed detections if they are too tight and false detections if they are too loose. In fact, a missed detection can not be fixed because there is no detection information. On the other hand, false detections still have opportunities to be removed in future processing.

Through the experiments, we have obtained some falsely detected objects. Some of the falsely detection boxes are smaller in sizes. Falsely detected objects are usually the results of different classifications, and they appear discontinuously in continuous videos. Therefore, we first process the detection box using very loose NMS parameters and then filter it with the following strategy:

- Filter the detection boxes that are not belong to a vehicle categories,
- Filter according a detection box size threshold, L_{min},
- Filter according a confidence threshold, C_{min}.

3.3 Trajectory Filtering Strategy

We estimate the traffic status scores by vehicle trajectories. The DeepSORT [14] is an extension of the Simple Online and Real-time Tracking algorithm (SORT) [15]. Central to the effectiveness of the DeepSORT algorithm are the appearance and movement models. We select the DeepSORT because of its effectiveness and quickness.

In DeepSORT, We use kalman filter based motion model and pre-trained appearance model from the MOT16 challenge dataset [16]. Apart from estimating the traffic status, the dynamically established trajectories are also used to estimate and create lane information at low budget. Because we use smaller models, we are able to achieve acceptable accuracy rates faster than more complex or larger models. As shown in Fig. 3, some obtained trajectories from live videos are not suitable for traffic status estimations. The more complex scenario in Fig. 4 is used here, rather than the simpler one in Fig. 2.

The better trajectories   The worse trajectories

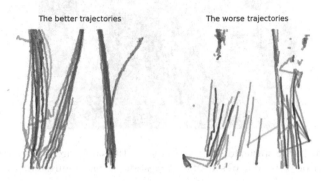

Fig. 3. Examples of created trajectories: each colored line is a trajectory.

Poorly created trajectories can lead to incorrect speed estimates. Therefore, we need to select trajectories with higher confidence. We define trajectory a set of points $\mathcal{T} = \{p_i\}, p_i = (i, x, y)$, where p_i is a point on the track detected from a video frame, the frame number is i, and the position of the point on the frame is (x, y). For a trajectory, i_0 is the first frame detected and i_n is the last frame detected. Then we add the following rules to determine whether a created trajectory can be accepted with high confidence:

- Trajectory length, $l = i_n - i_0$,
- Detected frame ratio, $r = \frac{|\mathcal{T}|}{i_n - i_0}$,
- A jumping trajectory, if exists, $|(p_{n-1}, p_n)|_2 > \gamma$, where γ is the distance threshold.

Through observations, the quality of the tracks at the edges is usually low, and those parts of the tracks near to the edges of frames are removed.

4   Traffic Status Estimation

4.1   Lane Separation

Different lanes in different directions on the same road may have different traffic status. Before calculating the traffic status, it is necessary to distinguish the traveling directions of traffic and calculate them separately. Although it is possible to identify lanes by simply manually marking with lane masks, this is in fact more costly when there are numerous cameras. Moreover, fixed lane masks do not fit lanes with sudden traffic controls, e.g., lanes with stopped traffic temporarily.

Fig. 4. Different traffic status for different lanes in the same directions: arrow indicates the travel direction, red indicates traffic congestion. (Color figure online)

Furthermore, the placements of the cameras are outside our control. If the light incidence angle of an camera is low, it may increases the degree of perspective of the camera. This allows parallel lanes of traffic to appear at different angles on the screen. We can use the track angle to determine different lanes. This process is automatic and therefore adapts automatically after a road change. By reducing the trajectory to a vector representation, $\langle p_0, p_n \rangle$, we can calculate its incidence angle, θ, with a unit vector, $\langle 0, 1 \rangle$.

Upon counting the trajectory angles over time, we can derive its distribution. We assume that the angle of travel for each lane always obeys a distribution, then the trajectory angles of N lanes should follow a set of N distributions. Based on this assumption, an angle-based lane separation mechanism is feasible. The minimal value of a trajectory angle distribution curve is used as the threshold for separating lanes. However, in practice, due to the limited number of lanes counted, the distribution function can be noisy and the statistics should be filtered before using the smallest value as the lane separation threshold (Fig. 5).

4.2   Traffic Status Score

We can quantify the traffic conditions of a lane by measuring the travel time of the trajectories, the travel time defined by the number of frames traversed. Historical data is being analyzed to determine the time required to go through a given lane on a video regularly. We use the previous day's lane tracking results to count the vehicle travel times, and take the median of the shortest 10% of the

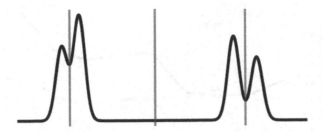

Fig. 5. Lane separation based on angle distribution: four lanes observed with the green line partitioning. (Color figure online)

travel times as the smooth travel times called t_{min}. Upon defining congested or slowly moving traffic, we define $t_{max} = \alpha * t_{min}$, where $\alpha = 1.6$ is set empirically.

We use the median travel time of all high-quality trajectories over a period of time t to calculate the traffic status score, which is defined as $\mathcal{S} = (t - t_{min})/(t_{max} - t_{min})$. If $\mathcal{S} < 0$, the traffic is clear or smooth. If $\mathcal{S} \geq 1$, there is traffic congestion.

5   Experimental Results

5.1   Vehicle Detection and Tracking

The inference speed is important to our system. Object detection models are often the bottleneck in MOT systems, because of the large computational cost associated with deep neural networks [17]. The appearance model is usually faster because it is smaller, which means that more images can be processed per batch using less inference time on the same device.

The deep neural network in our system is implemented by PyTorch, we use NVIDIA RTX2080Ti GPU for faster model inference. To find the best batch size for YOLOv5 on our device, we selected 9 different available batch sizes. The resolution of the selected video is 544×640 pixels, with 2500 frames. The results were shown in Fig. 6.

In contrast, YOLO was slower than expected, though we picked the faster YOLOv5l model. YOLOv5 achieved 196 fps (5.09 ms/frame) on our GPU. The object detection models usually generated many detection frames, but a vast majority of them were invalid. In order to reduce the usage of GPU transmission bandwidth, we used GPU for NMS calculations. Each GPU could support up to about 6 cameras for real-time vehicle detection, assuming that one camera generated 30 frames per second.

With GPU NMS, the inference speed was 177 fps (5.64 ms/frame). Regarding the NMS threshold issue, we used a two-stage NMS strategy. In the cases that it was impossible to pre-optimize the thresholds, our two-stage NMS strategy yielded acceptable results. It could filter a proportion of false detections as

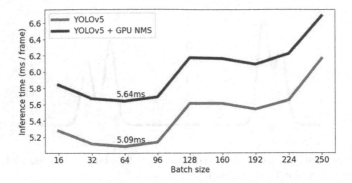

Fig. 6. YOLOv5 inference time with different batch sizes.

Fig. 7. Two-stage NMS result. Same scenario in Fig. 2

opposed to using a loose threshold only. The effect of the two-stage NMS strategy was shown in Fig. 7.

Through the DeepSORT algorithm, we could obtain many vehicle trajectories. However, not all trajectories were suitable for evaluating traffic status due to the fact that some trajectories were too short or broken. The ID switch, which was considered wrong in the field of target tracking, and had no influence on the detection of traffic status. Figure 8 showed the filtered trajectory, and each colored line represented a trajectory. The filtered trajectory on the right side was of higher quality than that on the left side. Our traffic status scores were calculated based on average travel time, and the high quality trajectory helped to obtain a more accurate estimate of traffic status.

5.2   Traffic Status Detection

Different lanes could have different traffic status. We used an angle-based approach to separate the lanes. In Fig. 9, an one-hour historical trajectory was used for lane separation. The blue bars indicated the number of occurrences of

Fig. 8. Vehicle trajectory. Left: raw data; Right: filtered. Same scenario in Fig. 4

different angles, the orange was the filtered smooth distribution function, and the green line showed the solved minima. These minima were the threshold values used for lane separations. In Fig. 10, the results of traffic lane separations in a camera were outlined.

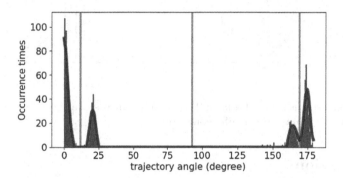

Fig. 9. Lanes by trajectory angle. Same scenario in Fig. 4

Our method allows for more flexible lane estimation than using the fixed lane. It can be deployed directly without additional annotation upon applying to a large number of cameras. However, it has a drawback that it takes some time to collect data for initialization and may not be put into use immediately.

After dividing the lanes, we can use traffic status score to estimate the traffic status. For the scenario in Fig. 4, we estimate the data for one lane for a day. The traffic status score of one lane from one camera was shown in Fig. 11. We randomly selected 500 videos to evaluate the accuracy of our method, these video clips have been manually tagged, half of these videos were traffic congestions. Our accuracy was 96.6%.

Fig. 10. Lane separation: a colored line represents a lane. Same scenario in Fig. 4 (Color figure online)

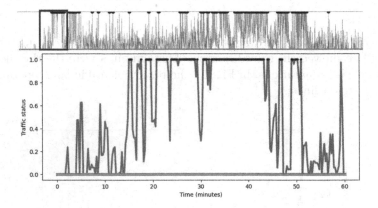

Fig. 11. Traffic status score of a lane, Top: a daily status score sheet; bottom: an hour score sheet (score 1 indicates traffic congestion).

6   Conclusion

Based on a set of deep learning algorithms, the YOLOv5, a 2-stage NMS, and the DeepSORT algorithms, we have proposed the design of a real-time multi-vehicle detection and tracking system. The system works with those online streaming videos provided by Macao Traffic Bureau. Through testing and observations, the proposed multi-vehicle tracking system works fast and satisfactorily. On average, it works harmoniously with 3 video cameras per GPU core. In our proposed design, the YOLOv5 model and a 2-stage NMS strategy are integrated to provide fast and acceptable detection results without the needs to run any manual NMS parametric adjustments. And the simple and fast DeepSORT algorithm is adopted for vehicular tracking. Through our proposed trajectory filtering strategy, high-quality trajectories can be generated for the road traffic status estimations. By calculating the travel times of vehicles per unit time, we obtain the traffic status scores for all lanes in videos in real-time. This information will be useful in future for finding recommended paths between any two locations in city. All in all, our proposed system works satisfactorily, and it can expands easily to handle large number of input videos.

References

1. Macao Transport Bureau: General traffic and land transport policy of MACAU (2011). http://www.dsat.gov.mo/ptt/pt/index.html. Accessed 30 May 2021
2. Macao Transport Bureau: Real-time road traffic videos (2021). http://www.dsat.gov.mo/dsat/realtime.aspx. Accessed 30 May 2021
3. Jocher, G., et al.: ultralytics/yolov5: v5.0 - YOLOv5-P6 1280 models, AWS, Supervisely and YouTube integrations (2021). https://doi.org/10.5281/zenodo.4679653
4. Lam, C., Gao, H., Ng, B.: A real-time traffic congestion detection system using on-line images. In: 2017 IEEE 17th International Conference on Communication Technology (ICCT), pp. 1548–1552 (2017)
5. Lam, C., Ng, B., Pun, I.: Analysis of traffic status using on-line traffic maps and real-time information of parking spaces. In: 2018 IEEE 18th International Conference on Communication Technology (ICCT), pp. 483–487 (2018)
6. Lam, C., Ng, B., Wang Chan, C.: Real-time traffic status detection from on-line images using generic object detection system with deep learning. In: 2019 IEEE 19th International Conference on Communication Technology (ICCT), pp. 1506–1510 (2019)
7. Redmon, J., Farhadi, A.: Yolov3: an incremental improvement. ArXiv abs/1804.02767 (2018)
8. Bui, K.H.N., Yi, H., Cho, J.: A multi-class multi-movement vehicle counting framework for traffic analysis in complex areas using CCTV systems. Energies (2020)
9. Datondji, S.R.E., Dupuis, Y., Subirats, P., Vasseur, P.: A survey of vision-based traffic monitoring of road intersections. IEEE Trans. Intell. Transp. Syst. **17**, 2681–2698 (2016)
10. Bochkovskiy, A., Wang, C.Y., Liao, H.: Yolov4: optimal speed and accuracy of object detection. ArXiv abs/2004.10934 (2020)
11. Redmon, J., Divvala, S., Girshick, R.B., Farhadi, A.: You only look once: unified, real-time object detection. In: 2016 IEEE Conference on Computer Vision and Pattern Recognition (CVPR), pp. 779–788 (2016)
12. Wojke, N., Bewley, A., Paulus, D.: Simple online and realtime tracking with a deep association metric. In: 2017 IEEE International Conference on Image Processing (ICIP), pp. 3645–3649. IEEE (2017). https://doi.org/10.1109/ICIP.2017.8296962
13. Liu, S., Huang, D., Wang, Y.: Adaptive NMS: refining pedestrian detection in a crowd. In: 2019 IEEE/CVF Conference on Computer Vision and Pattern Recognition (CVPR), pp. 6452–6461 (2019)
14. Wojke, N., Bewley, A., Paulus, D.: Simple online and real-time tracking with a deep association metric. In: 2017 IEEE International Conference on Image Processing (ICIP), pp. 3645–3649 (2017)
15. Bewley, A., Ge, Z., Ott, L., Ramos, F., Upcroft, B.: Simple online and real-time tracking. In: 2016 IEEE International Conference on Image Processing (ICIP), pp. 3464–3468 (2016). https://doi.org/10.1109/ICIP.2016.7533003
16. Milan, A., Leal-Taixé, L., Reid, I., Roth, S., Schindler, K.: Mot16: a benchmark for multi-object tracking. ArXiv abs/1603.00831 (2016)
17. Zou, Z., Shi, Z., Guo, Y., Ye, J.: Object detection in 20 years: a survey. ArXiv abs/1905.05055 (2019)

New Concepts to Improve Mobility by Digitization and Virtualization: An Analysis and Evaluation of the Technical Feasibility

Louis Calvin Touko Tcheumadjeu[1]([⊠]), Katrin Stuerz-Mutalibow[2], Janis Hoeing[2], Dennis Harmann[3], Julian Glaab[4], and Robert Kaul[1]

[1] German Aerospace Center (DLR), Institute of Transportation Systems, Rutherfordstr. 2, 12489 Berlin, Germany
louis.toukotcheumadjeu@dlr.de
[2] AVL Software and Functions GmbH, Im Gewerbepark B29, 93059 Regensburg, Germany
[3] Technical University Braunschweig, NFF Institut für Verkehr und Stadtbauwesen, Hermann-Blenk-Straße 42, 38108 Braunschweig, Germany
[4] Bliq GmbH, Mariendorfer Damm 1, 12099 Berlin, Germany

Abstract. Traffic infrastructures are one of the central elements of today's mobility. They are crucial for road traffic and offer road users space and orientation for mobility to move within public space. Road infrastructure is currently designed for non-autonomous vehicles. To be able to support new technologies and services related to autonomous driving, adaptation and enhancement of the capability of current traffic infrastructures is necessary. An innovative solution is the digitization and virtualization of conventional traffic infrastructures. In this paper, the possibilities of digitization and virtualization of current traffic infrastructure elements are presented and discussed in the form of an implementation concept. The paper illustrates the most significant use cases, where digitization and virtualization may lead to the improvements in the efficiency of traffic flow and management. Part of this contribution is also an analysis and evaluation of the technical feasibility of single-use cases for digitizing and virtualizing traffic infrastructures.

Keywords: Digitization and virtualization · Traffic infrastructure · Automated and connected driving · Mobility services

1 Introduction

The contribution presented in this paper describes the activities of the research project ViVre [1]. The integration of digitized and virtualized traffic infrastructure and automated driving functions for central traffic hubs in order to develop building blocks for innovative and sustainable mobility solutions is the aim of this project. In this context, stakeholders play an important role and need to be involved in the entire process (see Fig. 1).

The traffic infrastructure (TI) represents one of the central elements of today's mobility. It is decisive for road traffic and provides road users with space and orientation for

© ICST Institute for Computer Sciences, Social Informatics and Telecommunications Engineering 2022
Published by Springer Nature Switzerland AG 2022. All Rights Reserved
A. L. Martins et al. (Eds.): INTSYS 2021, LNICST 426, pp. 26–43, 2022.
https://doi.org/10.1007/978-3-030-97603-3_3

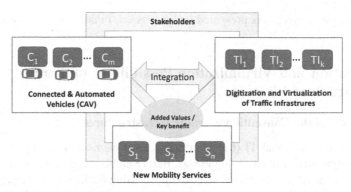

Fig. 1. Storyboard showing the integration CAV digitization and virtualization of traffic infrastructure and the generated mobility services

the realization of mobility to move within the public space. Currently, road infrastructure is designed for non-autonomous vehicles. However, with increasing progress in the field of autonomous driving and the spread of new forms of mobility, such as on-demand bus services, car-sharing or bicycle rental systems, the question arises whether the transport infrastructure in its current form is suitable for these new technologies and services or to what extent it can be adapted to their needs and potentials. Within the last years, many other studies investigated a change of road infrastructure due to new possibilities for connection and communication, i.e. [2–5]. However, still missing is an approach to assess whether certain infrastructure elements are still needed at all, regarding autonomous vehicles. The definition of the terms TI elements, digitization and virtualization are necessary for good understanding. Traffic infrastructure elements are all objects in road traffic that influence and control road traffic functionally and organizationally. The process of digitizing analogue information, i.e. converting it into a machine-readable form consisting of discrete values, is called digitization. The term virtualization refers to the transformation of digital information in such a way that it can be perceived by the user at an abstract level. From the definitions, it follows that virtualization presupposes digitization, but not vice versa. A digital instance of a traffic infrastructure element thus represents the information of an analogue (physical) traffic infrastructure element in an IT (information technology) system. A virtual instance maps this information to an abstraction level so that the structure, meaning and functionality of the element can be perceived by the user.

Under certain circumstances, a digital or virtual traffic infrastructure element no longer has a physical representation. Information can then only be exchanged with elements that are also integrated into or networked with the higher-level traffic management system.

The paper is structured as follows: The work is introduced in Sect. 1. In Sect. 2, the concept of the digitization and virtualization possibilities of traffic infrastructure elements is described. Next, in Sect. 3 the methodology for analyzing and evaluating the technical feasibility of the concepts developed in Sect. 2 is presented. After identifying the relevant aspects, evaluation criteria are developed in the form of research questions. In Sect. 4, the results of the technical feasibility assessment survey, which is based on the research question in Sect. 3 is presented and discussed. Finally, the work is concluded in Sect. 5.

2 Digitization and Virtualization Possibilities of Traffic Infrastructure Elements

2.1 Overview of the Conventional Traffic Infrastructures

The classic or conventional TI (traffic infrastructure) elements exchange information with the analogue driver in an analogue way. Before elaborating on the digitization and virtualization concepts, an overview of currently existing traffic infrastructure elements is provided first. The results are obtained using exploratory methods and research. The TI elements can be divided into five groups: A. stopping & parking, B. traffic signals, C. traffic signs, D. road users, and E. road network.

Each of these groups includes several elements, which in turn can be specified in different levels of details. An overview of the content thus identified is summarized as follows.

Group A: The stopping and parking group consists of parking lots in different categories (parking garage, roadside parking, underground car parking), the stops with special traffic function (e.g. bus stop) and loading area

Group B: The traffic signals group consists of traffic lights (TL) in different constellations (e.g. Three colours TL, pedestrian TL, bus and tramway TL, road works TL)

Group C: The Traffic Signs (TS) group can be categorized in traffic warning signs (e.g. pedestrian crossing), regulatory TS, guide TS, road surface marking (e.g. Boundary marking for stopping or parking prohibitions), or TS like lane marking and additional TS (e.g. boom gate)

Group D: The traffic participants/road users group consists of means of transport like vehicles (e.g. fire-fighting vehicle, police, motorized individual traffic, shuttle, ambulance) and vulnerable road users (VRU) including pedestrians, bicyclists

Group E: Road network group consists of traffic (e.g. traffic situation), roadway delimitation/boundary (direction separation, crash barrier), road (road damage, road surface, weather conditions) and traffic guidance (e.g. intersection/junction, tunnel, bridge, railroad crossing).

2.2 Concept of the Digitization and Virtualization of Traffic Infrastructure

Based on the existing conventional traffic infrastructure elements presented in the previous section, the next step is to develop the digitization and virtualization concepts. To this end, the following subsections outline how the information on the 'classic' analogue traffic infrastructure elements can be digitized and virtualized in the future and made accessible to road users. In this contribution, twenty-five mobility solutions related to the digitization and virtualization of TI elements have been proposed as use cases (see Table 1) and the concept of each use case has been described. The flow of information between the entities acting as system players, e.g. the connected/autonomous vehicle and a traffic sign, is illustrated graphically in each use case (see Fig. 2).

Table 1. Overview of the considered mobility solutions & use cases based on the digitization & virtualization of traffic infrastructure elements

UC No	Use case group	Mobilitys solution/Use cases (UC)	Digitization (D)/Virtualization (V)
UC1	A) Stopping & Parking [6, 12]	Digital mapping of stopping and parking places	D
UC2		Digital occupation monitoring	D
UC3		Digital payment and controlling of parking places	D
UC4	B) Traffic Lights (TL) [6, 13]	Traffic light prioritization control for connected (emergency) vehicles and busses	D
UC5		Digital constriction/bottleneck signalization	D
UC6	C) Traffic Signs (TS) [14–17]	Virtual pedestrian crossing	D&V
UC7		Digital traffic signs	D
UC8		Digital road work zone signs	D
UC9		Traffic signs without physical representation	D&V
UC10		Digital delineator	D
UC11	D) Traffic participants/Road Users [18, 25, 26]	Transparent wall	D
UC12		Digital turn signal/Digital brake light	D
UC13		Digital siren and blue light	D
UC14		Traffic jam warning	D
UC15		Connected warning triangle	D
UC16		Red light violation warning	D
UC17		Warning of pedestrian crossing	D
UC18		Cooperative adaptive cruise control ACC	D

(continued)

Table 1. (*continued*)

UC No	Use case group	Mobilitys solution/Use cases (UC)	Digitization (D)/Virtualization (V)
UC19		Public Transportation – Position and Capacity	D
UC20	E) Road Network (RN) [19–24]	Digital road traffic	D
UC21		Virtual lane and lane boundary	D&V
UC22		Digital road	D
UC23		Virtual traffic guidance	D&V
UC24		Digital construction zone	D
UC25		Digital local restricted traffic	D

The "Stopping and Parking" group (A) includes traffic infrastructure elements that serve the temporary or long-term parking of vehicles (e.g. cars, bicycles). Stopping places, parking spaces and loading zones could be identified as elements. While stopping places and loading zones are exclusively used for passengers to get on and off the bus or for loading and unloading vehicles, parking places also offer the possibility to park vehicles for a longer period.

The digital occupancy information of stops or parking spaces (UC2), which provide their availability at a certain time is decisive information for the use of parking or stop space. Within the scope of this concept, a "distributed" occupancy detection is to be carried out by a vehicle swarm. A vehicle swarm is understood to be the set of all vehicles that can detect parking and stopping possibilities by sensors (Camera-based occupancy detection for example). Thus, an overall view of the occupancy situation in an observed area can be generated. The advantages of the outlined concept for occupancy detection are the high scalability and the low costs per parking space compared to alternative solutions (e.g. LiDAR, Radar, ground sensor).

The "Traffic Lights" group (B) includes infrastructure elements traffic lights, which are used to control traffic efficiently and safely [5, 6], and pedestrian lights, which are used to enable pedestrians to cross roads safely. Warning signal, special signal and bottleneck signal systems also belong to this group and are used, for example, at railroad crossings, road work sites and dangerous locations to increase the attention of road users. In this group the digitalization concept of two use cases (UC 4 and 5) have been described.

The digital constriction/bottleneck signalization (UC5) is related to the transportable traffic signal systems ("road works traffic lights"), which are used to secure and regulate traffic at bottlenecks for a limited period, especially at road work sites. This means that each direction of travel can be cleared alternately to be able to drive safely through the bottleneck. If such a system is installed, the connected automated vehicle should be informed by the traffic management system about the location and the stop line of the traffic light and any associated changes in the traffic flow. The resulting delays can thus be considered when creating and selecting routes. If such a vehicle approaches a TL, the TL should inform the vehicle of its current and future status in advance.

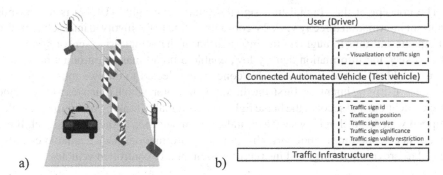

a)   b)

Fig. 2. a) Diagram showing how digital bottleneck signalling works b) Information exchange traffic signs without physical instance

The "Traffic Signs" group (C) comprises the infrastructure elements, which fulfil the task of communicating traffic rules to road users. In this group five use cases have been considered but only two have been described.

The concept of "digital traffic signs" (UC7) provides for the information inherent in traffic signs to be made available to vehicles directly in digital form, instead of being recognized by on-board cameras as was currently the case. In the case of a permanently installed traffic sign, its data can be integrated into a digital map that is stored in the vehicle's memory. This must be updated regularly if there are any changes to the signage. However, it can be assumed that shortly after a new sign is installed or an existing sign is changed, the map data cannot be updated immediately. It is therefore recommended that recently placed but permanently installed traffic signs be equipped for a certain period with a V2I transmitter unit that transmits data directly to surrounding vehicles. This data transmission concerns the traffic sign ID and its meaning, the position of the sign, the displayed value and any validity restrictions such as clock times.

The virtualization of traffic signs (UC9) without physical representation provides a lot of potentials, as traffic signs could be dynamically adjusted to traffic safety and traffic flow requirements. Permanently valid traffic signs can be stored on digital maps just as they are already in the concept of digital traffic signs. Updates to the map can be provided regularly as digital data networks become more powerful. For temporary traffic signs, it makes more sense to set up a V2I broadcast unit [7, 8] that provides an update for the region or route being travelled. However, since traffic signs are no longer installed, it is necessary to make them accessible to manually-controlled vehicles. For this purpose, the traffic signs must be virtualized for the drivers of these vehicles (e.g. using mobile phone application).

The "Traffic Participants or Road Users" group (D) makes the distinction between non-vulnerable and vulnerable road users. The first includes motor vehicles of all types. The second group (Vulnerable Road User, VRU) includes pedestrians, drivers of bicycles and very small electric vehicles. The digitization and virtualization concepts have been done for nine use cases (UC11 to UC19), and offer solution ideas for automated interaction within and between these two groups. But in this paper only the concept of two use cases has been presented.

The concept of the "digital turn signal/digital brake light" (UC12) is to transmit important information directly via V2V communication to the involved interacting traffic participants and thus to augment the information of the vehicle-side sensor system. In order to keep the information density low, enable a broad market introduction and be able to establish upgrade solutions, this concept is selected to the two most important indicators of driving intention. First, the direction indicator, which indicates a turn or lane change intention, and second, the brake light, which signals a braking operation. Vehicles equipped with this technology send a digital signal in addition to the visual signal. If the concept is extended to include virtualization, the information made available can also be used to provide warnings and instructions to manually controlled vehicles.

Fig. 3. Virtual traffic guidance in tunnel

The concept of the "connected warning triangle" (UC15) is to warn surrounding road users of a stationary vehicle on the route. However, this is not limited to the highway and can also be used on rural roads and in urban traffic in the event of a vehicle breakdown. If the vehicle user sets up a warning triangle in the event of a breakdown, this sends a warning to surrounding vehicles and its position. Approaching automated vehicles can thus brake or change lanes at an early stage, reducing the risk of accidents for people in and around the broken-down vehicle. If virtualization options such as HUD (head-up-display) or VR (virtual reality) are also available in non-automated vehicles, their drivers can be made aware of the situation much earlier than with conventional warning triangles and even in poor visibility conditions.

The "Road Network" group (E) comprises the infrastructure elements, which affect the roadway and its use. The infrastructure elements include the road surface, road boundaries and the course of the road, but also the traffic and the associated utilization of the road network.

The "digital road traffic" (UC21) is a more advanced form of digital traffic information in which all road users (e.g. CAV) are digitally recorded. Digitized road traffic also makes it possible to react flexibly to a changing traffic situation while driving. Routing programs can react ad-hoc to a changing traffic situation. The traffic information to be digitized can be divided into three categories: current traffic conditions (congestion information, traffic situation information), prediction information (congestion forecast) and traffic events (e.g. accidents, traffic situation during events).

Virtual traffic guidance (UC23), such as virtual markings on the ground in bridge and tunnel guidance (see Fig. 3) or in complex intersections, should offer the possibility to support the driver or the autonomous vehicle when confronted with complex traffic guidance dangerous situations (e.g., sharp or tight curves, uneven roadways, or steep gradients). Such virtual markers show only the road course that is relevant for the vehicle and can be displayed on the head-up display (HUD) for the driver. The driver is thus supported in finding his way by detailed information about the road layout. Traffic guidance information can be provided for such traffic infrastructure elements as tunnels, intersections, curves, road junctions, etc. There are various situations in which virtualized traffic guidance can support the user. At complex intersections for example, lane selection or lane changes can be prepared. Further examples are bridges, which indicate low permitted speeds and a maximum permitted total weight, as well as underpasses, which can lead to changing light conditions (change from light to dark and back) (also see [10]). In order for vehicles and drivers to be able to react to this complex situation, the corresponding symbols must be virtualized for the corresponding situation. The goal for the traffic management of the future will be that the traffic management centre (TMC) can control each vehicle and ensures that each vehicle receives the digital traffic guidance information based on the current trajectory and the vehicle profile (car, truck, motorcycle, etc.).

3   Method for the Analysis and Evaluation of Technical Feasibility

3.1   Identification of Relevant Aspects for the Evaluation

The implementation of digitization and virtualization concepts and the provision of the obtained information for road users before or during the journey as a contribution to the "traffic management of the future for connected and automated driving" (Traffic 2.0) is complex. It involves various stages in the realization and operation of such services. Figure 4 depicts the levels identified so far, which are required for the technical implementation. These are described briefly below:

Stage1: Identification of infrastructure elements and requirements analysis
In this stage, the individual transport infrastructure elements are systematically identified, digitized and/or virtualized. The question of the necessity and advantages of digitization and/or virtualization of the selected transport infrastructure elements is addressed here, including the problems that can be solved as a result. This step has already been outlined in Sect. 2.
Stage 2: Digitization and virtualization technology
This stage addresses the concept of digitization and virtualization of the selected transportation infrastructure element. This includes the processes for data acquisition, processing and generation of the digitized and virtualized information. It also looks at the technologies and standards used for digitization and virtualization solutions.

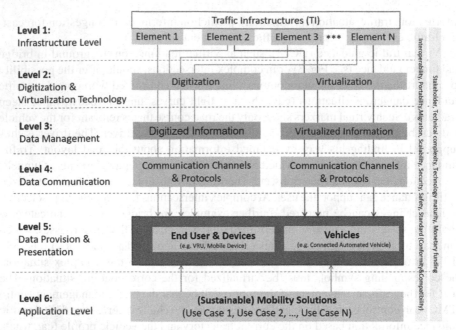

Fig. 4. Levels of technical implementation of digitization and virtualization of transport infrastructures on the data level

Stage 3: Data management
This stage addresses the concept of modelling, storing and managing the data in a digitized and virtualized form. Data protection and security (replicability, backup, access), data availability (24/7 operation) as well as the operation of the data (e.g. in the cloud platform, Big Data) and data quality (timeliness, validity, completeness, correctness, consistency) are addressed.

Stage 4: Data communication
This stage addresses the design and implementation of the communication interfaces to exchange digitized and virtualized information between data providers (e.g., the TMC) and data users (e.g., connected and automated vehicle). This includes securing the communication, the technologies used for the communication networks (e.g., LTE, Wi-Fi, 5G) and protocols (e.g., V2X, REST, SOAP, etc.), and the type and quality of data communication (data volume, data rate, real-time transmission).

Stage 5: Data provisioning and presentation.
This stage addresses the concept for receiving, interpreting (e.g., decoding), and displaying (e.g., visualizing) the digitized and virtualized information on end devices (e.g., virtual reality goggles), or in the connected and automated vehicle (human-machine interface (HMI)). The requirements for visualization devices are also being investigated. Since most services require information about the current position of the vehicle or road user (e.g., for navigation), GNSS technology is relevant for location.

In addition to the purely technical aspects, the cross-level factors - such as interoperability, financial feasibility and safety - also play an important role and must be considered in the design and realization of such intelligent transport systems.

3.2   Technical Realization of the New Mobility Services

The technical realization of the new mobility services listed in Table 1 is based on digitized and virtualized information about road infrastructure elements and requires the expansion and adaptation of the current services at the traffic management, infrastructure, vehicle (e.g., the adaptation of the automation function), terminal, and application levels. Figure 5 visualizes this relationship between the traffic management system, the traffic infrastructure elements as mobility applications, and the traffic infrastructures.

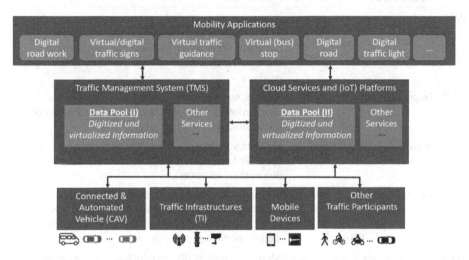

Fig. 5. System components of the mobility services

3.3   Stakeholder Participation

In addition, the need to involve various stakeholders in different areas and their interests must be considered. In the first step, the stakeholders that play an important (decision-making) role in the implementation of the mobility applications, or are involved in implementation processes, were identified. These include Road Authority, Automobile Manufacturers/Vehicle Developers, Municipalities, States, Federal Government, Traffic Data Operators, End Device App Developers, Police, Policy, Legislation, Road Users, End Users, Fire Services, Traffic Managers, Innovators & Authorities, Mobility Providers & Operators (public and private), Traffic Engineers & Planners, Consultants & System Integrators, Civil Engineers and Urban Planners, and Telecommunication Network Operators (also see [11]).

3.4   Formulation of the Added Values for the New Mobility Services

The digitization and virtualization of traffic infrastructures will supplement and expand the available traffic information. From the combination between intelligent traffic systems, improved traffic information and intelligent traffic management of the future, new added values (see Table 2) can arise, which contribute to sustainable mobility, such as: Increasing traffic safety, improving traffic flow, increasing traffic efficiency, increasing driving comfort, reducing emissions, driving new business models, and innovation potential.

Table 2. Overview of some selected added values

No	Added value	Description
AV1	Increasing traffic safety	Avoidance of conflicts/dangerous situations, e.g. by early execution of driving manoeuvres thanks to communication with other road users or by the information about road damage provided by the digital roadway
AV2	Improving traffic flow	Shortening or avoiding unnecessary routes or better distribution of traffic volumes (digital road works or traffic situation information)
AV3	Increasing traffic efficiency	Efficiency gains in the form of money saved (e.g. due to optimized driving behaviour) or time gained (time saved due to short distances)
AV4	Increasing driving comfort	The user can relax (stress reduction) or work and socialize while driving and does not need to worry about dangerous traffic situations (complex intersections or dangerous curves) while driving
AV5	Reduce of emissions	More environmentally friendly traffic by reducing emissions (optimized driving behaviour, shorter travel times)
AV6	Driving new business models	Digitization and/or virtualization provide an optimal framework for the "autonomous vehicle" and thus allow new business models to emerge (e.g., demand-oriented transportation service with virtual stops)
AV7	Innovation potential	Digitization and/or virtualization create the prerequisites for further developments and novel ideas

3.5   Formulation of the Evaluation Criteria

The approach developed in [9] served as the basis for the development of the evaluation methodology. Basically, after the development of a suitable target system, the evaluation criteria are determined. Depending on the characteristics, constraints and parameters are defined and possible alternatives are investigated. Furthermore, the data collection, the weighting of the evaluation criteria and the discounting of the costs may be necessary. In particular, the evaluation raises the question of which method category (non-formalized, partially formalized or formalized) is suitable for evaluating the technical feasibility of the digitization and virtualization of transport infrastructures and the resulting mobility services. Each of these method categories requires a certain degree of mathematization. While the non-formalized methods operate on an argumentative or qualitative level, the implementation of the formalized methods requires the determination of measurement and characteristic variables and the associated data collection in order to be able to make quantitative statements. Also, especially in the case of formalized methods, further components such as determination of the degree of target fulfilment, the definition of assignment rules, aggregation of the results and creation of a ranking are of importance.

Along with the process shown in Fig. 4, many research questions arose concerning the technical realization of digitization and virtualization of TI elements. The research questions including the indicators have been collected and grouped thematically in five evaluation criteria groups. An overview of the formulation of the evaluation criteria of each group is presented in Tables 3, 4, 5, 6, and 7.

Table 3. Technical Complexity (TC)

Research question		Rating
What is the complexity of the technical realization?		1 to 5
No	Indicators	Description
TC1	Networking	What is the degree of interconnection of the concept? Do several systems have to cooperate to realize the concept?
TC2	Number of systems	How many subsystems are required for the concept to function?
TC3	Information processing	Does the system need to be able to grasp and interpret complex relationships?
TC4	Structural changes	Are structural changes to the traffic infrastructure necessary to realize the concept?
TC5	Market penetration	How high must the market penetration of the technology be, for the concept to be useful?
TC6	Data users	For which road users must the digitized and/or virtualized information be made available? [Pedestrian, cyclist, motorcyclist, car driver, non-networked vehicle, networked or automated vehicle, car passengers, etc.]
TC7	Form of presentation	In what form is the digitized and/or virtualized information presented (on the vehicle or terminal side)? [textual, linguistic, visual, etc.]

Table 4. Technology Status (TS)

Research question			Rating
Can available technologies be used for the realization of the concept?			1 to 5
No	Indicators	Description	
TS1	Traffic infrastructure	Can existing traffic infrastructure be used for the concept?	
TS2	Additional sensors	Do additional sensors have to be integrated for the realization of the concept on the side of the vehicles and the traffic infrastructure?	
TS3	Technology status	Is it possible to integrate the concept into existing systems?	
TS4	New development	Are new developments in the area of hardware and software or traffic infrastructure required for the implementation of the concept?	
TS5	Standardization	Do technical standards exist on which to base the development of the concept?	
TS6	Data model	Can (standardized) existing data models be reused for modeling the digitized and virtualized information?	
TS7	Reuse of research results	Can existing research results (e.g. from previous systems or concepts) be used?	

Table 5. Funding and Monetization (FM)

Research question			Rating
How high are the costs for the realization of the concept to be estimated?			1 to 5
No	Indicators	Description	
FM1	Hardware costs	Is expensive hardware needed to realize the concept?	
FM2	Construction costs	Will construction costs be incurred as a result of structural changes to the transport infrastructure when the concept is implemented?	
FM3	Monetization concept	Are there attractive monetization concepts to compensate for high investment costs?	
FM4	Development effort	Are extensive efforts needed to realize the concept?	
FM5	Operating costs	What are the running costs (e.g. for monitoring the system, maintenance, servicing costs)?	
FM6	Scalability	Is there a chance that scaling effects can reduce the costs of implementing the concept?	

Table 6. Safety and Security (SS)

Research question		Rating
How high do you assess the risks in the area of safety and security and the associated need for appropriate countermeasures?		1 to 5
No	Indicators	Description
SS1	Personal data	Do personal data of the user have to be collected and stored for the realization of the concept/service?
SS2	Safety relevance	Does the concept influence safety-relevant functions of the vehicles (e.g. longitudinal or lateral guidance)?
SS3	Interfaces	Are interfaces to publicly available systems required for the concept?
SS4	Data storage	Can sufficiently secure storage be guaranteed for the volume of data (Big Data)?
SS5	Safety risk	Is there increased risk on the vehicle and user side if the system fails during real-time operation?

Table 7. Interoperability and Portability (IP)

Research question		Rating
How do you assess the interoperability and transferability of the concept?		1 to 5
No	Indicators	Description
IP1	Portability	Is the concept transferable to other traffic situations?
IP2	Data reuse	Can information/data from the concept be reused for other purposes?
IP3	Interoperability	Do you see the possibility of linking or extending the concept with other digital or virtual traffic infrastructure elements?
IP4	Extensibility	Is the concept easily extensible to a larger number of users or a different user group?

4   Presentation of the Evaluation Results

Based on the method and criteria for evaluating the feasibility of identified digitization and virtualization concepts of transport infrastructures presented in Sect. 3, a total of twenty-five online questionnaires were developed. One questionnaire per concept is available, covering all five research questions listed in the Tables 3, 4 and 5. The indicators associated with each research question are also listed in the questionnaires to alert participants to relevant aspects. The answer to each research question is to be given on a mandatory scale of 1 to 5, with 1 being the lowest (worst) score and 5 being the highest (best) score. In addition, a comment box is available where participants are encouraged to justify their decision. The questionnaires were made available to participants via an online link. Participants were not given a time limit for completion.

4.1 Participants Analysis

An online survey was conducted with experts in the area of mobility and transportation, both from industry and research. Twenty-five questionnaires were sent to 14 experts. Despite a few drop-outs and merely lurking participants, a total of 1030 valid ratings had been submitted. (see Fig. 6).

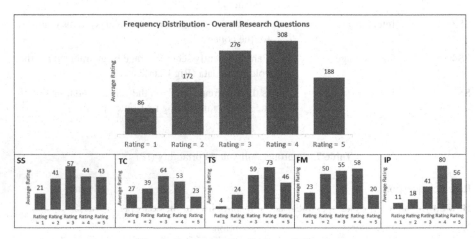

Fig. 6. Frequency distribution of all ratings

4.2 Overall Analysis

To make a final evaluation of the technical feasibility of the concepts presented, their performance across all research questions was analyzed. Instead of calculating the mean value across all ratings, it was looked at which concepts scored above or below average in many research questions. In this way, a bias due to strongly differing ratings in the research questions can be ruled out. The lowest and the highest rating for each use case between all research questions have been picked and presented.

Figure 7 shows the lowest rating of each concept across all research questions. The concepts of digital "turn signal and brake light" (UC12), "connected warning triangle" (UC15) and "construction site" (UC24), which are highlighted in green, thus achieved at least the value shown in the diagram in all research questions. These concepts are thus considered to have good technical feasibility.

In contrast, Fig. 8 shows the highest rating across all research questions. With the exception of the research question "Interoperability and transferability", the concepts "virtual pedestrian crossing" (UC6), "virtual lane & lane boundary" (UC21) and "digital

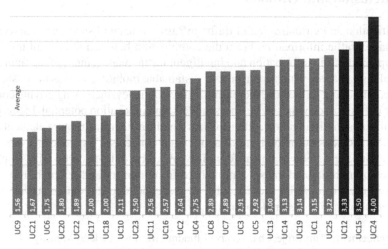

Fig. 7. Lowest rating result across all research questions

warning of pedestrian crossing" (UC17) each received a rating lower than 3.00 and arc marked in yellow. (Since all concepts scored above average in the Interoperability and Transferability research question, it was not considered for the overall rating). These three concepts are thus classified as costly in terms of technical feasibility.

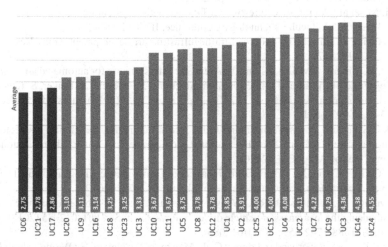

Fig. 8. Highest rating result across all research questions

5   Conclusion and Outlook

The digitization and virtualization of traffic infrastructures will supplement and expand the available traffic information. From the combination between intelligent traffic systems, improved traffic information and intelligent traffic management of the future, new added values can arise, which contribute to sustainable mobility, such as increasing traffic safety, improving traffic flow, increasing traffic efficiency, increasing driving comfort, reducing emissions, driving new business models, and innovation potential. In this paper, the possibilities for digitization and virtualization of traffic infrastructure elements were presented and discussed in the form of application concepts. First concepts were identified, which have a good technical feasibility by a first online survey with 14 experts in the area of mobility and transportation, both from industry and research. But further research is needed to verify these results. In a second step the online survey will be conducted using a bigger sample of participants.

Acknowledgement. This project has received funding from the Federal Ministry of Transport and Digital Infrastructure (BMVI). The authors would like to thank all project partners who also supported this work with their ideas and contributions. Special thanks go to Dr. Marek Junghans from DLR for reviewing this work.

References

1. ViVre Project, 2020–2022. https://verkehrsforschung.dlr.de/en/projects/vivre-virtual-stops-automated-traffic-future. Access 13 Sept. 2021]
2. Jerbi, M., et al.: An infrastructure-free traffic information system for vehicular networks. In: 2007 IEEE 66th Vehicular Technology Conference. IEEE (2007)
3. Zhankaziev, S.: Current trends of road-traffic infrastructure development. Trans. Res. Procedia **20**, 731–739 (2017)
4. Farah, H., Erkens, S.M.J.G., Alkim, T., Arem, B.: Infrastructure for automated and connected driving: state of the art and future research directions. In: Meyer, G., Beiker, S. (eds.) Road vehicle automation 4. LNM, pp. 187–197. Springer, Cham (2018). https://doi.org/10.1007/978-3-319-60934-8_16
5. Ranka, S., et al.: A vision of smart traffic infrastructure for traditional, connected, and autonomous vehicles. In: 2020 International Conference on Connected and Autonomous Driving (MetroCAD). IEEE (2020)
6. Guo, Q., Li, L., Ban, X.: Urban traffic signal control with connected and automated vehicles: a survey. Transp. Res. Part C: Emerg. Technol. **101**, 313–334 (2019)
7. Bhawiyuga, A., Sabriansyah, R.A., Yahya, W., Putra, R.E.: A wi-fi based electronic road sign for enhancing the awareness of vehicle driver. J. Phys. Conf. Ser. **801**, 012085 (2017). https://doi.org/10.1088/1742-6596/801/1/012085
8. Keong, T., Cano, J., Fernandez-Laguia, C.-J., Manzoni, P., Calafate, C.: Wireless digital traffic signs of the future. IET Networks, Bd. 8
9. Fornauf, L.: Entwicklung einer Methodik zur Bewertung von Strategien für das dynamische Straßenverkehrsmanagement. Technische Universität, Fachgebiet Verkehrsplanung und Verkehrstechnik, Darmstadt (2015)

10. Ebendt, R.: A flexibly linkable meta layer of geographic features supplementary for driving automation and simulation. In: Driving Simulation and Virtual Reality Conference and Exhibition, DSC 2020 EUROPE, pp. 19–26, 19th Driving Simulation & Virtual Reality Conference & Exhibition (DSC 2020 EUROPE VR), 9.-11. Sept. 2020, Antibes, France, ISBN 978-2-9573777-0-1, ISSN 2115-418X
11. Richter, A., Löwner, M.-O., Ebendt, R., Scholz, Michael, M.: Towards an integrated urban development considering novel intelligent transportation systems. Technol. Forecast. Soc. Change, **155**, 1–14. Elsevier (2020). https://doi.org/10.1016/j.techfore.2020.119970,ISSN0040-1625
12. Mathur, S., Jin, T., Kasturirangan, N.: ParkNet: drive-by sensing of road-side parking statistics. In: Proceedings of the 8th International Conference on Mobile Systems, Applications, and Services (MobiSys 2010), San Francisco (2010)
13. Gao, K., Han, F., Dong, P., Xiong, N., Du, R.: Connected vehicle as a mobile sensor for real time queue length at signalized intersections. Sensors, China, 1–22 (2019)
14. European Transport Safety Council (2019). https://etsc.eu/updated-euro-ncap-tests-reveal-advances-in-traffic-sign-recognition-technology
15. Saadna, Y., Behloul, A.: An overview of traffic sign detection and classification methods. Int. J. Multimed. Inf. Retrieval **6**(3), 193–210 (2017). https://doi.org/10.1007/s13735-017-0129-8
16. Wali, S., et al.: Vision-based traffic sign detection and recognition systems: current trends and challenges. Sensors, Bd. 19, Nr. 9 (2019)
17. Bhawiyuga, A., Sabriansyah, R., Yahya, W., Putra, R.: A Wi-Fi based electronic road sign for enhancing the awareness of vehicle driver. J. Phys. Conf. Series, Bd. 801 (2017)
18. Morold, M., Bachmann, M., Mathuseck, L., David, K.: Automated learning of pedestrian walking speed profiles. In Informatik 2019, Bonn (2019)
19. simTD: Sichere und intelligente Mobilität - Testfeld Deutschland. http://www.simtd.de. Accessed 20 July 2021
20. Autopilot. https://autopilot-project.eu/. Zugriff am 20. Juli 2020
21. Inframix: Road Infrastructure ready for mixed vehicle traffic flows. https://cordis.europa.eu/project/id/723016. Accessed 20 July 2021
22. Erhart, J., Harrer, M., Rührup, S., Seebacher, S., Wimmer, Y.: Infrastructure support for automated driving: further enhancements on the ISAD classes in Austria. In: Transport Research Arena TRA 2020, Helsinki (2020)
23. Mate, B., Apostolos, K., Konstantinos, M., Josef, E., Wen, X.: Connected roads of the future use cases, requirements, and design considerations for vehicle-to-everything communications. In: IEEE Vehicular Technology Magazine, 1556–6072/18, September 2018 (2018)
24. Guidance for day 2 and beyond roadmap CAR 2 CAR Communication Consortium. https://www.car-2-car.org/fileadmin/documents/General_Documents/C2CCC_WP_2072_RoadmapDay2AndBeyond.pdf
25. Sewalkar, P., Seitz, J.: Vehicle-to-pedestrian communication for vulnerable road users: survey, design considerations, and challenges. Sensors **19**(2), 358 (2019). https://doi.org/10.3390/s19020358
26. Morold, M., Nguyen, Q.-H., Bachmann, M., David, K., Dressler, F.: Requirements on delay of VRU context detection for cooperative collision avoidance. In: 2020 IEEE 92nd Vehicular Technology Conference (VTC2020-Fall)

An Unsupervised Approach for Driving Behavior Analysis of Professional Truck Drivers

Sebastiano Milardo[1](✉)(iD), Punit Rathore[1](iD), Paolo Santi[1](iD), Richard Buteau[2], and Carlo Ratti[1]

[1] Senseable City Lab, Massachusetts Institute of Technology, Cambridge 02139, USA
{milardo,prathore,psanti}@mit.edu
[2] Dover Corporation, Illinois 60515, USA
rbuteau@dovercorp.com

Abstract. Modern vehicles can generate up to several Gigabytes of data per day which are mostly used only for aspects directly related to the proper functioning of the vehicle itself. However, these data have an enormous value as they can be collected and analyzed to better understand additional aspects of the driving experience, such as classifying the driver's behavior and driving style.

In this paper, we present a simple yet novel unsupervised methodology that is able to classify the behavior of a driver in a certain geographical area on the basis of the data collected from all the drivers in the same area. The proposed methodology has been tested on two different datasets involving professional truck drivers and it has been verified using human labelled ground truth data. The results obtained demonstrate the feasibility of the proposed solution. To our knowledge, this is the first study to classify driving behaviours of professional truck drivers and validate their performance on such large-scale data with actual safety scores.

Keywords: Driving behaviour classification · Driving style recognition

1 Introduction

In recent years, driver behavior monitoring and characterization have evolved tremendously due to their importance in traffic safety. The emergence of smart and connected vehicles has amplified the need to understand and characterize driver's individual behaviors as driving behavior recognition is now seen as a fundamental step in the design of Advanced Driver Assistance System (ADAS).

Human driving behavior is a complicated concept and the common association of "driving behavior" with "driving style" complicates its definition even further. Specifically, driving behavior focuses solely on drivers' instantaneous decisions made in response to external environmental conditions such as road type, surrounding traffic, weather, etc. These instantaneous driving decisions

A. L. Martins et al. (Eds.): INTSYS 2021, LNICST 426, pp. 44–56, 2022.
https://doi.org/10.1007/978-3-030-97603-3_4

result from a complex fusion of different factors. Whereas, driving style concerns the way a driver chooses to drive i.e. individual driving habits. This article focuses on driving behaviour analysis.

Modern vehicles can collect massive amounts of data about the vehicle itself, the driver, and the surrounding environment [17]. Effective analysis of these data provides us opportunities to efficiently model driving behavior.

Many studies have focused on classifying driving behavior for road safety. Most of them are developed on the basis of classification models and/or extracted features. These classification techniques are usually implemented using either traditional machine learning algorithms on extracted feature sets, statistical models or a set of rules. In most studies, driving data were collected via controlled/simulated-based experiments or naturalistic driving studies with a few drivers. Moreover, many studies validate their classification models to classify individual driving events (e.g. harsh turn, harsh braking, etc.) rather than overall driving behavior of a driver (e.g. safe driver, harsh driver) as it is usually hard and time-consuming to manually evaluate actual driving behavior of a driver.

Although driving behavior classification from naturalistic driving data is well studied, their characterization is still an open problem which leads to a broader question of "what are the indicators that allow us to characterize a driving behavior as positive or negative?" In this sense, many studies answer this question through the absolute metrics of evaluation as contextualizing driving events is a difficult task. For example, excessive speed is generally associated with car accidents therefore it is logical to classify all speeding events as negative. Contrarily, a harsh braking can be correlated both to an aggressive driving style or a spontaneous reaction to avoid an unpredictable hindrance. Therefore, a context-aware study of driving behavior that goes beyond individual events is required.

In this paper, we move the focus from discrete evaluations, where every driving event is evaluated independently, to global evaluations of driving behavior, assuming that the (average) driving behavior of most drivers on a road segment under the same environmental conditions remains similar. There exists many studies on driving behavior analysis for taxi/car drivers; however, very limited work focused on truck drivers' behavior analysis through real-world driving data. Since most truck drivers usually drive for many consecutive hours in different traffic and weather conditions, unsafe driving behaviors are more likely to occur. Therefore, timely detection of a driver's driving style is fundamental. Developing a simple, explainable yet accurate approach for driving behavior classification is our primary objective here. The major contributions of this research are as follows:

- We present a simple unsupervised approach to classify driving behaviors of professional truck drivers by analyzing Controller Area Network (CAN) bus signals, such as speed, lateral (right and left movements) and longitudinal accelerations (acceleration and braking).
- We capture the behavioral evolution of drivers from their instantaneous response to overall driving habits. We categorize instantaneous driving behavior into four categories (scores): poor (0), average (1), good (2), and excellent (3). Then, the overall score for a driver as a driving habit is computed by con-

tinuously accumulating instantaneous classifications gathered from his/her previous trips.
- We validate the detected events (e.g. aggressive acceleration, harsh braking etc.) and overall driving behavior score for each driver (an indicator of driving habit) against the actual harsh driving events and actual driver safety scores, respectively. These events and scores were provided by a group of domain experts based on their routine observation for each driver over a period of 3 months. To our knowledge, this is one of the few datasets that provides realistic feedback about the driving behavior and driving events for validation.

Very few studies have focused on developing scoring functions that accurately reflect the actual driving behavior. Indeed, the choice of scoring function is very subjective due to the lack of large-scale and reliable datasets with actual behavior information. To the best of our knowledge, this is the first attempt to understand and classify driving behavior of professional truck drivers and validate their performance on the basis of large-scale data and actual safety scores. With a simple and explainable framework, our model not only contributes to academic research, but it can be of high relevance for the automotive industry.

The rest of the paper is organized as follows: Sect. 2 summarizes the literature on driving behavior analysis, particularly on unsupervised techniques. Section 3 describes the characteristics of the data collected. The proposed methodology is reported in Sect. 4, and the validation with the provided ground-truth data is detailed in Sect. 5. Finally conclusions are drawn in Sect. 6.

2   Related Work

A comprehensive survey on driving behavior analysis is provided in [4,12,19]. Most techniques on driving behavior classification can be divided in two categories: unsupervised and supervised. In the first type of approach, driving behavior is classified through statistical analysis or using unsupervised machine learning (ML) techniques, without the knowledge of actual classification. Whereas, in the second case, knowledge of actual driving behavior classification is used for training the underlying ML model. Since our presented method in this work is unsupervised, we restrict our discussion to the first type of approach, which we deem pertinent to this article.

Among unsupervised approaches, k-means, Gaussian mixture model (GMM), and Bayesian learning techniques have been used extensively for driving behavior recognition. Constantinescu *et al.* [5] approached two types of methods: hierarchical cluster analysis and principal components analysis (PCA). First, they employed Ward's hierarchical clustering method with Euclidean distance measure to identify groups of drivers based on similarities in the driving features. Then, they used PCA to project the original dataset onto a lower-dimensional space by extracting principal components (PCs). Further, they analyze the correlations between PCs and driving variables to estimate the significant PCs and plot data onto them to visualize clusters of different driving behaviors.

In [14], driver characteristics in car-following and pedal operational patterns were modeled using GMM and spectral analysis, respectively. The GMM model achieved 69% identification rate, while pedal spectral analysis achieved a classification rate of 89.6% in a simulated driving environment and 76.8% in a field test. Castigani *et al.* [3] presented a driving profiling platform, SensorFleet, to detect risky driving events from smartphone data using an adaptive profiling mechanism. Specifically, a fuzzy logic algorithm was implemented to compute the scores for different drivers using context information like road topology and weather. However, it was based on a 20 min calibration phase on a pre-defined path, which may not reflect naturalistic driving behavior.

Bender *et al.* [1] presented a Bayesian method for segmenting the naturalistic driving data into high-level driving behaviors. This study considered inertial data collected from a 13 minute drive by a single driver. Brambilla *et al.* [2] employed three unsupervised approaches: DP-means clustering, Hidden Markov Models (HMMs), and behavioral Topic Extraction, to detect different behavior along each trip and subsequently classify drivers based on their driving behavior profiles. Fugiglando *et al.* [8,9] used the k-means clustering algorithm to identify groups of similar drivers using CAN bus data based on the driving behaviors. A study on the stability of these groups was reported, however, no semantic explanation for the different resulting classes was provided.

Mudgal *et al.* [15] employed a hierarchical Bayesian regression technique to model instantaneous driving behavior at roundabouts. Similarly, McCall *et al.* [13] utilized Bayesian learning to analyze the driving behavior for braking assistance and collision avoidance. Experiments in these studies were either conducted in a simulated environment or they considered data from few drivers. Wang *et al.* [18] proposed a framework for driving style classification by using primitive driving patterns with the Bayesian nonparametric approaches. The features used in [18] were the vehicle longitudinal acceleration, speed, and the distance from the preceding vehicle.

Although extensive work has been done on driving behaviour analysis of car drivers, very limited studies have analyzed the driving behaviour of professional truck drivers provided that trucks have different vehicle and driving dynamics compared to cars and motorbikes. Linkov *et al.* [11] presented a study on the correlation between professional drivers' driving behavior and their personality traits using a truck simulator. This study [11] classifies the drivers based on their mean speed and mean lateral position from the center of the lane. However, the primary focus of this study [11] was on fuel efficiency [10] rather than driving behavior, which was considered as an auxiliary variable. In another similar study, Ferreira *et al.* [7] collected data from professional bus drivers in Lisbon, and applied Naive Bayes classifier to optimize fuel consumption and provide suggestions. Some suggestions such as "Minimize the use of acceleration" and "Minimize the use of braking" are generally related to both efficient fuel consumption and good driving behaviors.

3   Dataset

To classify the behavior of a driver using a statistical approach, it is fundamental to collect a meaningful and extended dataset. Fortunately, modern vehicles produce a huge amount of data that is rarely used outside of the activities needed by the vehicle itself. These data can be easily collected through the use of vehicular networks such as the CAN-Bus network. This standard, developed by Bosch, replaces the traditional point-to-point connections with a Bus topology in which a shared transmission medium is used to connect the electronic control units of the vehicle. This particular topology allows us to collect transmitted messages without interfering with the normal functioning of the vehicle. There are three main CAN-Bus standards used in modern vehicles:

- J1939: for heavy duty vehicles
- OpenCan, for robots and automation
- OBD2, for general vehicles

In this paper, as we focus mainly on trucks, we have leveraged the J1939 standard [17]. As different vehicles can produce different messages, we have decided to limit our analysis to the smallest set of common signals available from all the trucks in our dataset. We called this subset the *heartbeat* dataset.

This dataset contains information related to the GPS position of the vehicle, its speed, and the accelerations collected by the accelerometer mounted inside the cabin. The data is collected with a sampling rate 1 Hz. However, while the GPS is just sampled every second, the values reported for the acceleration are the averages of all the values measured during a second by an accelerometer working at a higher sampling rate (500 Hz).

The heartbeat data has been collected by professional truck drivers around the city of Trenton, NJ, USA during two different time intervals. The first dataset contains 54 million data points collected by 41 trucks and 34 drivers, from April 2019 to the end of June 2019, while the second dataset is made of 18 million data points collected during September 2020 from 37 vehicles and 22 drivers. In the remainder of this paper, we will refer to these datasets as *2019 dataset* and *2020 dataset* respectively. To validate the proposed solution we have used two different approaches:

3.1   2019 Dataset Ground Truth

The 2019 dataset includes a synthetic score for each driver. This score has been generated by domain experts based on values not contained in the analyzed dataset, but based on

- Number of tickets.
- Number of accidents.
- Direct observation of the drivers' behavior.

The scores assigned to the drivers are divided into 6 categories from A to F where A represents the best driving behavior and F the worst. In our dataset, there are no drivers with a score equal to E and there are only two drivers with a score equal to F. The distribution of the scores is reported in Fig. 1.

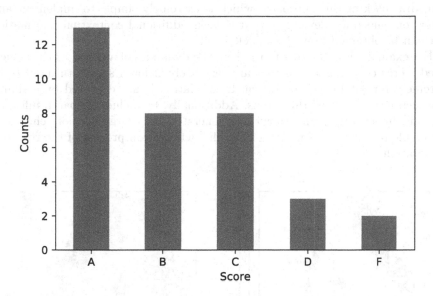

Fig. 1. Distribution of the Ground truth scores for the 2019 dataset.

3.2   2020 Dataset Ground Truth

The 2020 dataset provides a list of so-called *coachable events*. The activity of the drivers participating in the collection of the 2020 dataset was constantly monitored through cameras. When a trigger was fired (lateral acceleration >0.4 g or frontal acceleration >0.3 g), the video signal together with the accelerometric information were recorded and sent to the internal review process for manual verification by a supervisor. We call the data collected within a one minute window around the trigger event a *coachable event*. A summary of the list of coachable events is reported in Table 1.

Table 1. Coachable events available for 2020 Dataset

	Number of detected events
Harsh braking events	3638
Harsh turning events	436
Harsh acceleration events	274

4   Proposed Solution

The proposed approach is an evolution of a standard methodology used for the identification of harsh events based on thresholds [6]. Specifically, in [6], fixed predefined thresholds are used to classify each acceleration as safe or not. The main drawback of this approach, which is extremely simple to implement and deploy on embedded devices, is that it lacks additional contextual information that can be obtained from the vehicle itself.

For example, Fig. 2 shows that, given the dynamics of a truck, as the vehicle speed increases, accelerations that are very likely at lower speeds turn out to be extremely rare at higher speeds. Such correlation is not captured by a simple approach based on fixed thresholds. Additionally, by including spatial information and by leveraging the knowledge generated by a large fleet of vehicles, it is possible to improve even further the characterization process of the recorded accelerations.

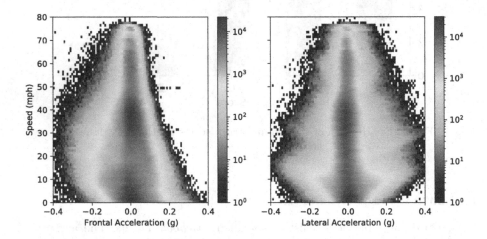

Fig. 2. Dataset 2019: Speed vs Frontal and Lateral accelerations

In fact, a lateral acceleration that can be considered acceptable on a curve may not be necessarily acceptable on a straight road segment and can therefore be considered an alarm or an event that should be investigated. In order to introduce crowd collected spatial information into this analysis, we developed a novel algorithm which, through the aggregation of information from different trucks, allows the creation of a geo-referenced model to classify the behavior of a driver.

The proposed solution is based on three different steps.

- Pre-processing
- Data Aggregation
- Scoring

4.1 Pre-processing

First, the collected data is filtered to remove errors or out of range values. For example, the GPS position can be inaccurate at the beginning of a recording or if there are not enough satellites. During pre-processing, the intervals when the vehicle is not moving are also removed from the dataset. Then, the dataset is segmented based on the path followed by the truck. To achieve this result, we used a geohashing algorithm.

Geohashes are a system used to encode a geographical position into a string. Each geohash algorithm ensures that:

- If two geohashes share a common prefix then the two points will be close.
- The longer the length of the prefix shared between the two points, the closer they will be.

In our proposed approach, we decided to use a geohash algorithm that aggregates GPS data points with a precision of 10m. This approach allows us to aggregate all the data points in our dataset on a $10m \times 10m$ grid, in a simple and efficient way. However, this simple aggregation method is optimal only on one-way road segments. In fact, more complex scenarios can result in the aggregation of data points collected by trucks moving on different paths.

An example is shown in Fig. 3. The upper two images show the 2D histogram of the frontal and lateral acceleration collected inside cell number 24745222599 for vehicles coming from cell number 24745222598 and moving towards cell number 24745222600. The bottom two images show the data points collected for vehicles moving in the opposite direction. As we will discuss it in detail in the subsequent paragraphs, we classify a driver based on how different his/her driving behaviour is from average behaviour of all the drivers in a cell.

In such a scenario, the average aggregated value for each driving attribute (such as speed, acceleration) will be different based on the routes followed by drivers as we mentioned above, and consequently, this may lead to conflicting results in our solution. Therefore, we compressed the path followed by a truck to a list of geohashes by removing consecutive duplicate geohashes and then associating a new feature to each data point in the dataset by concatenating the geohash at the current position with the previous and the next geohash in the path followed by the truck. We called this new feature *cell-ID*.

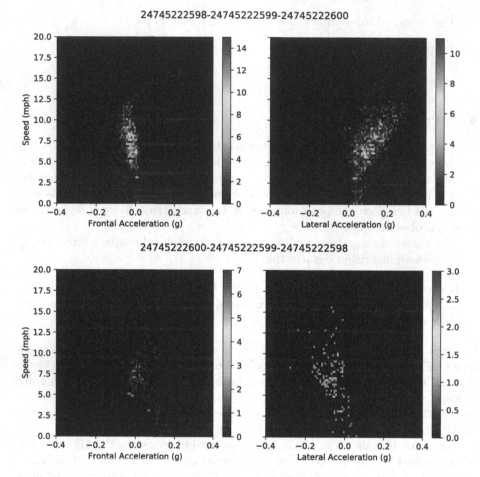

Fig. 3. Data points collected inside the same cell (24745222599) can show different characteristics based on the trajectory of the vehicle.

4.2 Data Aggregation

Next, we aggregate all the data points for each cell ID. This is done independently for the positive frontal acceleration, negative frontal acceleration, positive lateral acceleration, negative lateral acceleration, and speed signals. Specifically, the signals obtained from the frontal and lateral accelerations are divided according to speed in different bins. In particular, we created 8 bins equally distributed between 0 and 80 mph. This binned data is then used to calculate the mean and the standard deviation of each signal for each bin. At the end, the output of this step is a data structure containing the mean and standard deviation values of each signal for each bin for each cell ID. We call this data structure as *cell descriptor*.

4.3 Scoring

Once this data structure has been created, a model is trained on a given dataset that is used to classify the behavior of a driver within a given geographical area. In particular, in order to achieve a score that is representative of the driver's behavior and at the same time easy to interpret, we decided to transform each acceleration and speed value into a score between 0 and 3, following the *68-95-99.7 rule* on standard deviation, where 0 is assigned to values within one standard deviation from the mean of the data collected in the selected bin, and 3 for values outside the $[\mu - 3\sigma, \mu + 3\sigma]$ interval. Then, for each data point, we computed a maximum score that is equal to the maximum value among the scores collected for the signals analyzed. Finally, a trip (or a day) score of a driver is the weighted average of all the maximum scores obtained during the trip (or day). The weight used is a measure of the confidence for the specific score and it is equal to the number of points in the bin used to compute the score.

5 Evaluation

In order to verify the validity of the results obtained, we compared the scores calculated using the proposed method on the 2019 dataset with the scores assigned by the domain experts. For each hour in the dataset we computed the score and we normalized it between 0 and 5, where 0 corresponds to F and 5 to A. Then we matched these results with the ground truth by rounding the obtained score to the closest integer. The results are summarized in Fig. 4. As it is possible to notice, most of the drivers are scored correctly and the error is generally limited to the previous or next class. Of course there can be exceptions as the behavior of a driver can change over time but in general there is a good correlation between the computed and the provided ground truth score (MSE = 1.69).

However, to better understand the variability in the behavior of each driver, and to estimate the trade-off between the amount of data collected and the accuracy of the proposed solution we analyzed how the score changes when we analyze different amounts of data for a selected driver. Specifically, for each driver in the data set we randomly selected 10, 20, ...500 hours of driving, we repeated this process 1000 times and we computed the average score and the standard deviation. As it is possible to notice from Fig. 5, the standard deviation for all drivers in the dataset follows a power law, with exponent in the -0.3 ± 0.01 range. In general, after 200 hours of driving the score computed can be considered reliable.

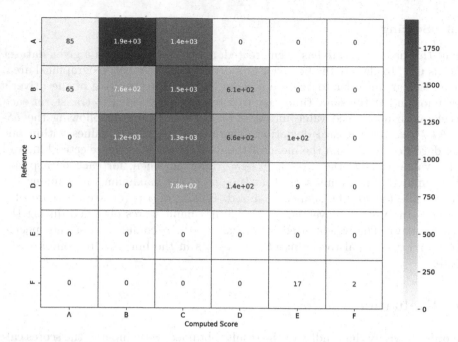

Fig. 4. The confusion matrix resulting from the comparison between the scores computed with the proposed solution and the reference scores for the 2019 dataset.

A further aspect that we addressed is the generalizability of the proposed solution. In fact, once the model is created, we verified that this model can be used to classify a different dataset collected over the same spatial region. Therefore, to verify this hypothesis, we classified the 2020 dataset by using the cell-descriptor generated using the 2019 dataset.

As the 2020 dataset does not contain a synthetic score (as ground truth) for each driver, we compared the proposed solution with the coachable events by computing how many coachable events are correctly detected. Specifically, all 4348 coachable events (shown in Table I) were correctly classified as harsh events (score ≥ 2), while the number of false positives was equal to 648, thus resulting in a precision of 0.87, a recall of 1 and an $F1$ score equals to 0.93.

Finally, it is important to emphasize that the proposed approach heavily relies on the availability of data for a specific area. As reported in [16], few vehicles moving randomly in an urban area can cover most of it in a relatively small amount of time but some areas might remain uncovered for longer periods. However, in the case of the data analyzed in this paper, the trajectories followed by trucks are not random, and the paths followed by the drivers allowed us to easily collect enough data from multiple drivers for each location in our dataset.

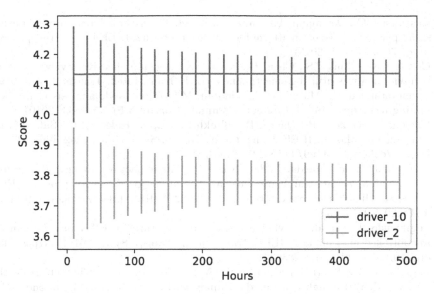

Fig. 5. The average and standard deviation of the computed scores derived by selecting different amounts of data for two sample drivers.

6 Conclusions

In this paper, we have presented a simple yet novel solution to classify the driving behavior of professional truck drivers using an unsupervised approach. We verified through the use of coachable events and synthetic scores that our methodology is generalizable and is able to detect and classify both instantaneous and global behaviors. Additionally, by aggregating the data collected from the vehicles using geographical information, the proposed approach allows not only to classify and model driving behavior but at the same time it can be used to map and underline dangerous or challenging road segments.

As shown in this paper, while the data collected allow us to detect events and label the behavior of drivers, our future works will focus on obtaining higher resolution data and additional signals, such as the steering wheel angle or the pedal position, in order to characterize and aggregate micro-events (e.g. minor steering wheel corrections) in order to focus on additional dangerous behaviors, such as distracted driving,

References

1. Bender, A., Agamennoni, G., Ward, J.R., Worrall, S., Nebot, E.M.: An unsupervised approach for inferring driver behavior from naturalistic driving data. IEEE Trans. Intell. Transp. Syst. **16**(6), 3325–3336 (2015)
2. Brambilla, M., Mascetti, P., Mauri, A.: Comparison of different driving style analysis approaches based on trip segmentation over GPS information. In: 2017 IEEE International Conference on Big Data (Big Data), pp. 3784–3791. IEEE (2017)

3. Castignani, G., Derrmann, T., Frank, R., Engel, T.: Driver behavior profiling using smartphones: a low-cost platform for driver monitoring. IEEE Intell. Transp. Syst. Mag. **7**(1), 91–102 (2015)
4. Chan, T.K., Chin, C.S., Chen, H., Zhong, X.: A comprehensive review of driver behavior analysis utilizing smartphones. IEEE Trans. Intell. Transp. Syst. (2019)
5. Constantinescu, Z., Marinoiu, C., Vladoiu, M.: Driving style analysis using data mining techniques. Int. J. Comput. Commun. Control **5**(5), 654–663 (2010)
6. Fazeen, M., Gozick, B., Dantu, R., Bhukhiya, M., González, M.C.: Safe driving using mobile phones. IEEE Trans. Intell. Transp. Syst. **13**(3), 1462–1468 (2012). https://doi.org/10.1109/TITS.2012.2187640
7. Ferreira, J.C., de Almeida, J., da Silva, A.R.: The impact of driving styles on fuel consumption: a data-warehouse-and-data-mining-based discovery process. IEEE Trans. Intell. Transp. Syst. **16**(5), 2653–2662 (2015). https://doi.org/10.1109/TITS.2015.2414663
8. Fugiglando, U., et al.: Driving behavior analysis through CAN bus data in an uncontrolled environment. IEEE Trans. Intell. Transp. Syst. (2019). https://doi.org/10.1109/TITS.2018.2836308
9. Fugiglando, U., Santi, P., Milardo, S., Abida, K., Ratti, C.: Characterizing the "driver DNA" through can bus data analysis. In: Proceedings of the 2nd ACM International Workshop on Smart, Autonomous, and Connected Vehicular Systems and Services, pp. 37–41. CarSys 2017, Association for Computing Machinery, New York, NY, USA (2017). https://doi.org/10.1145/3131944.3133939
10. Hlasny, T., Fanti, M.P., Mangini, A.M., Rotunno, G., Turchiano, B.: Optimal fuel consumption for heavy trucks: a review. In: 2017 IEEE International Conference on Service Operations and Logistics, and Informatics (SOLI), pp. 80–85, September 2017. https://doi.org/10.1109/SOLI.2017.8120974
11. Linkov, V., Zaoral, A., Řezáč, P., Pai, C.W.: Personality and professional drivers' driving behavior. Transp. Res. Part F Traffic Psychol. Behav. **60**, 105–110 (2019)
12. Marina Martinez, C., Heucke, M., Wang, F., Gao, B., Cao, D.: Driving style recognition for intelligent vehicle control and advanced driver assistance: a survey. IEEE Trans. Intell. Transp. Syst. **19**(3), 666–676 (2018). https://doi.org/10.1109/TITS.2017.2706978
13. McCall, J.C., Trivedi, M.M.: Driver behavior and situation aware brake assistance for intelligent vehicles. Proc. IEEE **95**(2), 374–387 (2007)
14. Miyajima, C., et al.: Driver modeling based on driving behavior and its evaluation in driver identification. Proc. IEEE **95**(2), 427–437 (2007)
15. Mudgal, A., Hallmark, S., Carriquiry, A., Gkritza, K.: Driving behavior at a roundabout: a hierarchical Bayesian regression analysis. Transp. Res. Part D: Transp. Environ. **26**, 20–26 (2014)
16. O'Keeffe, K., Santi, P., Wang, B., Ratti, C.: Urban sensing as a random search process. Phys. A Statist. Mech. Appl. **562**, 125307 (2021)
17. Simma Software Inc: Understanding SAE j1939 (2021). http://www.simmasoftware.com/j1939-presentation.pdf
18. Wang, W., Xi, J., Zhao, D.: Driving style analysis using primitive driving patterns with Bayesian nonparametric approaches. IEEE Trans. Intell. Transp. Syst. **20**(8), 2986–2998 (2019). https://doi.org/10.1109/TITS.2018.2870525
19. Wang, W., Xi, J., Chen, H.: Modeling and recognizing driver behavior based on driving data: a survey. Mathematical Problems in Engineering 2014 (2014)

Blockchain and Disaster Management

Wine Traceability and Counterfeit Reduction: Blockchain-Based Application for a Wine Supply Chain

Ulpan Tokkozhina[1,2] (iD), Joao C Ferreira[1,3,4] (iD), and Ana Lúcia Martins[1,2(✉)] (iD)

[1] Iscte - Instituto Universitário de Lisboa, 1649-026 Lisbon, Portugal
{ulpan_tokkozhina,jcafa,almartins}@iscte-iul.pt
[2] Business Research Unit (BRU-IUL), Lisbon, Portugal
[3] ISTAR-IUL, Lisbon, Portugal
[4] Inov Inesc Inovação—Instituto de Novas Tecnologias, 1000-029 Lisbon, Portugal

Abstract. With the growing number of counterfeits in food supplier chains, one of the most important subjects to a final consumer is the assurance of product legitimacy and safety to consume. In this paper, we develop an approach towards wine traceability, with main objectives on combating counterfeit and increasing brand reputation by assuring the origin of wine to the final consumer. We build an architecture for a blockchain-based system to track and record all the main transactions between the supply chain participants from the moment the grapes are harvested until the moment when the final consumer is making a decision to purchase the wine. This application shows the enormous potential of blockchain technology to reduce counterfeiting levels and assure the final consumer with the origin of the wine, potentially avoiding health risks that counterfeit wine can cause, and thus increasing the wine brand reputation.

Keywords: Blockchain · Supply chain · Wine counterfeiting

1 Introduction

In recent years, major organizations such as technology firms and financial entities have made significant investments in blockchain-based technologies with the goal of fundamentally transforming business applications and move towards decentralization of processes. Blockchain technology (BCT) can be characterized as a distributed ledger, where all the historical transactions are tamper-proof and transparent to all the network participants; at the same time all the information within the ledger is immutable, which makes it secure [1]. BCT is based on a decentralized nature, which implies a high level of transparency [2], and can be implemented to facilitate the execution of safe corporate procedures and the automation of inter-company transactions.

Additionally, BCT represents a significant potential for small and medium-sized businesses who lack the resources necessary to engage in new technologies and are often left behind when a technological leap happens. Various sectors were studied as

A. L. Martins et al. (Eds.): INTSYS 2021, LNICST 426, pp. 59–70, 2022.
https://doi.org/10.1007/978-3-030-97603-3_5

possible examples for BCT implementation starting from healthcare [3, 4], e-government [5, 6] and food traceability [7, 8], to fashionable products [9], diamond authentication [10, 11] and property rights tokenization [12].

Unique features of BCT bring an enormous potential to modern supply chains (SCs), allowing to build well established business processes that bring innovativeness in terms of transparency and enhanced trust between stakeholders [13]. Small and medium businesses may innovate and gain an advantage via blockchain transformation by using BCT-based services and developing their own applications, such as decentralized applications, or DApps. Some examples of application cases may include marketplaces for renting or selling properties on BCT-based peer-to-peer platforms (real estate); managing claims (insurance); monitoring and tracking freight movement (logistics); addressing security (IoT); and ensuring food safety via IBM's Food Trust Network, which connects distributors, retailers, producers, and regulators in the food industry [14].

Regarding enhanced transparency of business processes, BCT poses a great potential to reduce counterfeit in various sectors for different types of products, such as drugs [15], luxury products [16], food fraud [17] etc. One of the products that is facing a high volume of counterfeit and fraud scams is wine. For instance, European Union is facing with nearly 1.3 billion Euros of counterfeit wine trade per year, which makes 3.3% of the whole industry and is causing such consequences as economic level damage, brand reputation loss and potential health issues of final consumers [18]. Thus, this study is focused on a wine industry and the potential benefits that BCT-based application can bring to it.

Thus, the purpose of this paper is to investigate the ability of a BCT-based solution in providing a safe and veritable wine to the final consumer. The goal of this study is therefore to explore the potential counterfeit reduction and traceability enhancement enabled by BCT application throughout the SC by proposing an architecture of a smart contract for a wine distribution SC. This paper is built as following: Sect. 2 reviews the current literature and identifies current state of the art – SC principles for BCT and the types of BCT existing. Section 3 is dedicated to the wine production and counterfeiting; it also shows the current architecture of a wine SC and defines the quality and traceability standards for food industry. Section 4 talks about methodology applied, and Sect. 5 introduces the implementation itself. Section 6 provides the conclusion and future gaps that can be addressed.

2 Literature Review

BCT is a Distributed Ledger Technology (DLT), which is an immutable database of information about each transaction that is shared across a network of participants [19]. This technology is based on the concepts of decentralization and disintermediation, which means that data may be collected, stored, and updated in a dispersed way by all network participants [20]. This kind of architecture enables actors to store and exchange data in a synchronized manner, at the same time guaranteeing their integrity via consensus-based validation procedures and cryptographic signatures [21]. The governance is based on a broad and dispersed system of mutual trust in which no actor may assert dominance and in which decision-making is consensus-based [22].

2.1 Supply Chain Principles Based on Blockchain

BCT is an integrative technology designed to defragment SCs by synchronizing the data captured along it. More precisely, each product is defined by a processing cycle involving many actors. Each actor is assigned a unique digital identity (supplied by an accreditation provider) and is responsible for documenting (tracking) critical information about the product's (or service's) development procedures and status throughout the network. Each product is given a unique digital identity via the use of a unique tag (a barcode, RFID or QR Code). This tag is a one-of-a-kind digital cryptographic identification that links the physical product to its network-based virtual identity, allowing any actor to access all or any related information. To safeguard the process against theft and counterfeiting, BCT entails the generation of a digital token linked with the digital identity whenever the product/service is manufactured or transferred amongst SC actors [23]. As a result, the ultimate product recipient (e.g. a final consumer) may verify the token and trace the item's history back to its inception [24].

When transferring (or selling) a product to another actor, both parties have to sign a digital contract to verify the transaction [25]. Once all parties have signed the contract, the transaction's information will be kept. The actors' privacy may be adjusted according to the subject's preferences: they can stay anonymous, but their identity must be verified by the trust-building certifiers [23]. Thus, BCT's fundamental features that are essential for the business processes improvement of SC's are as follows:

- **Transparency:** Any network participant may see all recorded transactions at any time [26], that is why BCT is considered as a trustworthy technology.
- **Immutability:** BCT guarantees that all data is completely unalterable and uncorruptible. The sole exception is when a node's control exceeds 51% [27].
- **Decentralization:** By its nature, BCT eliminates a need in a central entity, who is usually responsible for transaction verifications [28].
- **Autonomy:** BCT is a consensus-based system that is available to all networks participants and guarantees same information access and visibility throughout all the participants [29] and may be changed only with the agreement of all members.
- **Anonymity:** Both the data transmission and the individual transaction may be anonymous, as long as the person's blockchain address is known [30].
- **Security:** Data security in terms of information sharing is guaranteed for BCT-based applications [31] as it is a tamper-proof technology.
- **Authenticity:** BCT enables access to verified information and data about transactions[32] and protects SCs from counterfeiting and fake assets [33].

Although the principles of transparency, fair trade, and sustainability are increasingly important in customers' purchasing decisions, most companies still deal with complex, non-integrated SCs with high exposure to risks towards, but not limited to counterfeit, human rights abuses, and other illegal practices. Implementation of BCT in SC cases enables organizations to manage business processes is a more active and efficient way [34], guaranteeing the truthfulness of the transaction data and a possibility to trace backwards the production of a particular product [35].

2.2 Types of Governance in Blockchain and Smart Contracts

BCT architecture may be permissioned or permissionless from a governance perspective. The permissioned (private or authorized), chain is an alternate development to the unauthorized chain (the one where anybody may join) [36] with Bitcoin and Ethereum serving as examples. Transparency is limited to authorized participants in this instance, making it impossible to handle data that need some level of privacy [37]. There are two kinds of roles in this sense: (1) **participants** - who are restricted to using the system (2) **validators** - who have access to the system and a copy of the current ledger. Validators are in charge of the distributed consensus process [38].

Permissionless BCT systems (public or unauthorized), vice versa, do not need owners and allow for the ownership of a copy of the updated ledger to be shared among all participants. Participants may also act as validators in this scenario, and are therefore accountable for both the distributed consensus process and the system's integrity [39].

From an immutability standpoint, public blockchain transactions are much more difficult to manipulate due to the increased number of participants who keep the records.

The primary distinction between the three blockchain types is that the public blockchain is fully decentralized, while the consortium blockchain is partly decentralized. The private blockchain, on the other hand, is wholly centralized and managed by a single node.

One of the biggest innovations that BCT brings is the automation. Transactions can be automatically triggered between the nodes, when predefined criteria are met; this is enabled with the use of smart contracts, which can be described as digital protocols that automatically execute contract terms [40]. The use of smart contracts eliminates the need in third-parties, that usually execute transactions and, as a result, improves SC efficiency [41]. Like this, smart contracts provide transparency, thus improving trust among stakeholders [42].

3 Wine Production and Counterfeiting

Wine production includes all kinds of activities that allow the transformation of grapes into wine. There are five basic stages when making wine: (1) Harvesting; (2) Crushing; (3) Fermentation; (4) Pressing; (5) Aging; and finally (6) Bottling. It all starts at the "raw material" stage, which is the grape harvesting, then it goes throughout all the necessary procedures in order to produce wine and give it to the bulk wine distributor. This is only the wine production flow, but after that more stakeholders are involved in processes like bottling, transportation, warehouse and retailing points distribution etc.

The current architecture of a wine SC is based on a barcode system (GS1) and according to the Standards defined by GS1, stakeholders have to fill in some mandatory information throughout each stage of the SC flow, which includes the following [43]:

Grape Grower - Name and address of the vineyard, plot map reference, size of plot/number of wines, wine variety, contract details.

Wine Producer - Identification of the wine producer, product identification, shipping container identification, quality of wine dispatched, batch number of each product.

Bulk Distributor - wine container Serial Shipping Container Code (SSCC).

Transit Cellar - identification of the transit cellar; identification of a container; product identification; quality of the wine dispatched; batch number of each product.

Distribution - SSCC of the inbound pallet, SSCC of the outbound pallet, links between the SSCC of the created pallet and the SSCC of the pallets used in its creation, Global Location Number (GLN) of the retail location to which the pallet is dispatched.

Retail - Global trade item number; lot number; packaging date; batch/lot number [43].

3.1 Wine Counterfeit

Wine counterfeiting itself has many edges, from production fraud to wine investment fraud; when talking about production fraud/counterfeit, final consumers have an impression of buying a specific good quality wine, when in reality the drink can be harmful and dangerous to health [44]. This counterfeiting poses very serious problems for society, implying not only into financial losses but also human losses.

Human losses –Earlier this year, 26 people died and 80 had a heavy poisoning after consuming counterfeit alcohol in Dominican Republic [45]. In Turkey, due to a rise on alcohol taxes, homebrewing became popular and in the end of 2020, 44 people died after consuming counterfeit bootleg liquor with ethyl alcohol [46]. More than 700 people died in Iran in 2020 due to a deadly methyl poisoning of a counterfeit alcohol [47].

Financial losses: There is around €2.8 billion sales losses every year across EU because of counterfeit wine and other spirits [48], which leads not only in sales loss per se, but to consequences such as workplace reductions for registered manufacturers.

Under these circumstances, BCT as a transparent and tamper-proof technology with an ability to address and reduce counterfeiting levels, is inducing growing interest from the side of wine producers and wine related SCs.

3.2 Quality and Traceability

In general, defining the quality of a product is difficult since it is dependent on a variety of variables and may take on a variety of meanings based on the perspective of the SC players. While the term "quality" is often linked with goods, it really refers to processes and material flows. Indeed, according to [49]. Quality refers to both the physical characteristics of the meal and the methods by which those properties were obtained. The capacity to trace the whole route used to get the final result is critical for ensuring its quality, for example, by detecting mistakes in real time and halting the process if it does not comply with criteria.

[49] established a list of categories for formalizing the quality standards or quality control systems used in agri-food production. We accept the fundamental definition given by the International Standards Organization (ISO), specifically ISO 8402:1994 [50], which defines quality as "the sum of a product's or service's features and qualities that affect its ability to fulfill expressed or inferred customer requirements." In simpler terms, a product is considered to be of high quality if it meets a variety of criteria and meets the user's specifications.

Quality is also associated with maintaining provenance, or information about the area in which the product was produced. Typically, knowledge regarding the origins and producers of the product is lost as the commodity travels downstream from the farmer [51]. As a result, a product may be difficult to track in future. [52] found in their research that both quality and safety may contribute to customer trust, and both are related to traceability. The findings, particularly in Italy, demonstrated significant correlations between traceability as a tool for food safety by offering recall and food quality mechanisms. Another fundamental issue that must be addressed is the traceability of a product. Numerous definitions of traceability and traceability system may be found in the literature [53–56] and [57]. [53] offer a generic definition for traceability that may possibly be applied to any product: "the capacity to obtain any or all information related to that which is being considered, across its full life cycle, through documented identifications."

Given the International Organization for Standardization's definition of traceability in ISO 22005:2007, a specific standard for traceability in the food and feed chain, as "the ability to follow the movement of a feed or food through specified stages of production, processing, and distribution"[58], a traceability system based on product labeling must conform to this definition. According to [53], traceability of food items is the ability to ensure that goods traveling through the food supply chain meet specified criteria.

The installation of traceability systems is essential for wine SCs, as current systems are not able to fully protect final consumers from fraud. Typically, the food and beverages SCs are less digitalized, and are mainly built on paper documentation and private databases, which may be easily altered and counterfeited. Innovation and innovative techniques for product-based traceability systems are required.

4 Methodology

In order to meet the goal of this study a collaborative environment, which includes SC scholars and technical specialists, was built. First of all, literature was reviewed to understand the current state of BCT applications and the acuteness of the anticounterfeit solution for alcohol. Based on the state of the art, the need in a traceable and trusted solution for wine production and distribution was highlighted.

Thus, in order to start, the architecture of a SC and definition of the main participants of wine SC need to be performed by identifying each stakeholder and its role. Our proposal to the implementation of the traceability of the wine is the use of smart contracts that were programmed in DAML [59], that represents an open-source smart contract language and in terms of the virtual shared ledger, it identifies who may write what events, and to whom these events would be distributed.; hence, the next step is the smart contract flow architecture creation and adaptation to the wine application. The goal is to enhance the transparency and traceability levels of wine SCs, at the same time reducing counterfeit chances and improving the brand reputation, which would allow final consumers to gain more trust in wine by tracing its origins.

5 Implementation

The global structure of the SC for this application is represented in the Fig. 1, we identified four main stakeholders of wine production and distribution process that will take part in the BCT network, which are:

Manufacturer – the party that is responsible for the wine processing and bottling of the ready wines.

Warehouser – the party that keeps packed bottles of wines until retailing points request a new consignment of wine.

Transporter – the party that is responsible for the wine transportation from manufacturer further to next parties.

Retailer – this party includes various retailing points where wine will be further sold straight to the final consumer.

It is very important to note, that as can be seen in Fig. 1 these are just the central stakeholders, but not the only ones. In practice, wine changes ownership more times during the production and distribution process, including stakeholders that are responsible for: grape harvesting and collection, packing, transitioning, wholesaleing, etc. It is also crucial to understand, that the final consumer is not a participant of a BCT network in terms of creating a new block, here the final consumer will only be able to trace backwards all the records of the production and distribution process, thus gaining confidence in the origins of the wine. We decided to focus on the four main stakeholders for this application in order to show a comprehensive implementation of a smart contract and its architecture.

As presented in Fig. 1, the main goal is to track all the records and stages through which wine goes until it gets to the final consumer, this is done based on BCT-enabled hash system, where each consecutive hash of a new block contains the hash of a previous one. Like this, for every transaction that is taking place throughout the SC, a new hash in the new block is created, allowing tracking wine at any stage and moment of the cycle. In our application, the traceability starts at the level of the manufacturer, where

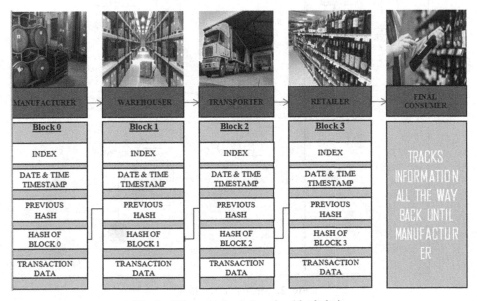

Fig. 1. Wine supply chain using blockchain

wine is processed and bottled and can be traced backwards at the moment when the final consumer is making a decision of purchasing ready bottle of wine in the retail point.

For the smart contract implementation, we built a DAML language template with the following parties: Manufacturer, Transporter and Owner. The owner role can be explained as any consecutive party in the SC, and if the application has more than four stakeholders, any party that is going to take the ownership of the wine at its own stage, can be considered as an owner and the logic of Fig. 2 would be implemented.

The general smart contract architecture for our application looks as following: starting from the moment that wine is processed and the physical bottle is created, Manufacturer transfers the ownership to the Owner by the use of the smart contract. In our case, the next Owner of wine would be a warehouse. Once warehouser accepts the ownership transfer, it would change the holder to the Transporter, who further accepts the holdership, transits wine to the next stakeholder, registers the delivery and assigns it to the next respective Owner. In our application, the next Owner would be a retailer, who receives ready bottles and further sells it to the final consumer. Thus, the last block would be created by the retailer, and the final consumer would be able to trace all the records of ownership change and transactions that took place, starting from the production stage. Like this, the final consumer can be assured with the origins of each particular bottle that can be found at the shelves of the retailing point and check that it is not a counterfeit wine.

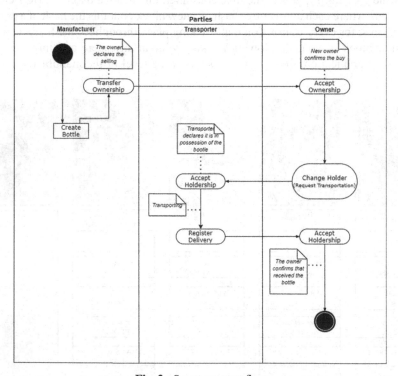

Fig. 2. Smart contract flow

The use of BCT-enabled smart contracts in the wine SC case enables a possibility to make wine traceable and creates a full visibility for the final consumer to see the origins of wine, which brings improvements of several factors.

First of all, anticounterfeiting measures would be met, since smart contract is triggering and recording transactions that meets a predefined protocol, the assurance of wine safety and originality can be guaranteed. As claimed in [60] consortium blockchain and smart contract use creates a decentralized environment, with robust level of guarantees on the integrity of stored and recorded data.

Secondly, it improves the visibility of the final consumer, where final consumer can trace backwards the full production and distribution related transactions that are stored on the BCT networks records and due to the immutable nature of the technology [61] it improves the credibility and trust towards the product from the perspective of the final consumer.

The third improvement that decentralized and trusted wine distribution process potentially brings is the strengthening of a brand reputation. As mentioned in [24], veridical data of each product that can be traced backwards by the final consumer is potentially able to improve the satisfaction level, thus reinforcing an overall brand reputation.

6 Conclusion

With our proposal of implementation, we can conclude that the use of the smart contracts (DAML language) can actually bring advantages in terms of its simplicity: to see all the transactions and clearly track the final product since the moment that it was just a raw material. However, this language is early iterations, contributing to a diffuse documentation and some conflicts with IDE's, with that we can say that this language needs to be a little more community enrollment.

The main contribution of this study is the universal smart contract architecture introduction, which can be used for specific applications. This study also contributes in practical terms, as it shows the potential boost in trust of final consumer when using BCT-based products. Our blockchain-based system helps to track and record all the main transactions between the SC participants in wine production and distribution industry shows a great potential of BCT-based solutions to reduce counterfeit levels and assure the final consumer with the origin of the wine. The origin knowledge further avoids health risks chances that counterfeit wine can cause. Like this the traceability may even boost an increase in overall wine brand reputation.

As BCT solutions for SCs are still in an infancy stage, it represents a great opportunity for the future of SC applications. This technology guarantees immutability and irreversibility, making it possible to control the entire supply chain from the producer to the final consumer. For future research, we suggest applying the proposed system to see the actual level of an end consumer trust and satisfaction with the feature.

Acknowledgement 1. We would like to thank ISTAR-IUL students Carlos Lourenço, David Inglez, Gonçalo Martins, Inês Carvalho and Joana Ascenso for contribution in DAML prototype development.

Acknowledgement 2. This work was supported by EEA Grants Blue Growth Programme (Call #5). Project PT-INNOVATION-0045 – Fish2Fork.

References

1. Berdik, D., Otoum, S., Schmidt, N., Porter, D., Jararweh, Y.: A survey on blockchain for information systems management and security. Inf. Proc. Manag. **58**(1), 102397 (2021)
2. Wan, P.K., Huang, L., Holtskog, H.: Blockchain-enabled information sharing within a supply chain: a systematic literature review. IEEE Access **8**, 49645–49656 (2020)
3. Ukanah, O., Obimbo, C.: Blockchain application in healthcare. In: International Conference on Computational Science and Computational Intelligence (CSCI), pp. 1167–1172, IEEE (2020)
4. Shuaib, M., Alam, S., Alam, M.S., Nasir, M.S.: Self-sovereign identity for healthcare using blockchain. Mater. Today: Proc. (2021, in press)
5. Ahmad, D., Lutfiani, N., Ahmad, A.D.A.R., Rahardja, U., Aini, Q.: Blockchain technology immutability framework design in e-government. Jurnal Administrasi Publik : Pub. Admin. J. **11**(1), 32–41 (2021). https://doi.org/10.31289/jap.v11i1.4310
6. Fallucchi, F., Gerardi, M., Petito, M., De Luca, E.W.: Blockchain framework in digital government for the certification of authenticity, timestamping and data property. In: Proceedings of the 54th Hawaii International Conference on System Sciences, p. 2307 (2021)
7. Bumblauskas, D., Mann, A., Dugan, B., Rittmer, J.: A blockchain use case in food distribution: Do you know where your food has been? Int. J. Inf. Manag. **52**, 102008 (2020)
8. Stranieri, S., Riccardi, F., Meuwissen, M.P.M. Soregaroli, C.: Exploring the impact of blockchain on the performance of agri-food supply chains. Food Control **119**, 107495 (2021)
9. Choi, T.-M.: Supply chain financing using blockchain: impacts on supply chains selling fashionable products. Ann. Oper. Res. **1**, 23 (2020). https://doi.org/10.1007/s10479-020-03615-7
10. Choi, T.M.: Blockchain-technology-supported platforms for diamond authentication and certification in luxury supply chains. Trans. Res. Part E: Logist. Trans. Rev. Elsevier **128**(April), 17–29 (2019)
11. Thakker, U., Patel, R., Tanwar, S., Kumar, N., Song, H.: Blockchain for diamond industry: opportunities and challenges. IEEE Internet of Things J. **8**(11), 8747–8773 (2021). https://doi.org/10.1109/JIOT.2020.3047550
12. Garcia-Teruel, R.M., Simón-Moreno, H.: The digital tokenization of property rights. A comparative perspective. Comput. Law Security Rev. **41**, 105543 (2021)
13. Chang, S.E., Chen, Y.: When blockchain meets supply chain: a systematic literature review on current development and potential applications. IEEE Access **8**, 62478–62494 (2020)
14. Wu, H., et al.: Data management in supply chain using blockchain: challenges and a case study. In: Proceedings 28th International Conference on Computer Communication and Networks (ICCCN), pp. 1–8 (2019)
15. Adsul, K.B., Kosbatwar, S.P.: A Novel Approach for Traceability & Detection of Counterfeit Medicines Through Blockchain (2020)
16. Li, G., Fan, Z.-P., Xue-Yan, W.: The choice strategy of authentication technology for luxury e-commerce platforms in the blockchain era. IEEE Trans. Eng. Manage. **1**, 14 (2021). https://doi.org/10.1109/TEM.2021.3076606
17. Leung, H.W., Chapman, A., Fadhel, N.F.: Identifying Food Fraud using Blockchain (2021)
18. Counterfeit products steal 1.3 billion euros from the EU wine market. https://winenews.it/en/counterfeit-products-steal-1-3-billion-euros-a-year-from-the-eu-wine-market_438742/. Accessed 20 Oct 2021
19. Tian, F.: A supply chain traceability system for food safety based on HACCP, blockchain & internet of things. In: IEEE 2017 International Conference on Service Systems and Service Management, pp. 1–6 (2017)

20. Monteiro, M.: Blockchain: tecnologia da bitcoin está a chegar a múltiplas indústrias, MaisTic (2018)
21. Adam, V., Ankit A.S., Robert, K., Sophia, M.: Using blockchain to drive supply chain innovation. https://www2.deloitte.com/us/en/pages/operations/articles/blockchain-supply-chain-innovation.html. Accessed 20 Oct 2021
22. Deloitte Homepage, Continuous interconnected supply chain. https://www2.deloitte.com/content/dam/Deloitte/lu/Documents/technology/lu-WP-Supply-Chain-Blockchain-181020 17.PDF. Accessed 20 Oct 2021
23. Selinko Homepage, Anti-counterfeiting study wines and spirits market.docx. https://selinko.com/. Accessed 20 Oct 2021
24. Tokkozhina, U., Martins, A.L., Ferreira, J.C. :Adopting blockchain in supply chain – an approach for a pilot. In: Lecture Notes of the Institute for Computer Sciences, Social-Informatics and Telecommunications Engineering, LNICST, vol. 364 LNICST, pp. 125–141 (2021)
25. Abeyratne, S.A., Monfared, R.P.: Blockchain ready manufacturing supply chain using distributed ledger. Int. J. Res. Eng. Technol. 5(9), 1–10 (2016)
26. Min, H.: Blockchain technology for enhancing supply chain resilience. Bus. Horiz. 62(1), 35–45 (2019)
27. Vyas, N., Beije, A., Krishnamachari, B.: Blockchain and the Supply Chain: Concepts, Strategies and Practical Applications. Kogan Page Publishers (2019)
28. Esmaeilian, B., Sarkis, J., Lewis, K., Behdad, S.: Blockchain for the future of sustainable supply chain management in Industry 4.0, Resour. Conserv. Recycl. 163, 105064 (2020)
29. Gonczol, P., Katsikouli, P., Herskind, L., Dragoni, N.: Blockchain implementations and use cases for supply chains-A survey. IEEE Access 8, 11856–11871 (2020)
30. Lu, Y., Tang, Q., Wang, G.: Zebralancer: private and anonymous crowdsourcing system atop open blockchain. In: 2018 IEEE 38th International Conference on Distributed Computing Systems (ICDCS), pp. 853–865 (2018)
31. Leng, K., Bi, Y., Jing, L., Fu, H.C., Van Nieuwenhuyse, I.: Research on agricultural supply chain system with double chain architecture based on blockchain technology. Futur. Gener. Comput. Syst. 86, 641–649 (2018)
32. Perboli, G., Musso, S., Rosano, M.: Blockchain in logistics and supply chain: a lean approach for designing real-world use cases. IEEE Access 6, 62018–62028 (2018)
33. Cui, P., Dixon, J., Guin, U., Dimase, D.: A Blockchain-based framework for supply chain provenance. IEEE Access 7, 157113–157125 (2019)
34. Sternberg, H.S., Hofmann, E., Roeck, D.: The struggle is real: insights from a supply chain blockchain case. J. Bus. Logist. 42(1), 71–87 (2020). https://doi.org/10.1111/jbl.12240
35. Kamble, S., Gunasekaran, A., Arha, H.: Understanding the blockchain technology adoption in supply chains – Indian Context. Int. J. Prod. Res. 57(7), 2009–2033 (2019)
36. Namasudra, S., Deka, G.C., Johri, P., Hosseinpour, M., Gandomi, A.H.: The revolution of blockchain: state-of-the-art and research challenges. Arch. Computat. Methods Eng. 28(3), 1497–1515 (2021)
37. Ameyaw, P.D., de Vries, W.T.: Transparency of land administration and the role of blockchain technology, a four-dimensional framework analysis from the Ghanaian land perspective. Land 9(12), 491 (2020)
38. Jalal, I., Shukur, Z., Bakar, K.A.A.: A Study on Public Blockchain Consensus Algorithms: A Systematic Literature Review (2020)
39. Li, Z., Barenji, A.V., Huang, G.Q.: Toward a blockchain cloud manufacturing system as a peer to peer distributed network platform. Robot. Comput. Integ. Manuf. 54, 133–144 (2018)
40. Wang, Y., et al.: Making sense of blockchain technology: how will it transform supply chains? In: International Journal of Production Economics. Elsevier B.V., 211(February), pp. 221–236 (2019)

41. Kamble, S.S., Gunasekaran, A., Sharma, R.: Modeling the blockchain enabled traceability in agriculture supply chain. Int. J. Inf. Manag. Elsevier **52**, 101967 (2019). https://doi.org/10.1016/j.ijinfomgt.2019.05.023

42. Omar, I.A., et al.: Automating procurement contracts in the healthcare supply chain using blockchain smart contracts'. IEEE Access **9**, 37397–37409 (2021)

43. GS1: Wine Supply Chain Traceability GS1 Application Guideline. https://www.gs1us.org/DesktopModules/Bring2mind/DMX/Download.aspx?Command=Core_Download&EntryId=660&language=en-US&PortalId=0&TabId=134. Accessed 20 Oct 2021

44. The fake wine epidemic. https://wisermarket.com/blog/the-fake-wine-epidemic/. Accessed 20 Oct 2021

45. Deaths in Dominican Republic linked to tainted alcohol. https://www.foodsafetynews.com/2021/04/deaths-in-dominican-republic-linked-to-tainted-alcohol/. Accessed 20 Oct 2021

46. Turkey: Dozens dad in bootleg alcohol poisoning. https://www.dw.com/en/turkey-dozens-dead-in-bootleg-alcohol-poisoning/a-55255560, Accessed 20 Oct 2021

47. Bouscaren, Pandemic's deadly side effect: Global rise in bootleg alcohol poisonings (2020). https://www.pri.org/stories/2020-10-20/pandemic-s-deadly-side-effect-global-rise-bootleg-alcohol-poisonings. Accessed 20 Oct 2021

48. Whitworth: Wine and spirits one of top sectors affected by counterfeiting – EUIPO (2018). https://www.foodnavigator.com/Article/2018/06/25/EUIPO-assesses-counterfeiting-cost-in-spirits-and-wine-category. Accessed 20 Oct 2021

49. Morris, C., Young, C.: Seed to shelf' teat to table' barley to beer' andwomb to tomb': discourses of food quality and quality assurance schemes in the UK. J. Rural Stud. **16**(1), 103–115 (2000)

50. Quality management and quality assurance Vocabulary (1994)

51. Galli, F., Bartolini, F., Brunori, G., Colombo, L., Gava, O., Grando, S., et al.: Sustainability assessment of food supply chains: an application to local and global bread in Italy. Agricult. Food Econ. **3**(1), 21 (2015)

52. Van Rijswijk, W., Frewer, L.J.: How consumers link traceability to food quality and safety: an international investigation. Technical report 736-2016-50767, pp. 2–7 (2006)

53. Olsen, P., Borit, M.: How to define traceability. Trends Food Sci. Technol. **29**(2), 142–150 (2013)

54. Bosona, T., Gebresenbet, G.: Food traceability as an integral part of logistics management in food and agricultural supply chain. Food Control **33**(1), 32–48 (2013)

55. Galli, F., Gava, O., Bartolini, F., Marescotti, A., Brunori, G.: Global and Local wheat-to-bread supply chains. Glob. Local Food Asess. **104** (2015)

56. Karlsen, K.M., Dreyer, B., Olsen, P., Elvevoll, E.O.: Literature review: does a common theoretical framework to implement food traceability exist? Food Control **32**(2), 409–417 (2013)

57. Dabbene, F., Gay, P., Tortia, C.: Traceability issues in food supply chain management: a review. Biosys. Eng. **120**, 65–80 (2014)

58. Traceability in the Feed and Food Chain—General Principles and Basic Requirements for System Design and Implementation (2016). https://www.iso.org/standard/36297.html

59. DAML. https://daml.com. Accessed 20 Oct 2021

60. Aniello, L., Halak, B., Chai, P., Dhall, R., Mihalea, M., Wilczynski, A.: Towards a supply chain management system for counterfeit mitigation using blockchain and PUF. arXiv preprint arXiv:1908.09585

61. Ferreira, J.C., Martins, A.L.: Building a community of users for open market energy. Energies **11**(9), 1–21 (2018)

Open Market for Reusing Auto Parts with Blockchain

Daniel Cale[✉] [iD]

ISTAR-IUL, Instituto Universitário de Lisboa (ISCTE-IUL), 1649-026 Lisboa, Portugal
ddces@iscte-iul.pt

Abstract. The evolution of technologies in recent years has allowed many advances in various areas, such as robotics, the Internet of Things, Big Data, Blockchain, among others.

These advances have allowed to solve many of the problems we face nowadays, such as today, for example, they have been used recently in the fight against Covid-19 which has affected and continues to affect people and organizations around the world.

Taking advantage of the advancement of these technologies, the circular economy concept has been successfully implemented in various spheres of society and in various countries, with the aim of transition from linear economy ideas (produce, consume, and dispose) to more sustainable models (recycle, reuse, and reduce), keeping products and raw materials in circulation if possible, while adding value for society and business.

In this paper we will address how Blockchain can leverage the ideals of the circular economy, analysing and implementing a prototype Blockchain network in the used car parts market.

The structure of this work is based on bibliographical research that served as a basis to collect data and information relevant to the themes in question, as well as the practical implementation of the concepts in the case of the reuse of used parts.

Keywords: Circular economy · Blockchain · Ethereum network · Open market

1 State of the Art

1.1 Blockchain

The ideas behind blockchain are not new, in 1991, Stuart Haber and W. Scott Stornetta introduced a computational solution for digital documents in a way that that they could not be altered. Because of the ease in which digital easily manipulated, they believed it was necessary to create a "time stamp", i.e. date and time on digital documents, allowing to know the period of changes to them. They believed that, to achieve this, two steps were needed steps:

The first is to find a way to stamp the data without being dependent on the characteristics of the physical medium that stores them, making it impossible to change one

A. L. Martins et al. (Eds.): INTSYS 2021, LNICST 426, pp. 71–84, 2022.
https://doi.org/10.1007/978-3-030-97603-3_6

without changing the other. The second step is to create a way that it is impossible to stamp a document with a date and time other than the original (Haber and Stornetta 1991).

In 2004, Hal Finney created a system that is the precursor to Bitcoin, the Reusable Proof of Work. This system receives "hashcash" as a Porf of Work token, in return it creates tokens signed by the RSA2 cryptographic system, which can be transferred from person to person and exchanged for new RPOW's at each step. Until then, the cryptographies of digital currencies had a major problem of double spending, which was the risk that a coin could be spent twice. The RPOW solves this problem by keeping the ownership of tokens registered on a trusted server.

In 2008, a person or an entity named Satoshi Nakamoto, published an article describing a decentralized digital currency based on peer-to-peer technology and in January 2009 Bitcoin was launched. The most important thing about Bitcoin is that it is a technology that not only has a decentralised system behind it, but all transactions are stored in an immutable ledger, where there is no financial behind it, relying more on the network than a central entity (Satoshi Nakamoto 2008).

The blockchain can be defined as a decentralised network in which transactions take place transactions occur between its members transparently and openly without the assistance of intermediaries (Mougayar and Buterin 2016).

One of the most important components of the blockchain system are Smart Contracts, applications that run on a blockchain network and are a set of rules that help in the process of streamlining transactions.

The concept of Smart Contracts was first introduced by Nick Szabo in 1994 but had a long time in inactivity because there was no platform that could implement these rules. That changed with the creation of Bitcoin and since then, Smart Contracts have gained a lot of popularity and are essential today in any Blockchain network (Mougayar and Buterin 2016).

Swan (2015) states that what makes Smart Contracts different from other types of agreements are the existence of three elements, autonomy, self-sufficiency and decentralisation. Autonomy, means that after start-up, they do not need human interventions. Self-sufficiency means that Smart Contracts have the ability to gather sufficient resources to be able to function, for example processing power processing power. And finally, decentralisation allows these rules to be executed in several nodes in the network.

Another important concept in blockchain technology is the consensus algorithm, allowing different participants to agree to validate transactions that are requested in a blockchain network. Mougayar and Buterin (2016) states that consensus is the first layer of a decentralised architecture such as blockchain; users do not need to know how that algorithm works, despite the dependency, trust and security that it offers. This allows that there are never repeated values in the same transaction.

1.2   Benefits of a Blockchain Network

The benefits of blockchain technology go beyond Bitcoin or other implementations of cryptocurrency. Its applications are many and already help in the resolution of real problems that can be found in the political, social, environmental, scientific, among others.

According to Mougayar (2016) Blockchain brings benefits at the level of cost reduction, greater transparency between the parties involved, less risk in transactions, greater productivity, greater efficiency in solving tasks, higher quality and by consequently, more gains and growth.

1.3 Challenges in Implementing a Blockchain Network

Despite the benefits that can be achieved in the long term mentioned above, Blockchain presents some challenges nowadays. Mougayar (2016) mentions that Blockchain just like so many other technologies will take some time to be widely accepted due to various challenges and barriers, whether technical or human.

The same author cites some factors such as infrastructures in developmental stage, scarcity of skilled human talent, scalability problems, that is, the ability to accommodate increases in users in a network such as Bitcoin, privacy issues, cryptocurrency volatility, initial implementation costs, lack of understanding of the potential of Blockchain, distrust between members of a network, among others.

2 Circular Economy

The current business landscape is changing extremely fast, bringing to the fore new challenges that force organisations to be more adaptive and innovative. With the scarcity of resources, air and sea pollution, and an increased concern about climate change, social actors are becoming increasingly aware of the need to implement sustainable, renewable and long-lasting measures in order to avoid irreparable damage for future generations. Many companies are following the changes in governmental laws and customer's consumption habits, adopting measures such as the use of recycled materials and/or cutting down on the use of plastics.

In this context, the circular economy emerges as a new approach to face the challenges that the current world proposes us, transforming them into added value for the society and business, offering the ability to redesign a positive and sustainable future.

The circular economy offers a new pathway and a new way of making use of used products, extracting as much value as possible through reuse and recycling before they are safely disposed of in nature (MacArthur 2013).

The major goal of the circular economy is to make the transition from the linear economy that is based on the principles of producing, consuming and disposing products to an approach of reusing recycle and reduce in the consumption of materials and raw materials, i.e. keeping products in a looping stage for as long as possible. Essentially, the circular economy eliminates the idea of waste, changing the way we produce and consume, creating a healthy and thriving ecosystem for society and the economy (Lacy et al. 2020).

The same authors maintain that although many efforts have already been made, much remains to be achieved because companies focus more on instant gains and programmes that can be regressed to current business models. They feel that the way to achieve the potential of the circular economy is to underpin it with the technologies of the fourth industrial revolution in ways that capture new business opportunities and strengthen core businesses. That is, to analyse the waste that is operations, rethink the life cycle of products or services in order to optimise their use and eliminate waste. Another thing to improve is the organisational culture, that is, to root the principles of circularity in the new practices and procedures.

2.1 Benefits of a Circular Economy

The potentials of the circular economy are still being discovered, and although they are limited geographically, it is estimated that the values of savings in consumption of materials and products could be as high as USD 700 billion globally (MacArthur 2013).

According to studies by the Ellen Macarthur Foundation, the benefits of savings can be found on a number of fronts, notably in the UK catering industry, where processing waste in line with the principles of the circular economy principles can generate a profit of $1.5 billion annually, while at the same time providing new business opportunities for local community and investors. The same study mentions that another opportunity can be found in the fashion industry, where clothes at the end of their life cycles can be reused to produce other types of products or recycle the yarns for future production.

Lacy and Rutqvist (2015) state that another benefit of the circular economy can be identified in product packaging. They use the example of the Carlsberg Circular Community, which is an initiative that relies on the creation of future generation packaging bottles optimised for recycling and reuse, while delivering added value and quality to customers. The aim of this initiative is to encourage customers that these bottles are not materials to be wasted, but rather to be reused for a long period of time, in the most correct way possible.

2.2 Challenges in Implementing the Circular Economy

P. Lacy et al. (2020) state that despite the gains made in recent years, there are still barriers that hinder the application of the circular economy still exist. They say that societies culture or habit of consumption, i.e. many people are still attached to the idea of buying, using and disposing of products. For example, smartphones that may have 4 or 5 years of useful life, but the demand for new models and trends, limit the ability to use used parts or sell second-hand products.

Other barriers that hinder the implementation of the circular economy are the policies and regulations of governments in many countries. According to the report "Paving the way for a circular economy: insights on status and potentials" by the European Environment Agency (EEA) countries use regulation basically for recycling, waste management and energy recovery. On the other hand, the ideas of reuse, consumption and green development have fewer demanding rules and are usually just campaign labels (EEA Report, no. 11/2019).

3 Application of Blockchain in Circular Economy

Blockchain and the circular economy are two emerging and disruptive concepts that promise to transform the social, economic and technological lives of social actors.

Kouhizadeh et al. (2020) state that blockchain offers capabilities in the implementation of the principles in various ways, such as transparency of information, verifying the origin of a product and tracking its life cycle as well as showing the users involved in the operations. One of the most practical use of blockchain in the circular economy is the application of the principles of transparency in supply chain management. Participants in this network can track and verify the life cycle of a product from the origin of raw materials to the final manufacture.

The same authors state that despite the advantages already mentioned, the use of blockchain in the circular economy in supply chain management, may bring some drawbacks such as, as the sharing of confidential information of the network members, as well as other information that the members do not want to share.

Another advantage that blockchain offers is the Reusable Proof of Work used in ledgers, which reduce the risks of failure of blockchain networks and cyber-attacks.

But on the other hand, this has a cost which is the power consumption in the computations required (Mougayar and Buterin 2016).

Another difficulty is the lack of exchange of information between companies in a given industry, as these often prefer to focus on their own customers (Kouhizadeh et al. 2019).

The use of blockchain in the circular economy encourages changes in habits and consumer behaviours. This can be achieved through rewards on the purchases of products that build on the ideas of the circular economy. Rewards that can be tokens or cryptocurrencies for customers (Kouhizadeh et al. 2020).

Finally, we can conclude that despite the benefits that can be found in the adoption of blockchain in the circular economy, these two concepts are still nascent and not all successful applications end up serving all sectors of society. It takes a lot of work and engagement among communities, entrepreneurs, governments, and investors to overcome the barriers that prevent the widespread use of circular economy principles based on the potentials that blockchain can offer.

4 Traceability for Blockchain-Based Circular Economy

Blockchain technology allows its authorised users to send data and validate information that cannot be manipulated by anyone. Therefore, when there is a record of the occurrence of an event and the associated data is recorded in the chain, that event is immutable and a record of the event occurrence can be viewed on the allowed networks, based on the agreed privacy settings.

This means that we can reconstruct the entire history of the object in the supply chain, keeping a validated event log available to users with the touch of a smartphone. This functionality is relevant and useful for the recycling of automotive parts and beyond, as it provides a fundamental basis for any verifiable and defensible statement that can be made about products.

If industries are effectively moved from a linear to a circular economy, the interconnectedness of data may be the revelation that catalyses them towards self-perpetuation. Within these new ecosystems, traceability mechanisms and Chain of Custody (CoC) models can substantiate any assertion of content that value chain stakeholders may wish to make. Points of evidence generated through these models and mechanisms provide evidence that recycled material remains active, i.e. in use as an ongoing resource and not ending up in storage.

While evidence of responsible handling and validated claims is important, traceability important, traceability mechanisms can support insights by connecting data that was previously isolated. When we allocate a digital identity to materials at the batch or component level and trace it through a value chain, we are able to capture information from primary production through use and ultimately its future disposal or reuse.

4.1 Sustainability

By having visibility of all actors involved in the handling of this material, we can gather sustainability credentials and allow primary stakeholders the opportunity to assess and report on their appointed suppliers approach to human and environmental sustainability factors.

The additional transparency of material flows can allow industry and entities to access more data to build reliable life cycle analyses and assess the environmental impacts of a product or value chain with more accurately.

4.2 Efficiencies

Blockchain, can use smart contracts to track and automate transactions without the need for a centralised authority. There is untapped potential to increase efficiency and reduce costs with blockchain applications across industries for their supply chains. The transparency that blockchain offers also supports more data insights into material flows, making it easier to prevent fraud.

5   Traceability for Automotive Parts Chains

To deal with the supply of spare parts the blockchain technology proposes to permanently record all movements, modifications, restorations and ownership details of spare parts in a transparent and tamper-proof distributed ledger. Furthermore, the transparency of transaction records (e.g. frequent component maintenance) increases the trust of customers and regularity authorities. Using immutable transaction records, blockchain technology helps identify counterfeit parts, minimise fraud, reduce component maintenance costs and delays, and establish asset provenance based on the traceability feature. Still, the track and trace service help keep track of a component or document during its shipment.

Validated traceability enables in today's more transparent and responsible economy. What if change could be catalysed by enabling waste producers to connect to second life outcomes, including recycling and beyond? If consumers and industry were given the opportunity to consume their own waste through validated material circularity, perhaps we can improve our current trajectory.

BMW is one of the first groups in the automotive industry to use technology blockchain to improve transparency in its global supply chain, specifically targeting the parts and raw materials procurement segment. To a huge entity like BMW, the use of blockchain can help optimise its operations and increase traceability in its supply chain, while at the same time ensuring that shared data is tamper-proof. The main objective is focused on providing seamless traceability of components and will provide immediate data transparency.

One of the BMW Group's latest projects, PartChain is to enable the collection of tamper-proof and consistently verifiable transaction data in the BMW's supply chain.

In 2019 BMW started a project to track parts via blockchain, involved BMW's plants in Spartanburg, South Carolina and Dingolfing, Germany, as well as three locations of its supplier, Automotive Lighting. The aim is to achieve complete traceability of raw materials with its suppliers.

6 Case Study

Nowadays, consumption is increasing more and more, reaching extremely of products that are only used once and then thrown away. This effect is due to the increase in people's quality of life and also to the increase in consumers purchasing power.

In this way, the importance of reusing products is gaining more and more space in our lives. Most of the industries have implemented policies of recycling and reuse of products, and in the car parts market the scrap yards are places where they collect used parts and consequently sell them at lower prices than at the manufacturers.

The job of the scrap yard is to collect end-of-life vehicles, dismantle and store the parts that can still be reused, so that they can later sell them second-hand at a lower price than a new part would cost. In this sense, they practice a circular economy model, where they reuse products that are practically thrown away or that are at the end of their life.

Although prices are lower for second-hand items, the present system of selling used parts brings many uncertainties to the final consumer. This is notably due to the fact that there is no guarantee when purchasing the product, lack of information uncertainty of the condition of the part and its origin are the main disadvantages that of second-hand products today.

The studies around Blockchain technology have been growing in the last years, presenting revolutionary results in various markets and departments. An implementation of this technology in the used parts market will bring more transparency, information and trust to the final consumer, and as a consequence, the practice of stimulate the practice of circular economy in various entities of this industry.

6.1 Blockchain Applied to the Case Study

The car scrapping centres, or the so-called scrap yards have been the subject of several polemics, many entities operating illegally are pointed out as an environmental problem, processing the parts incorrectly, polluting and damaging the environment. Moreover, the demand for second-hand parts has generated a lot of uncertainty by the consumer at the time of negotiation, the lack of guarantees by the seller, results in an obstacle in the evolution of circular economy in these entities.

The implementation of Blockchain architecture in this used parts market would be the resolution of the problems previously reported. In this way, the acquisition process of a second-hand part will be transparent and secure, generating more trust and value information at the time of purchase. It would be impossible to manipulate and change the information about the origin of the piece. Furthermore, the constant verification on the part of the brands that produced the pieces will facilitate the auditing process by other entities.

Since this is a project based on the circular economy methodology, the whole process of validation and acquisition of used parts will have two types of verifications. Each time that a person wants to get rid of an old car, he will have to deliver it to a certified entity, this transaction will be verified by the public institute for modality and transport that is part of the indirect administration (IMT) in order to be able to cancel the registration and stop paying taxes on the vehicle. Then, the car will be disassembled, and the parts will be registered in the Blockchain, where the brands themselves will validate the information such as serial number, year of production and the type of the part.

This system of validating information on used parts allows greater transparency for the end consumer. On the other hand, scrap shops and workshops, which will implement the Blockchain architecture will automatically become certified entities, where they will be able to sell parts above the normal market average (Table 1).

Table 1. Comparison between traditional processes and Blockchain processes.

Current process	Blockchain process
Lost information - In huge second-hand markets, scrapyards and workshops, customers do not know the origin of the parts, their actual condition	The pieces will be related to their origins, whether they are white label or parts that have never been altered since the year of manufacture of the car. The brands that produced the parts will have to validate information such as part type, year of production and serial number
Non-certified entities - There are scrapyards and workshops operating illegally polluting the environment	All entities will be automatically certified, increasing the quality of their services and consequently the demand
There are stolen cars that are dismantled in scrapyards and illegal workshops, where they are later sold for parts in second-hand markets	With the IMT entity as the validator of ownership, nobody will be able to deliver a stolen car to be sold for parts
Illegal scrap shops that dismantle cars have no authority to cancel a registration. This way people risk losing their car and continue to pay the Single Road Tax. circulation tax	The registration of ownership will be automatic passed to the scrap yard or workshop certified
A process with many polemics and little valid information	Transparent and safe process

6.2 Implementation

After analysing our case, what implications it would have to bear, we moved on to the implementation phase. To implement this solution, we establish the different nodes and actors of our Blockchain network and represented the actions between them.

Nodes: Workshops and Scrap Metal.

Actors: Workshops and Scrap Metal, IMT, Brands, Customer (Fig. 1).

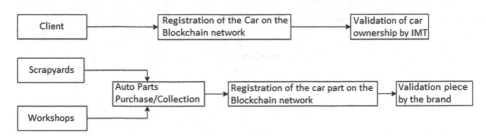

Fig. 1. Information flows.

As we can see in the previous figure, the goal of our Blockchain network is to allow in a sustainable way the reuse of the different parts of the different cars according to a circular economy concept.

Initially the user requests the registration of his car before the validator entity that in this case is the IMT. With this registration the client can later sell his car so that the parts in good condition and viably functional can be used and reused. This IMT registration also allows to guarantee the ownership of the vehicle, so that someone doesn't try to sell a stolen car.

Regarding the scrapyards and workshops, they can opt for the purchase process of the parts that a particular car includes. The parts are collected and registered on our Blockchain network. All this data is then validated by the brand so that no one tries, for example, to insert adulterated parts.

6.2.1 Implementation Objectives and Requirements

The following objectives and requirements have been defined for the functional application of our Blockchain network:

1. Allow the input of information about cars and parts in a secure and transparent way.
2. Automatic registration of ownership.
3. Creation of validating entities that confirm the veracity and integrity of the information.
4. Traceability and origin of all cars and their parts.

6.2.2 Tools and Technology Used

We use Ethereum technology to implement our solution. Ethereum is a decentralized platform capable of executing smart contracts and decentralized applications using blockchain technology.

For the development of smart contracts, we used the Solidity language. This high-level language was created with the intention of allowing the implementation of smart contracts that guarantee and govern the behaviour of our Blockchain network.

The following image illustrates the architecture of our system (Fig. 2):

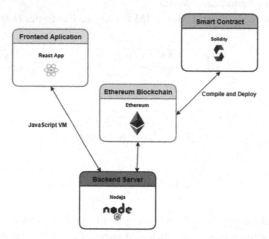

Fig. 2. System architecture.

6.3 Smart Contracts

6.3.1 Smart Contract Cars_BC

Before explaining the reason for implementing this Smart Contract, it is first, important to clarify and define what information our Blockchain network will contain about each car.

The following figure lists the data that the contract will contain and which methods existing (Fig. 3).

This smart contract will contain all the data about the car in question, such as brand, model, engine, and serial number, it will be possible to input all this information into the Blockchain network.

Add Car() Function: Function that allows adding a new car to the Blockcahin network. For this, it is entered data such as the brand, model, engine, other fundamental about the status and ownership of the vehicle. In this transaction is also registered the current owner of the car that is obtained through the "address" present for the user in the network (Fig. 4).

Function Validate_IMT_Car(): Function that allows to supply the supplied information. In case the information is correct, true is returned. If the information is incorrect false is returned. In this case the validating entity is the IMT, and this has its own address that allows distinguee of all other actors of our Blockchain network.

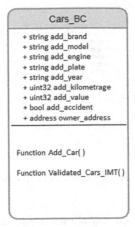

Fig. 3. Smart contract Cars_BC

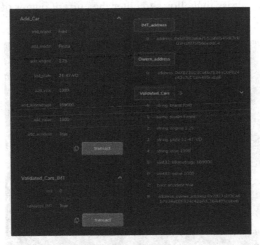

Fig. 4. Function Add_Car().

6.3.2 Smart Contract Parts_BC

As was the case with the smart contract for cars, for parts the method and implementation thinking were similar. The aim is that consultation and information about the different components of each car and that this information is validated by a trustworthy agent, which in this case was chosen to be the brand itself (Fig. 5).

Fig. 5. Smart contract Parts_BC.

AddPiece() Function: Function that allows adding a new piece to the Blockcahin network. Are the different data of the piece are entered as the brand, model, engine and other fundamental data about the state and characteristic part. In this transaction is also registered the owner_adress that allows to enter the current owner of the part (Fig. 6).

Fig. 6. Function Add_Part().

Function Validate_Mark_Piece(): As it happened previously for the case of the car this function allows to validate each one of the pieces through a Boolean variable (True/False). The integrity of this information is performed by the brand through its address in our Blockchain network.

Function Buy_Parts(): Method invoked when a transaction occurs in which the owner of the auto parts is changed. Using the msg.sender function, the address of the caller of this function is obtained and the information is updated in the Blockchain network.

6.3.3 Smart Contract Deploy Contracts

This contract has the function of allowing the 'deployment' of the remaining contracts, i.e., it can be seen as the contract that triggers the first block of our blockchain network. This first block in a Blockchain network can be configured using the genesis.json file and allows different configuration parameters to be set.

In this case the Cars_BC and Parts_BC contracts are created and invoked and added to a list of implemented contracts (Fig. 7).

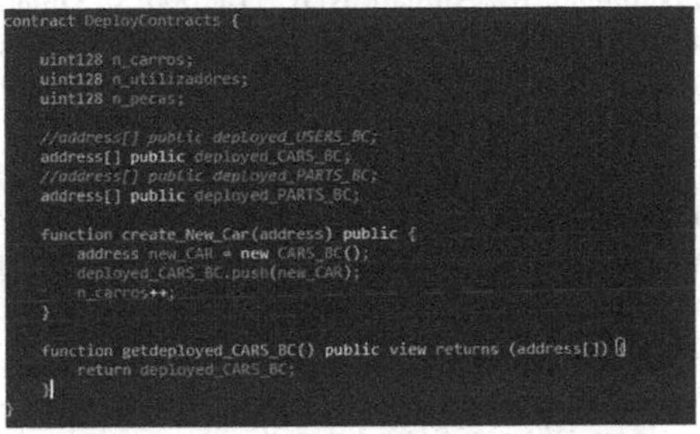

```
contract DeployContracts {

    uint128 n_carros;
    uint128 n_utilizadores;
    uint128 n_pecas;

    //address[] public deployed_USERS_BC;
    address[] public deployed_CARS_BC;
    //address[] public deployed_PARTS_BC;
    address[] public deployed_PARTS_BC;

    function create_New_Car(address) public {
        address new_CAR = new CARS_BC();
        deployed_CARS_BC.push(new_CAR);
        n_carros++;
    }

    function getdeployed_CARS_BC() public view returns (address[])
        return deployed_CARS_BC;
}
```

Fig. 7. Smart contract deploy contracts.

7 Conclusion

The main objective of this work is the connection of blockchain technology with the concept of circular economy. The model was implemented for a car scrapping network, including scrapyards and workshops, where used parts will be registered and reused by consumers. The demonstration part allows used parts to be added to the network associated with its original car, facilitating access to information for both consumers as well as producers and suppliers.

When implementing this project, we identified a number of possible improvements that blockchain could bring to today's societies. Knowing the life cycle life of products and their origins, consumers will have a greater motivation to practice the concept of the circular economy in their daily lives.

Based on pillars such as accessibility, reliability and immutability our work above all aim to encourage society to think outside the box and no longer third parties simply to certify a fact and encourage the community to develop self-sufficient and scalable solutions.

However, technologies like Blockchain have challenges to be optimized as high consumption of energy spent for its operationalization, as well as mistrust of actors and competition with other business models.

However, we are sure that the application needs improvements to be adapted to the real context, but our main intention is to generate debate on the important circular economy, a disruptive issue in itself, allied to blockchain aiming at having a big impact in the in the next years in the way we live, think and consume products.

Funding. This work is partially funded by national funds through FCT - Fundação para a Ciência e Tecnologia, I.P., under the project FCT UIDB/04466/2020.

Data Availability. Link to the implementation: https://github.com/ddces-iscteiulpt/Blockchain-CircularEconomy-2021.git.

References

Hasan, H.R., Salah, K., Jayaraman, R., Ahmad, R.W., Yaqoob, I., Omar, M.: Blockchain-based solution for the traceability of spare parts in manufacturing. IEEE Access **8**, 100308–100322 (2020). https://doi.org/10.1109/ACCESS.2020.2998159

Haber, S., Stornetta, W.S.: How to time-stamp a digital document. In: Menezes, A.J., Vanstone, S.A. (eds.) CRYPTO 1990. LNCS, vol. 537, pp. 437–455. Springer, Heidelberg (1991). https://doi.org/10.1007/3-540-38424-3_32

Robson, C., Watanabe, Y., Numao, M.: Parts traceability for manufacturers. In: Proceedings - International Conference on Data Engineering, May, pp. 1212–1221 (2007). https://doi.org/10.1109/ICDE.2007.368980

Mougayar, W., Buterin, V.: The Business Blockchain: Promise, Practice, and Application of the Next Internet Technology. Wiley (2016). https://www.wiley.com/enae/The+Business+Blockchain%3A+Promise%2C+Practice%2C+and+Application+of+the+Next+Internet+Technology-p-9781119300311

Lacy, P., Long, J., Spindler, W.: The Circular Economy Handbook: Realizing the Circular Advantage. Palgrave Macmillan, London (2020)

MacArthur, E.: Towards the Circular Economy: Opportunities for the Consumer Goods Sector, pp. 1–112. Ellen MacArthur Foundation (2013)

Böckel, A., Nuzum, A.K., Weissbrod, I.: Blockchain for the circular economy: analysis of the research-practice gap. Sustain. Prod. Consum. **25**(December 2020), 525–539 (2021). https://doi.org/10.1016/j.spc.2020.12.006

Kouhizadeh, M., Sarkis, J., Zhu, Q.: At the nexus of blockchain technology, the circular economy, and product deletion. Appl. Sci. (Switzerland) **9**(8), 1712 (2019). https://doi.org/10.3390/app9081712

Monti, M., Rasmussen, S.: RAIN: a bio-inspired communication and data storage infrastructure. Artif. Life **23**(4), 552–557 (2017). https://doi.org/10.1162/ARTL_a_00247

Swan, M.: Melanie Swan (2015)

Kouhizadeh, M., Zhu, Q., Sarkis, J.: Blockchain and the circular economy: potential tensions and critical reflections from practice. Prod. Plann. Control **31**(11–12), 950–966 (2020). https://doi.org/10.1080/09537287.2019.1695925

Enabling Citizen-Centric ITS Services Through Blockchain and Human Incentives

Sofia Martins[✉], António Costa, Zafeiris Kokkinogenis,
and Rosaldo J. F. Rossetti

Laboratório de Inteligência Artificial e Ciência de Computadores (LIACC),
Departamento de Engenharia Informática (DEI), Faculdade de Engenharia da
Universidade do Porto (FEUP), Rua Dr. Roberto Frias, 4200-465 Porto, Portugal
{up201606033,up201609065,zafeiris.kokkinogenis,rossetti}@fe.up.pt

Abstract. Given the increasing migration of populations from rural to metropolitan areas, it is imperative to make urban mobility more efficient in order to mitigate traffic, pollution and degradation of the quality of life. In this paper, we propose a system that attempts to influence drivers to follow a certain route by means of an incentive. The proposals are put forward based on predefined urban traffic network indicators in need of optimization, such as the carbon dioxide emissions in a specific route or another equally compatible with our model. Our hypothesis is that influencing drivers' behaviours can lead to the optimization of such indicators. The accumulated incentives are registered in a Blockchain network in order to ensure the unchanging and reliable registration of route proposals accepted by drivers. Additionally, we describe an application developed as a proof of concept and as a basis for future work.

Keywords: UVAR · Urban vehicle access regulations · Blockchain · ITS · Intelligent transport systems

1 Introduction

In 2018, 55% of the world's population lived in urban areas, as opposed to only 30% in 1950, and it is estimated that by 2050 more than two thirds will be living in urban centres [19]. This growth has been accompanied by an increasing need for mobility in urban centres, resulting in traffic congestion, emergencies and unforeseen accidents, and requiring significant changes in transport infrastructure. Inefficiencies result in lost time, reduced safety for both vehicles and pedestrians, high pollution, degradation of the quality of life, and waste of non-renewable fossil fuels [5].

Therefore, many cities and towns struggle to balance traffic congestion, noise levels, air pollution, accessibility, habitability and other pressures of urban life. One way to solve these issues is to regulate the vehicles or journeys access to urban infrastructure, balancing the need for vehicles accessing an area with a

A. L. Martins et al. (Eds.): INTSYS 2021, LNICST 426, pp. 85–94, 2022.
https://doi.org/10.1007/978-3-030-97603-3_7

reduction in the total number of vehicles. Three motivations stand out in the adoption of these measures: environmental aims, raising revenues, and reduce congestion [16].

This paper re-examines these issues and proposes an architecture based on Blockchain technology, in an attempt to mitigate them. The Blockchain is one type of Distributed Ledger Technology (DLT) which has become disruptive in recent years. More specifically, it serves as a digitized, decentralized public ledger of data, assets and all pertinent transactions that have been executed and shared among participants in the network [15]. Blockchain networks are categorized into public and private Blockchains; the difference between the two resides in the fact that public Blockchains allow anyone to join the network and execute transactions (as is the case of the Bitcoin application), whereas the latter enforces a controlled environment through participants' authentication that enables different access permissions. Today, there are various Blockchain frameworks available, offering functionalities that fit either (or both) private and public networks. Hyperledger Fabric[1] and Openchain[2] are just two examples of these frameworks, which promote the design and implementation of private Blockchain networks.

Key to the Blockchain technology is the concept of Smart Contracts, which are designed by the Blockchain developer and encapsulate the logic behind a value transaction within the network. These are automatically executed upon the fulfilment of certain conditions, therefore automating business processes by eliminating the need of a third-party intermediary for overseeing the transaction in real-time [15]. Moreover, ongoing studies have attempted to expand on their features, namely to embed them with pro-active behaviour [2], as well as agreement technologies in Multiagent Systems in the context of autonomous negotiations [3,17].

In this paper, we propose the adoption of a Blockchain architecture that manages rewards issued to drivers. The architecture encompasses two main components: a Server and a Client Application. We envision the latter to be deployed at mobile devices running on vehicles during commutes. Within those periods, drivers accept or reject route proposals issued by the Server and subsequently presented on the mobile device. The route proposals may incur some degree of inconvenience for the driver, such as added commute time, so a proper incentive mechanism needs to be employed. We adopt a reward-based incentive, which could include, for example, free tickets to access the cities' public transportation system. As a consequence, we expect these rewards to be determined by each municipality. We hypothesize that these incentives can lead to improvements in various indicators, including those related to carbon emissions and traffic congestion, as the Server establishes the proposals considering a specific objective: the optimization of those indicators. In addition, we rely on Blockchain technology for the distribution of rewards with added transaction transparency and reliability of drivers' compliance with accepted proposals, using Smart Contracts.

The remaining sections of this paper are organized as follows: Sect. 2 briefly describes the state of the art concerning Urban Vehicle Access Regulation

---

[1] Hyperledger Fabric, https://www.hyperledger.org/use/fabric.
[2] Openchain, https://www.openchain.org.

(UVAR); Sect. 3 elaborates on the technical aspects of the proposed architecture; Sect. 4 presents a proof of concept (PoC) that we have designed and implemented, and highlights preliminary findings collected from our experiments on the PoC; finally, Sect. 5 gathers conclusions and outlines relevant future approaches.

2   State of the Art

The main objective of the Urban Vehicle Access Regulation (UVAR) is to regulate the access of certain vehicles to specific areas, based on their class or purpose, mainly for air quality reasons, but also for long-term policies and objectives such as reducing congestion, noise and carbon emissions, improving the quality of life, and the attractiveness of urban and tourist centres [7].

Several techniques and typologies have been adopted to implement UVARs, either by physical restriction of access, such as physical barriers or traffic signs, or through application of circulation charges in reserved areas, toll rings or area license-based fees; such charges may vary according to the time of day, distance or duration of the journey, or type of vehicle [16].

The concept of Tradable Credits Scheme (TCS) was proposed as a way to manage daily traffic congestion by pre-scheduling the departure time in a competition among commuters to reduce travel costs [10], but also as a way to control emissions by encouraging users to switch from internal combustion to zero-emission vehicles in an approach where a central authority determines TCS parameters, such as credit and charging models by vehicle type [14]. Emissions Trading has been implemented by many governments to comply with international agreements and protocols. The transport sector has a large share in emissions. By implementing a *cap and trade* scheme at road user level, with distribution of future emissions among individuals, Blockchain technology can play a key role by increasing security, end-user control and transparency [6].

Over the past few years, the concept of gamification has been approached as a mean of promoting engagement and behaviour change, with positive and playful experiences, in non-game contexts [4]. Using information technologies embedded into everyday tasks and services [1], users are given support in creating global value [9]. Within the field of transport it is suggested to implement this concept to encourage more energy-efficient behaviour, based on the accumulation of rewards and creating competition between "players" [18], or for motivating driver cooperation in lane-changing scenarios [13]. Studies indicate that, at least in the first phase, a reward strategy should be used to encourage pro-social behaviour, rather than punishment, which plays a more appropriate role in maintaining it [8].

3   Proposed Approach

The main motivation for the development of the proposed system is to render cities more efficient and sustainable, leading vehicles to follow alternative routes rather than others that include roads with special characteristics that may be momentary, such as rush-hour congestion, or persistent, such as those where efforts are made to reduce carbon dioxide emissions. We define the latter route roads as *exclusion* roads.

Different vehicles may coexist within this system. We consider, for example, the distinct roles of a typical passenger vehicle and an emergency vehicle; undoubtedly, the latter should have indiscriminate access to any road, regardless of it being an *exclusion* road or not. In this setting, drivers of regular vehicles are motivated to follow one of the routes proposed by the system. We designate this set of routes with common *origin* and *destination* addresses as the *Special proposal set*.

Influencing driver's behaviour change, that is, leading the driver to select one of the *special proposal* routes instead of the fastest route is not sufficient without a proper incentive since, most often, the former will not overlap with the latter specially considering the sustainable driving factors. The choice of a proper incentive should be managed by a municipality and could vary from monetary incentives to free tickets to access the cities' public transportation system; in the latter case, the incentive alone would also foster the city's environmental sustainability.

3.1   The Android App, The MSP and The CA

The proposed architecture, as depicted in Fig. 1, includes an Android App component; the assumption being made is that each vehicle has associated a mobile device, where the Android App is installed. Drivers may register their vehicles through a Membership Service Provider (MSP), which is responsible for requesting to a Certification Authority (CA) the public and private keys that uniquely identify the vehicle and prove its identity. Each vehicle is registered with the MSP through its License Plate. Having a mapping of the cryptographic hashes generated from these License Plates to the vehicle category, the MSP is able to recognise to which category each vehicle belongs.

3.2   The Server

Upon registration within the Android application, the driver may access its navigation mode and select an origin-destination pair for its upcoming trip, as in all navigation applications that are available in the market. The Server's REST API provides the list of available locations along with this first request from the Client Application. It then submits the list of alternative routes, some of which may include *exclusion* roads according to their momentary or persistent characteristics, which are properly monitored by the Server. The set of routes that do not traverse any *exclusion* road comprise the *special proposal* set and provide the means to influence the driver's route selection strategy.

The incentive mechanism, in turn, motivates the need for a system that is capable of properly managing the set of incentive transactions that occur whenever the drivers opt for one of the *special proposal* routes. Among the possible candidate solutions to address this need, one stands out today: the Blockchain.

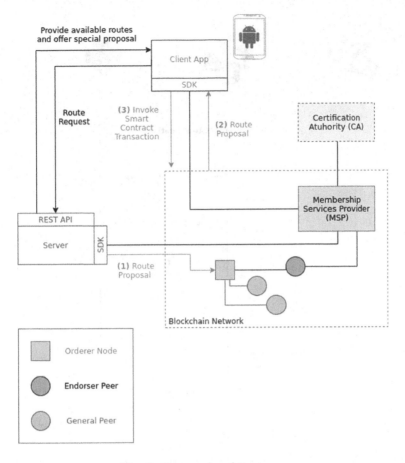

Fig. 1. Proposed architecture.

3.3   Blockchain System

Any DLT system – such as Blockchain – enables the proper transfer of value, namely through immutability, consensus and security. Within the scope of the proposed system, the Blockchain provides the means to record drivers' compliance with accepted proposed routes, which have inherent value in the form of incentives.

In Fig. 1 we can observe the interplay of the Server, the Client App and the Blockchain Network; the previous component follows a similar architecture as the one implemented by the Hyperledger Fabric framework. Whilst the Server replies to the Client App with a set of *special proposal* routes it also issues one transaction proposal for each of those routes, through the SDK. The proposal is signed by the Server using its private key (since it is also registered with the MSP). Upon this stage, the proposal enters the Blockchain network and is passed to the Orderer Node, which asks the Endorser Peer to validate the Server's key by

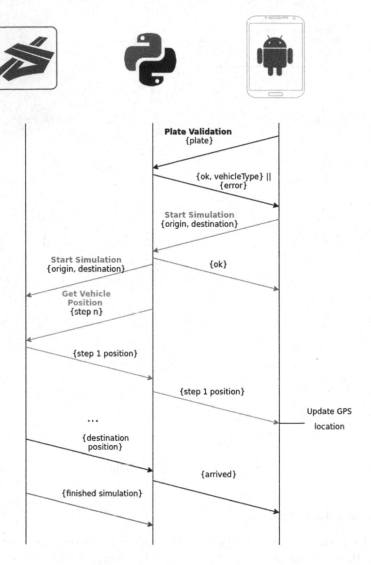

Fig. 2. Experimental setup.

consulting the MSP. If the proposal is successfully validated (the key is accepted, that is, it is recognized by the MSP and belongs to the one possible proposal initiator – the Server) then it is delivered to the Client App through the SDK. Finally, if the driver accepts one of these proposals, its private key is used to sign the proposal and invoke the proper Smart Contract execution (that encapsulates the transaction conditions) to the Blockchain Network. Again, the Orderer Node initiates the validation of the last signature and, upon receiving the confirmation of the validity of the proposal, it generates a transaction block and delivers it to the General Peers, which record it, thereby maintaining the integrity of the network and ensuring the immutable recording of the transaction.

4   Proof of Concept

The demonstration of the Proof of Concept was conducted using SUMO (Simulation of Urban MObility), an open source microscopic and continuous multi-modal traffic simulation package [11], enabling us to individually model each vehicle and its dynamics [12]. The city of Porto, together it is usual traffic flow, compose our experimental scenario. Figure 3 illustrates this scenario on our SUMO environment, which is based on OpenStreetMap. The TraCI (Traffic Control Interface) API enables access to the simulated vehicles and manipulation of their behaviour in real time. A route was considered between Campo dos Mártires da Pátria and Rua de Camões, with a reserved access area in Rua dos Clérigos.

A Python application is employed as a middleware between the traffic simulator and an emulated Android mobile device. It acts as a logical unit to control the driver's decisions. In addition, it exchanges the vehicle's geolocation with the respective Android device, that is, mocks the Android device's GPS location, as given in Fig. 2. In turn, the Android device executes an application through which drivers can accept or reject route proposals, as expected from a real-world deployment in which the driver would be assisted by the application running in its mobile phone during commute. Figure 4 depicts some *screens* of the application we have developed and emulated in our simulations. Also, for simplicity of the experiment, it takes on the role of the CA and the MSP depicted in Fig. 1, with information about the classes of vehicles and the restricted access zones. As a result, it carries out class authentication of the vehicle, distinguishing between a private passenger vehicle and a priority emergency vehicle.

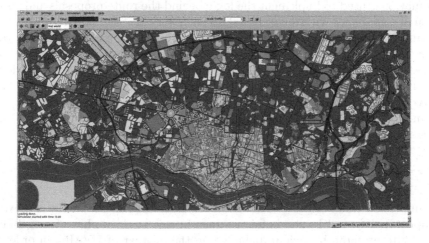

Fig. 3. Porto city map in SUMO.

Fig. 4. Application screens: *login* and *navigation*.

The Android application issues the identification of the vehicle to the system for validation of the registration and vehicle type (*emergency* or *passenger*), by means of the MSP and the CA, mimicked by the middleware as in Fig. 2. This information is used to implement the logic behind the route proposals and verification of compliance with the proposals. The driver chooses an origin-destination pair and has the possibility to choose between two routes, one of which will avoid the exclusion zone, subject to an incentive, and will receive a bonus by accepting the proposed alternative route and following it until reaching the preset destination. However, when entering the exclusion zone, emergency vehicles will only receive a notification as navigational information, whereas passenger vehicles, encouraged to change their behaviour, will receive a warning of breach of the proposed agreement.

5   Conclusions and Future Work

The implementation of the UVARs has been essentially a task in the context of European policy and local administrations. In this work, we have focused on a strategy to promote behavioural change, in the context of UVARs, in order to encourage more sustainable practice in urban centres and to remove car traffic from the most sensitive areas. The prospect of being able to achieve this goal, serves as a continuous incentive for future research.

We have proposed an architecture for a system that addresses the interplay of gamification, the pervasiveness of mobile devices and the Blockchain technology. In addition, we have presented a proof of concept, by means of an urban mobility simulator, which aimed at illustrating the client-level implementation of this system.

Future work will focus on the Distributed Ledger-level of the system, through the deployment of an Hyperledger Fabric-based network, operating through programmable Smart Contracts to ensure compliance with the conditions regarding route acceptance, leading to incentive recognition and auditing. In addition, further development of the system will rely on the current experimental setup, using the *Mock GPS* functionality.

Acknowledgment. This work is a result of project DynamiCITY: Fostering Dynamic Adaptation of Smart Cities to Cope with Crises and Disruptions, with reference NORTE-01-0145-FEDER-000073, supported by Norte Portugal Regional Operational Programme (NORTE 2020), under the PORTUGAL 2020 Partnership Agreement, through the European Regional Development Fund (ERDF). This research has been developed within the Artificial Intelligence and Computer Science Laboratory, University of Porto (LIACC), FCT/UID/CEC/0027/2020, funded by national funds through the FCT/MCTES (PIDDAC).

References

1. Bui, A., Veit, D., Webster, J.: Gamification - a novel phenomenon or a new wrapping for existing concepts? In: Thirty Sixth International Conference on Information Systems, Fort Worth, December 2015
2. Ciatto, G., Maffi, A., Mariani, S., Omicini, A.: Smart contracts are more than objects: pro-activeness on the blockchain. In: Prieto, J., Das, A.K., Ferretti, S., Pinto, A., Corchado, J.M. (eds.) Blockchain and Applications, pp. 45–53. Advances in Intelligent Systems and Computing, Springer, Cham (2020). https://doi.org/10.1007/978-3-030-23813-1_6
3. Ciatto, G., Mariani, S., Omicini, A., Zambonelli, F.: From agents to blockchain: stairway to integration. Appl. Sci. **10**, 7460 (2020). https://doi.org/10.3390/app10217460
4. Deterding, S., Dixon, D., Khaled, R., Nacke, L.: From game design elements to gamefulness: defining gamification. In: Proceedings of the 15th International Academic MindTrek Conference: Envisioning Future Media Environments. MindTrek 2011, vol. 11, pp. 9–15. Association for Computing Machinery, September 2011
5. Dimitrakopoulos, G., Demestichas, P.: Intelligent transportation systems. IEEE Veh. Technol. Mag. **5**(1), 77–84 (2010). https://doi.org/10.1109/MVT.2009.935537
6. Eckert, J., López, D., Azevedo, C.L., Farooq, B.: A blockchain-based user-centric emission monitoring and trading system for multi-modal mobility. In: 2020 Forum on Integrated and Sustainable Transportation Systems (FISTS), pp. 328–334, November 2020. https://doi.org/10.1109/FISTS46898.2020.9264892

7. Enei, R.: Vehicle types, exemptions and (cross-border) enforcement of successful urban vehicle access regulations (UVARs) schemes across Europe. Technical Report, European Commission, Directorate-General for Mobility and Transport, April 2017
8. Góis, A.R., Santos, F.P., Pacheco, J.M., Santos, F.C.: Reward and punishment in climate change dilemmas. Sci. Rep. **9**(1), 16193 (2019). https://doi.org/10.1038/s41598-019-52524-8
9. Huotari, K., Hamari, J.: Defining gamification: a service marketing perspective. In: Proceedings of the 16th International Academic MindTrek Conference, pp. 17–22. MindTrek 2012, ACM, New York, NY, USA, October 2012
10. Liang, L., Xu, M.: Using tradable credit scheme for morning commuting congestion Management with an activity-based approach. In: 2019 IEEE Intelligent Transportation Systems Conference (ITSC), pp. 962–967, October 2019. https://doi.org/10.1109/ITSC.2019.8916997
11. Lopez, P.A., et al.: Microscopic traffic simulation using sumo. In: The 21st IEEE International Conference on Intelligent Transportation Systems. IEEE (2018). https://elib.dlr.de/124092/
12. Lopez, P.A., et al.: Microscopic traffic simulation using SUMO. In: The 21st IEEE International Conference on Intelligent Transportation Systems, pp. 2575–2582. 2019 IEEE Intelligent Transportation Systems Conference (ITSC), IEEE, Maui, HI, November 2018. https://doi.org/10.1109/ITSC.2018.8569938
13. Lütteken, N., Zimmermann, M., Bengler, K.J.: Using gamification to motivate human cooperation in a lane-change scenario. In: 2016 IEEE 19th International Conference on Intelligent Transportation Systems (ITSC), pp. 899–906, November 2016
14. Miralinaghi, M., Peeta, S.: Promoting zero-emissions vehicles using robust multi-period tradable credit scheme. Transp. Res. Part D: Transp. Environ. **75**, 265–285 (2019). https://doi.org/10.1016/j.trd.2019.08.012
15. Nawari, N.O., Ravindran, S.: Blockchain and the built environment: potentials and limitations. J. Build. Eng. **25**, 100832 (2019). https://doi.org/10.1016/j.jobe.2019.100832
16. Ricci, A., et al.: Study on urban vehicle access regulations. Final Report, European commission, directorate-general for mobility and transport, April 2017
17. Rúbio, T.R.P.M., Kokkinogenis, Z., Cardoso, H.L., Rossetti, R.J.F., Oliveira, E.: Regulating blockchain smart contracts with agent-based markets. In: Moura Oliveira, P., Novais, P., Reis, L.P. (eds.) Progress in Artificial Intelligence. pp. 399–411. Lecture Notes in Computer Science, Springer, Cham (2019). https://doi.org/10.1007/978-3-030-30241-2_34
18. Shreenath, V.M., Kornevs, M., Raghothama, J., Meijer, S.: A feasibility study for gamification in transport maintenance: requirements to implement gamification in heterogeneous organizations. In: 2015 7th International Conference on Games and Virtual Worlds for Serious Applications (VS-Games), pp. 1–7, September 2015
19. United Nations, Department of Economic and Social Affairs, Population Division: World urbanization prospects: the 2018 revision (2019)

Relay Communication Solutions for First Responders

Tiago Rocha da Silva[✉], Luís Fernandes, José Gonçalves, Paulo Chaves, and Vasco Bexiga

INOV Instituto de Engenharia de Sistemas e Computadores Inovação, Lisboa, Portugal
{tiago.r.silva,luis.fernandes,jose.goncalves,paulo.chaves,
vasco.bexiga}@inov.pt
https://www.inov.pt/

Abstract. First Responders (FRs) frequently intervene in dangerous environments, result of natural catastrophes, technological disaster or terrorist attacks, for that it is crucial to maintain their protection and operational effectiveness, namely their capacity in terms of situational awareness and communication in adverse situations. In the event of a disaster, communication networks may not be available at all, different reasons e.g. infrastructure collapse, denial of service or even the area of the incident may not be covered by communication services. This paper presents innovate project to respond to emergencies, focus on a resilient network solution easy to be deployed, to mitigate this problem and extent the existent communication networks. The solution uses nodes to relay communications from the nearest point to a farthest point with live communications, permitting long range communication of FR's wearable sensor data. The nodes can be installed in UAVs (Unmanned Aerial Vehicle), mounted on the ground on tripods or even on UGVs (Unmanned Ground Vehicle), the solution is modular and auto-configurable. The core/backbone of the Wireless Resilient communication network is supported in Mesh topology (802.11s), that provides any-to-any connections between nodes, these nodes can be dynamically added or removed, the network will always try to find a path to deliver data, each node is also simultaneously Wi-Fi Access Point (802.11n).

Keywords: Mesh network · First Responder · Resilient network · Relay communication · Extending the communication · Transmitting wearable data · 80211s

1 Introduction

First responders (FRs) are the people who are among the first to arrive and provide assistance at the disaster scene. They are typically professionals with specialized training, including law enforcement officers, firefighters, emergency medical personnel, rescuers, K9 units, civil protection authorities and other related organizations [3].

© ICST Institute for Computer Sciences, Social Informatics and Telecommunications Engineering 2022
Published by Springer Nature Switzerland AG 2022. All Rights Reserved
A. L. Martins et al. (Eds.): INTSYS 2021, LNICST 426, pp. 95–112, 2022.
https://doi.org/10.1007/978-3-030-97603-3_8

Due to the nature of their work, FRs are often operating in risky and hazardous environments, including collapsed, burning or flooded buildings, darkness, smoke, heat, and broken communications. Furthermore, FRs may experience health incidents (e.g. sudden illness, dizziness or exhaustion strokes) during operations, which can prevent them from completing their mission, and, more importantly, put their own life at risk. FRs may often not notice early signs or choose to ignore them in favor of accomplishing their mission, which can lead to become additional casualties of the disaster [2].

FASTER [1] is a research and innovation project, funded by the European Commission, that aims to address the challenges associated with the protection of FRs in hazardous environments, while at the same time enhancing their capabilities in terms of situational awareness and communication. FASTER's overall concept is illustrated in Fig. 1, where it shows that at the heart of FASTER's concept lie the FRs that will be supported by a set of ergonomic and non-intrusive wearable devices that comprise sensors, actuators and displays, as well as artificial intelligence capacity. These will be responsible for assessing the situation, be it either individualized bio-monitoring of the FRs or local environmental sensing. Their purpose will be to deliver information either in a peer-to-peer (P2P) manner among FRs or centralized points of presence. The distinction made between these two schemes is necessary as disasters can manifest in various - typically uncontrollable - ways, necessitating the employment of centralised, decentralised and distributed (P2P) management schemes. To that end, FASTER will

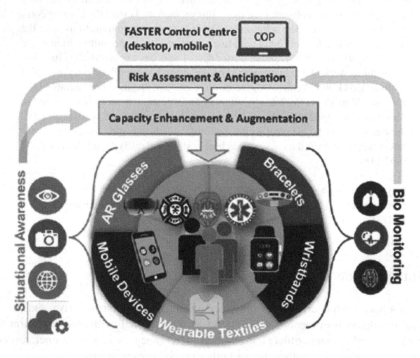

Fig. 1. FASTER core FRs capacity enhancement and augmentation [4].

consider both edge-based and cloud-based processing and analysis technologies to realize a risk assessment and anticipation system that will reach decisions and analyse the overall situation to provide targeted information and instructions to FRs. These will be delivered by the same wearable devices to augment and enhance their operational capacities [4].

The whole system will be facilitated by tools for Resilient Communications Support featuring opportunistic relay services, emergency communication devices and 5G-enabled communication capabilities (the Primary network). A FR secondary network, a relay network was developed, to mitigate any degradation of the primary network.

2 FASTER Secondary Network

The FASTER secondary network is composed by secondary network, several relay nodes, which can be deployed installed in Unmanned Aerial Vehicles/Unmanned Ground Vehicles (UAV/UGV - UxV) or for example in tripods a swarm of UAVs can be deployed at the event scene with radio relays payloads constitutes a resilient network.

The UxV Relay for extended communication implements a resilient communication service, employing common devices that will provide, in the worst-case scenario, a degraded service offering the minimal acceptable network performance in order to provide the basic services (FR localization and biometric data) in a crisis scenario. This service ensures communications even in inaccessible areas through the deployment of relay nodes, which will extend the existent communication network by utilizing UxVs to relay communications from the nearest point with live communication.

During the deployment procedures of the sites, after a disaster, the means of communication resources are evaluated and in case of a total disruption or of a high probability of losing the main communications, in this case 4G/5G, a secondary communication structure should be deployed in order to mitigate the loss of the primary communications. In this case, the secondary UxV relay communication structure is deployed, allowing the FR, K9 and other personnel or structures deployed on site to operate without any disruption of its operations.

The relay nodes are based on communication technologies, which work on the 2.4 and 5 GHz unlicensed bands. The transmit power limitations imposed by regulatory requirements limit the range (coverage) that can be achieved by WLANs (Wireless LAN) in these bands. However, the demand for "larger" wireless infrastructure is emerging, ranging from office/university campuses to city-wide deployments.

The wireless local area network standard IEEE 802.11 using the 2.4 GHz unlicensed band it is a low-cost data service and easy solution to deploy, the same hardware (HW) can in simultaneous support two networks, 802.11s and 802.11n:

- Mesh Point (MP), where the 802.11s address the aforementioned need for multi-hop communication introducing wireless frame forwarding and routing capabilities at the MAC layer and brings new interworking and security [5]; and
- Mesh Access Point (MAP), where the 802.11n protocol is used with Multiple-Input and Multiple-Output (MIMO) (2 antennas) to increase throughput over single antenna systems or to improve range of reception, depending on the environment by default the "back compatible" is enable with 802.11 b/g [6, 7].

In Fig. 2, is an example of Wi-Fi UxV relay network deployed in "Flood in urban environment (natural disaster)" is presented. Each node of secondary network has dual functionality, act in simultaneous as:

- Mesh Point, the core network, (802.11s); and as
  Mesh Access Point for FRs (802.11n).

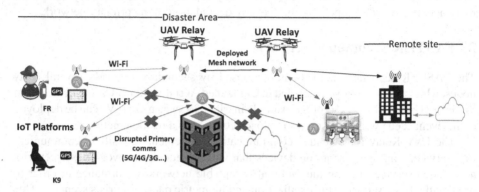

Fig. 2. Overview FASTER secondary network.

3   FASTER Secondary Network Components

One of the objectives of the UxV relay network is to install network nodes in the payload of UAVs and use a swarm of UAVs to deploy the communication network in order to cover the disaster area. A gateway is deployed as well at remote site, which will permit the assets at the disaster area to access the Internet, this solution is based on open source Debian/Linux. The relay networks can be installed in UAVs and on the ground in UGV or over tripods.

3.1   Relay Node

The Relay node (RNode), is composed by a hardware processing unit based on "open-hardware" SBC [8], a GNSS receiver, several sensors, a Wi-Fi radio and supporting elements like a battery, user buttons and LEDs and plastic box for protection and fixation on the UAV itself (or UGV).

The GNSS receiver tracks the position of the UAV. The Wi-Fi radio enables connection to the mesh network and provides a local WiFi network access for the ground elements to connect. The following figure, Fig. 3, represents a node with the main hardware modules and presents the payload of the UxV.

The node's weight and dimension were key factors when designing the hardware and box enclosure, because it would be part of the payload of an UAV, which mandates also that it needs to be battery powered (with an aprox. 3 h 50 m of autonomy). In line

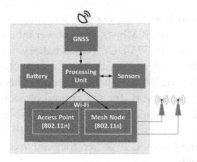

Fig. 3. Diagram of FASTER secondary network RNode and UxV payload.

with these requirements the WiFi hardware is based on the TI/WL1835MOD (WiLink™ 8 single band combo 2.4 GHz 2 × 2 MIMO Wi-Fi®, Bluetooth® & Bluetooth Smart module) [10]. This device acts simultaneously as a Mesh Access Point and a Mesh Point. Open-source Linux device drivers are available. In Table 1 an overview of WLAN specification is presented.

Table 1. Relay node - WLAN specification (overview).

WiFi interface	Wireless mesh	Wireless access point
Protocol	802.11s	802.11n
Frequency	2.4 GHz (24000–2483.5 MHz)	
Channel used (by default)	1	
Authentication[a]	Simultaneous Authentication of Equals (SAE)	WPA2[a] Pre-Shared Key (WPA2-PSK)
Encrypt Method	CCMP	CCMP
Using modulation DSSS and bitrate 1 Mbps		
Max. TX power:	17.3 dBm	
Max. Sensibility	−96.3 dBm	
Antennas[b] (2.4 GHz)	Wireless mesh	Wireless access point
Type	Omnidireccional dipole	
Gain	5 dBi	

[a] WPA3 is also supported
[b] Other type of antennas can be used (e.g. in UGV configuration).

3.2 Relay Gateway

The Relay Gateway (RGw) diagram, Fig. 4 represent the gateway with the main hardware modules, is similar to the RNode diagram (Fig. 3), a hardware processing unit based on "open-hardware SBC [9], and the RGw is supposed to work in ground in a fixed position and connect to a local network, it support more functionalities, features and interfaces and elements than the RNode: an Ethernet interface (10/100Mbps), POE power module (fully IEEE 802.3af compliant, input voltage (input 36-37VDC), buffer battery, user buttons and LEDs, USB Client and Host ports, Bluetooth and plastic box for protection and mechanical fixation. As for the RNode, in RGw the Wi-Fi radio are used to connect to the mesh network and to generate a local Wi-Fi network for the ground elements to connect to, plus a data concentrator for the data provided by the RNodes, Table 2 present antenna specification. The Ethernet interface is used to communicate with the local network switch that will provide access to the Internet. Together, they are used to create a bridge between the mesh network and the internet.

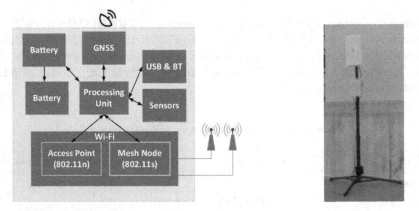

Fig. 4. Diagram and view of secondary network Relay Gateway (RGw).

Table 2. Gateway node – RGw WLAN antenna specification.

Wi-Fi (2.4 GHz)	Wireless mesh
Antenna[a]:	
Type	MIMO Sector
Gain	H:14dBi/60° V:12dBi/70°

[a] Other type of antennas can be used

3.3 Network Laboratory Tests

To verify the functionality and performance of this solution, the test setup presented in Fig. 5 was deployed in laboratory with the following components:

- STA - Client Station (Laptop or a Smartphone);
- MAP - Mesh Access Point
- MPP – Mesh Portal (RGw)

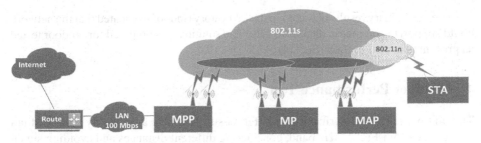

Fig. 5. Secondary network the test setup.

- MP – Mesh Points.

The Table 3 presents the result of test scenario A, using a Laptop 802.11ac as STA and iPerf - an open-source network performance tool for TCP, UDP and SCTP [11] (iper3 v.3.6 [11]) as network analyzer. The iperf tool version 3 was used to assess the wireless network performance. In the receiving node an iperf3 server instance was started in background with the command "iperf3 -s -D", while in the transmitting node a client instance was started in two different ways. The first one used TCP packets to assess the network throughput with the command "iperf3 –c <ip_server> -t30". The second one used UDP packets to assess network stability with the command "iperf3 -u -b <bitrate> -c <ip_server> -t30". The bitrate selected for the UDP test was bellow or equal to the bitrate measured for the network throughput in the TCP test in the same test conditions. Both tests used a randomly generated data block during a 30 s interval. The TCP test used a 128 KB data block, while the UDP test used a 8 KB data block. With the same test setup, another test was performed, the Scenario B – Video Streaming, were a smartphone was used as STA from where the VLC app was launched to access an IP TV service. The smartphone was connected to the MAP node and an HD (1080p) channel was selected for viewing. As a result, the channel view was fluid but with occasional stutters in the video and sound.

Table 3. Lab test – network performance.

Network section		Protocol	Throughput [Mbits/s]
A	External network → MPP	Ethernet*	34.1
	MPP → External network		81.7
B & C	MPP → MP	802.11s	12.2
	MP → MPP		11.7
D	MAP → STA	802.11n	72.1
	STA → MAP		81.7

* Using a BeagleBone Green Wireless Adaptor USB2.0 to RJ45 Ethernet Network.

The preliminary results obtained in the laboratory (indoor) indicated that the network could support the biometric data from FRs. The solution was prepared for outdoor tested as presented in next section (Sect. 4).

4   Outdoor Performance Tests

The outdoor tests were performed in different situation near a small city with medium or rare use of Wi-Fi 2.4 GHz band, considering different distances and avoiding signal obstacles. The network configuration deployments were based on two RNodes and a Client (one MPP, one MAP and one STA, see Fig. 5).

4.1   Link Viability

An overview of power model in a wireless system between two points is presented in Fig. 6.

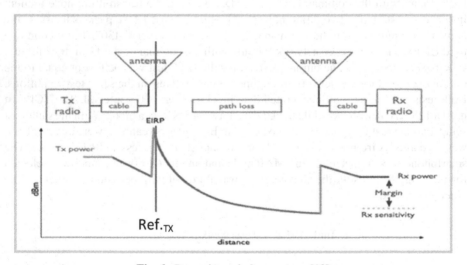

Fig. 6. Power in a wireless system. [12]

Where:

- Path loss, free space loss [12]:

$$Lp \, (\mathrm{dB}) = 32.5 + 20 \, log_{10}(d \, [\mathrm{Km}]) + 20 \, log_{10}(f \, [\mathrm{MHz}]) \qquad (1)$$

In a simplified model objects, interference between channels, ellipsoid Fresnel interruption, other temperature etc. are not considered. All wireless mesh network interconnection (RNodes) are stationary (speed 0 Km/h) as well as the mobile clients (FR). All RNodes have to support client connections, i.e., the need to be simultaneously a Mesh Point and a Mesh Access Point.

- Reference points:

  i) Ref. $_{TX}$ = EIRP, Equivalent Isotropic Radiated Power. (@Antenna Output)
     EIRP$_{MAX}$ = 20 dBm, for Wi-Fi 2400,0–2483,5 MHz (2.4 GHz) - both trans-
     mitters are limited, on TX Maximum Radiated Power the power must not exceed
     100 mW E.I.R.P. (20 dBm) [16].
     All RNodes are configured to be according with this rule, the TX Maximum
     Radiated Power to not exceed 100 mW E.I.R.P. (20 dBm).
  ii) Rx power, power received at radio receiver.
  iii) Rx sensibility, the minimum signal strength that a receiver can detect.
  iv) Cable, include all signal loss, like pigtails, cables, connectors.

- Fresnel Clearance, the area around the line-of-sight (LoS), where the radio waves
  spread out into after leave the antenna the maximum value [17]:

$$Fresnel\ Radius_{max}[m] = 17.31*\sqrt{\frac{D[Km]}{4*f[GHz]}} \tag{2}$$

Any obstruction of Fresnel Zone must be less than 20%, and, in ideal conditions the
Fresnel Zone must be without any obstruction. The Fig. 7 present at graphic of Max.
Radius Fresnel versus the link distance at 2.4 GHz.

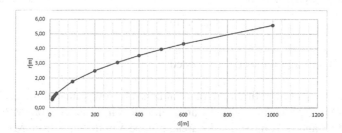

Fig. 7. Wi-Fi 2.4 GHz Max. Radius Fresnel & link distance.

4.2 Outdoor Test

These tests were performed near a small city, were the signal strength of other Wi-Fi
network near the MPP (RGw, GPS coordinates "38.643546, −9.222945" area (Viewpoint) is less than −80 dBm. In all scenarios it was guaranteed LoS between RNodes
(MPP and MAP). Note that these tests were performed in a public area, with movement
of people that could affect the test results (see in Fig. 8 and Fig. 9). The Wi-Fi CH1 was
selected (2.412 GHz).

MPP   MAP   STA

Fig. 8. Test A: network devices

Two different STA devices as been considered an iPhone 4S [13] on link viability analysis and on test field test a laptop HP ProBook 450 G6 Notebook was been used.

Map view (Google Earth)   Py and Pz areas

Fig. 9. Test – map.

Three different topologies of tests tested:

- Test A: All devices at "Miradouro dos Capuchos" (viewpoint): altitude 92 m;
- Test B: MAP and STA moved to Py area: altitude 3 m distance from MPP 526 m;
- Test C: MAP and STA moved to Pz area: altitude 5 m distance from MPP 393 m.

On Test B and Test C, the MPP antenna was aligned with the equidistant point of the remote sites (Py and Pz).

The test conditions in Table 4 software modules installed in MPP and MPA (*hostapd* and *wpasupplican*t updated in project) are presented, software tools in Table 5 and wireless protocols in Table 6.

Table 4. Test – software version installed on MPP and MPA components.

SW modules	Name	Version
OS	Debian	10.9 (Buster)
Kernel	Linux	4.19.94-ti-r59
Driver Wi-Fi	wl18xx	R8.8
Firmware Wi-Fi	wl18xx	8.9.0.0.86
Host Access Point Daemon	hostapd	2.9.0-21-inov3[a]
WPA Supplicant for Linux	wpasupplicant	2.9.0-21-inov3[a]

[a] Updated in the project

Table 5. Test – software tools used.

Tool name	Description	Version
Wi-Fi Analyser [14]	Android application to analyze Wi-Fi signal	3.0
iw [15]	Tool for configuring Linux wireless devices	5.9
iperf [11]	Internet Protocol bandwidth measuring tool	3.6

Table 6. Test – FASTER Wi-Fi SSID.

RNode	Network interface	SSID
MPP (GW)	Mesh (802.11s)	hidden
	AP (802.11n)	FASTER GW
MAP	Mesh (802.11s)	hidden
	AP (802.11n)	UAV01

The network diagram model adapted from Fig. 6 is presented in Fig. 10, where the locations of MAP and STA have the same elevation, and where d_{MAP} and d_{MSTA} are, respectively, the distance between nodes MAP and MPP (RGw) and between the STA (Client) and the MAP node. The height of the MPP antenna is adapted according to the topology of the locations:

$$h_{MPP}[m] = \langle Antenna\ Size_{MPP}[m]\rangle + Antenna\ Size_{MPP} > [m] - Elevation_{MAP} \qquad (3)$$

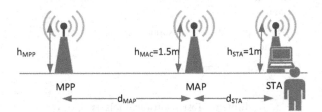

Fig. 10. Test: network deployment diagram.

As mentioned before the *iperf* tool was used to assess the wireless network performance using the same procedure used on Network Laboratory Tests (see Sect. 3.3).

Test A – Miradouro dos Capuchos (Viewpoint)
The Test A, performed at Miradouro dos Capuchos, with all network elements installed at same elevation (Fig. 11).

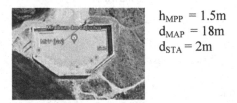

$h_{MPP} = 1.5m$
$d_{MAP} = 18m$
$d_{STA} = 2m$

Fig. 11. Test A - network devices deployment.

Monitoring the ISM band of 2.4 GHz with the "WiFi Analyzer" tool no other Wi-Fi networks were detected, according with the results presented by the Channel Chart and Time Line Chart of that tool (Fig. 12).

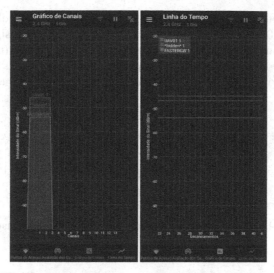

Fig. 12. Test A: Wi-Fi channel chart and time line chart.

This field test, the first to be performed is also useful to verify that all devices and software of the relay network are working properly, run this scenario is a pre-requirement to perform Test B and Test C. The result of field tests is presented in Table 9.

Test B – MPP and STA in Area Py

Monitoring the Wi-Fi of ISM band of 2.4 GHz, in Py area, with the Wi-Fi Analyser tool other Wi-Fi networks where detected near the MAP and STA locations, according with the output, Wi-Fi Channel Chart and Time Line Chart reports (see Fig. 13), only another one Wi-Fi network in CH1 was detected with $S > -70$ dBm (and less -60 dBm), all other

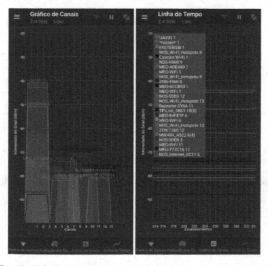

Fig. 13. Test B: Wi-Fi channel chart and time line chart near the MPP (Py).

networks where detected with inferior signal strength, less than −70 dBm, the FASTER Wi-Fi networks (802.11s and 802.11n) where detected with higher signal strength, the signal received from MPP (RGw) is received approx. with −50 dB (more 20 dB). The wireless link represented in a map and h_{MPP} and link distance values are characterized in Fig. 14. View from MPP to MAP and from MAP to MPP is presented respectively in Fig. 15.

$h_{MPP} = 90.5m$
$d_{MAP} = 526m$
$d_{STA} = 10m$

Fig. 14. Test B: map view (google maps), h_{MPP} and link distances.

Fig. 15. Outdoor test B: MPP and MAP view.

The result of link viability is present in Table 7.

Table 7. Rural test B – link viability analysis.

Link (2.4 GHz/CH1)	STA[a] → MAP	MAP → MPP	MPP → MAP	MAP → STA[a]
D [m]	10	526	526	10
Ref. $_{TX}$ [dBm]	13.5 [13]	20.0	20.0	20.0
Path loss	−60.1	−94.5	−94.5	−60.1
G. Antenna Rx [dBi]	5	14	5	0
Cable [dB]	−2.5	−5	−2.5	0
Sensibility[b] [dBm]	−96.3	−96.3	−96.3	−83
Margin Rx [dB]	38.7	30.8	24.3	42.9

[a] STA for reference using a mobile phone: iPhone 4S) d = 86m → Margin Rx (STA → MAP) = 20 dB
[b] Value at bitrate = 1 Mbps (Max. Sensibility)

The result of field tests is presented in Table 9.

Test C – MPP and STA in Area Py

Monitoring the Wi-Fi of ISM band of 2.4 GHz, in Pz area, with the Wi-Fi Analyser tool other Wi-Fi networks where detected near the MAP and STA locations, according with the output, Wi-Fi Channel Chart and Time Line Chart reports (see Fig. 16), the gap between the signal strength between the FASTER networks (802.11s and 802.11n) and other Wi-Fi networks detected is higher compared with the gap detected on Test B. View from MPP to MAP and from MAP to MPP is presented respectively in Fig. 15. The link viability is present in Table 8 (Fig. 17).

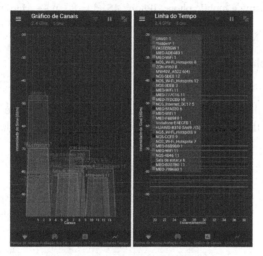

Fig. 16. Test C: Wi-Fi channel chart and time line chart.

$h_{MPP} = 89.5m$
$d_{MAP} = 396m$
$d_{STA} = 8m$

Fig. 17. Test C: map view (google maps), h_{MPP} and link distances.

The result of link viability analysis is present in Table 8.

Table 8. Test C – link viability analysis.

Link (2.4 GHz/CH1)	STA[a] → MAP	MAP → MPP	MPP → MAP	MAP → STA[a]
D [m]	8	386	386	8
Ref. $_{TX}$ [dBm]	13.5 [13]	20.0	20.0	20.0
Path loss	−58,2	−91.8	−91.8	−58,2
G. Antenna Rx [dBi]	5	14	5	0
Cable [dB]	−2.5	−5	−2.5	0
Sensibility[b] [dBm]	−96.3	−96.3	−96.3	−83
Margin Rx [dB]	40,64	33.5	27.0	44.8

[a] STA for reference using a mobile phone: iPhone 4S) d = 86 m → Margin Rx (STA → MAP) = 20 dB
[b] Value at bitrate = 1 Mbps (Max. Sensibility)

The result of field tests is presented in Table 9.

Field Test Results

The Field Tests results are summarized in Table 9, where the Bitrate, Packet Loss, Jitter are presented as well for MAP and MPP nodes the receiver power level and margin.

Table 9. Field test – results.

Link	Bitrate [Mbits/s]	Packet loss	Jitter [ms]	MAP power Rx/Margin[a] [dBm]/[dB]		MPP power Rx/Margin[a] [dBm]/[dB]	
Test A							
MAP → MPP (d = 18 m)	39.4	0/25898 (0%)	0.907	–		−50	24.9
STA → MAP (d = 2 m)	65.5	0/25898 (0%)	0.080	−47	27.9	–	
STA → MAP → MPP	23.6	0/25896 (0%)	1.140	−47	27.9	−50	24.9
Test B							
MAP → MPP (d = 526 m)	2.16	3/2590 (0.12%)	4.986	–		−73	23.3
STA → MAP (d = 10 m)	39.7	N/A	N/A	−62	12.9	–	
STA → MAP → MPP	1.47	4/2590 (0.15%)	6.731	−62	34.3	−67	29.3
Test C							
MAP → MPP (d = 396 m)	1.57	1/2590 (0.039%)	3.361	–		−68	28.3
STA → MAP → MPP	1.46	0/2590 (0%)	3.070	−73	23.3	−68	28.3

[a] Using as reference, modulation DSSS and bitrate 1 Mbps, Max. Sensibility: −96.3 dBm (see Table 1) and −74.9 dBm for results tests with bitrate > 11 Mbits/s (reference value at 54 Mbits/s)

In all situations the margin reported of signal received at RNode, MPP and MAP (mesh network elements), is higher than 23 dB, what give us an indication of the stability of the link of mesh network at these conditions. Remarks:

- For the Wi-Fi clients connect to the MAP/802.11n, in real situation using a stationary UAV, about 10 m to 15 m from the ground and close as possible to the Wi-Fi clients (STA/FRs) to receive information from biometric sources, the signal strength received at MAP is strong enough to establish the data wireless link.
- The bitrate in Test B was higher than in Test C, between MAP and MPP (RGw). An explanation for this is the fact that the wind level at the MPP site was relatively high during the realization of Test C, with strong gusts of wind, which forced extra care on the fixation of the MPP support tripod. Unfortunately, it was not possible to completely eliminate the oscillation of the MPP (RGw) antenna. On all Test Scenarios, the bitrate is enough to support biometric data service (vital data, e.g. temperature, heartbeat).

5   Conclusions and Next Steps

To maintain the FRs protection and operational effectiveness, namely their capacity in terms of situational awareness and communication in adverse situations, result of natural catastrophes, technological disaster or terrorist attacks, event of a disaster, communication networks may not be available at all, different reasons e.g. infrastructure collapse, denial of service or even the area of the incident may not be covered by communication services.

Although the Relay communication solutions for FRs, a resilient network solution easy to be deployed, to mitigate this problem and extent the existent communication networks. The solution allows FRs in network's shadow zones to be networked and at least vital biometric data to continue to be transmitted. The possibility that network nodes can be installed in UAVs or even in UGVs (UxVs) allows a fast and efficient repositioning of each network node and with this change the network coverage on the ground.

The next step, following the positive assessment by the FRs and other FASTER stakeholders, the solution will be deployed using UxVs and carry out the field tests in relevant environment, and plus the validation of a new algorithm for node repositioning to improve network coverage (the result be available to the UxV operator(s) in realtime).

In future this solution can also evolve to interact or support other types of networks as Low Power Wide Area Networks (LPWAN) IoT (as LoRa [18]).

Acknowledgements. This work has received funding from the European Union's Horizon 2020 (H2020) programme under grant agreement No: 833507.

References

1. CORDIS: First responder Advanced technologies for Safe and efficienT Emergency Response Homepage. https://cordis.europa.eu/project/rcn/222619/factsheet/en. Accessed 7 June 2021

2. Hall, B.: Don't Be a Dead Hero. SLATE Homepage (2013). https://slate.com/techno logy/2013/05/rescuers-turning-into-victims-lessons-from-first-responders-on-saving-peo ple.html. Accessed 5 June 2019
3. Georgiou, H.: FASTER: first responder advanced technologies for safe and efficient. In: SafeCorfu 2019 – 6th International Conference on Civil Protection & New Technologies SafeCorfu 2019 Proceedings (2019). ISSN 2654-1823
4. Dimou, A., et al.: FASTER: First Responder Advanced Technologies for Safe and Efficient Emergence Response. In: Mediterranean Security Event 2019 (MSE 2019), Fodele Crete (2019)
5. Hiertz, G., et al.: IEEE 802.11s: the WLAN mesh standard. IEEE Wirel. Commun. 17(1), 104–111 (2010). (E-ISSN 1558-0687)
6. Paul, T., Ogunfunmi, T.: Wireless LAN comes of age: understanding the IEEE 802.11n amendment. IEEE Circ. Syst. Mag. 8(1), 28–54 (2008). https://doi.org/10.1109/MCAS.2008. 915504. e-ISSN: 1558-0830
7. Halperin, D., Hu, W., Sheth, A., Wetherall, D.: Tool release: gathering 802.11n traces with channel state information. ACM SIGCOMM Comput. Commun. Rev. 40(1), 53–53 (2010)
8. BeagleBone Green Wireless Homepage. https://wiki.seeedstudio.com/BeagleBone_G reen_Wireless/. Accessed 9 June 2021
9. BeagleBone Green Gateway Homepage. https://wiki.seeedstudio.com/BeagleBone-Green-Gateway/. Accessed 9 June 2021
10. TI Homepage. https://www.ti.com/product/WL1835MOD?qgpn=wl1835mod. Accessed 9 June 2021
11. iPerf Homepage. https://iperf.fr/. Accessed 14 June 2021
12. Pietrosemoli, E.: Link budget calculation. In: School on Applications of Open Spectrum and White Spaces Technologies, Trieste, Italy, 3–14 March 2014
13. Cisco iphone 4S detail radio information Homepage. https://www.cisco.com/c/dam/glo bal/cs_cz/assets/ciscoconnect/2013/pdf/T-VT1-HighDensity-RF-design-Alex_Zaytsev.pdf. Accessed 24 Apr 2021
14. Gitbub-WiFiAnalyser Homepage. https://vremsoftwaredevelopment.github.io/WiFiAnaly zer/. Accessed 9 June 2021
15. Linux Wireless Trace-iw Homepage. https://wireless.wiki.kernel.org/en/users/documentatio n/iw. Accessed 9 June 2021
16. ANACOM Homepage. https://www.anacom.pt/streaming/dec0107_en.pdf?categoryId= 53809&contentId=86109&field=ATTACHED_FILE. Accessed 244 Apr 2021
17. Frolic, K.: Wireless links. PAGERPOWER Homepage (2020). https://www.pagerpower.com/ news/fresnel-zone/. Accessed 15 June 2021
18. Luca, D., Emanuele, P., Gianluigi, F.: Hybrid LoRa-IEEE 802.11s opportunistic mesh net-working for flexible UAV swarming. Drones 5(2), 26 (2021). https://doi.org/10.3390/drones 5020026

Data-Driven Disaster Management in a Smart City

Sandra P. Gonçalves[1], Joao C Ferreira[1($\boxtimes$)], and Ana Madureira[2]

[1] Instituto Universitário de Lisboa (ISCTE-IUL), ISTAR, Lisbon, Portugal
{sandra_goncalves,jcafa}@iscte-iul.pt
[2] 2ISRC, Instituto Superior de Engenharia do Porto - Politécnico do Porto, Porto, Portugal
amd@isep.ipp.pt

Abstract. Disasters, both natural and man-made, are extreme and complex events with consequences that translate into a loss of life and/or destruction of properties. The advances in IT and Big Data analysis represent an opportunity for the development of resilient environments once the application of analytical methods allows extracting information from a significant amount of data, optimizing the decision-making processes. This research aims to apply the CRISP-DM methodology to extract information about incidents that occurred in the city of Lisbon with emphasis on occurrences that affected buildings, constituting a tool to assist in the management of the city. Through this research, it was verified that there are temporal and spatial patterns of occurrences that affected the city of Lisbon, with some types of occurrences having a higher incidence in certain periods of the year, such as floods and collapses that occur when there are high levels of precipitation. On the other hand, it was verified that the downtown area of the city is the area most affected by occurrences. Finally, machine learning models were applied to the data and the predictive model Random Forest obtained the best result with an accuracy of 58%.

Keywords: Disaster management · Data mining · Machine learning · Smart city

1 Introductions

Disasters, both natural and man-made, have been occurring more frequently around the world with damaging consequences that are reflected in the loss of human life and material/facilities damage [1]. In fact, in the last ten years, 3 751 natural disasters such as earthquakes, tsunamis, and floods were detected worldwide, representing total damages of $1 658 billion and impacting more than 2 billion people [2]. In this way, it becomes crucial to implement disaster management techniques to minimize the risks associated.

Disaster management can be characterized as a multifaceted process where the primary goals is to avoid, reduce, respond, and recover from disaster impact in the system. Due to the complexity of these events, disaster response involves different organizations such as governmental, public, and private organizations as well as different layers of authority [3]. The involvement of different entities in the disaster management processes

© ICST Institute for Computer Sciences, Social Informatics and Telecommunications Engineering 2022
Published by Springer Nature Switzerland AG 2022. All Rights Reserved
A. L. Martins et al. (Eds.): INTSYS 2021, LNICST 426, pp. 113–132, 2022.
https://doi.org/10.1007/978-3-030-97603-3_9

highlights the need for collaboration and coordination mechanisms since these agencies, to be effective in a disaster situation, need to communicate, coordinate, and collaborate with each other. Some factors may difficult the communication between stakeholders, such as lack of situational awareness or difficulty in adopting technological systems for disaster response since they represent high costs [4].

The increase in population density in cities and the increase in the frequency of disasters in recent years arise the need for cities to provide better services and proper infrastructures to their population. In this context, the concept of Smart City (SC) emerges, considered the ideal solution to overcome the challenges brought by globalization and urbanization [5]. Cities that aim to become a SC use digital and networked technologies to address different types of problems, such as improving the quality of services, becoming more sustainable, growing the local economy, improving the quality of life, and increasing the safety, and security of their inhabitants [6].

In a SC, electronic devices and network infrastructures are incorporated to obtain high-quality services and as cities get the latest network infrastructure, smart devices, and sensors, a substantial amount of data is generated, known as Big Data (BD). This data can contain large amounts of information that can be contextual, spatial, or temporal [7].

In the case of disaster situations, BD plays an important role in disaster management processes since it is possible to apply data mining (DM) and analysis techniques to analyze patterns and predict disasters, allowing the development of appropriate disaster management strategies from the data collected that have occurred in the past [6]. In this way, the application of BD technologies assists agents in the decision-making process, since they enable identifying potential risks and, consequently, the development of appropriate strategies to cope with disaster situations, thus increase the resilience of the SC [2].

This research aims to apply a data-driven approach to extract information about disasters in the context of a SC to contribute to improving the way the city is managed.

The objective is to perform a descriptive and predictive analysis of the data provided by the Lisbon City Hall that contains information regarding incidents that occurred in the city. This analysis is going to be performed using two different data sources: data regarding occurrences registered by firefighters between the years 2011 and 2018 both descriptive and predictive analysis are going to be carried out. The second dataset, where only a descriptive analysis of the data is going to be conducted, comes from the application "*Na Minha Rua Lx*" [8], which is an application for intervention request management in the city of Lisbon. In both cases, the analysis was conducted in two phases, where in a first moment a general analysis of the reported occurrences was carried out and in a second moment the analysis focused on occurrences that affected buildings in the city.

2 State of the Art

Data-driven disaster management is a recent area that has been undergoing an evolution due to the number of works that have been developed [9]. In this sense, a survey and critical appreciation of the literature related to the proposed theme were performed by applying the Preferred Reporting Items for Systematic Reviews and Meta-Analyses (PRISMA) methodology [10] in accordance with the Systematic Literature Review steps proposed by Okoli and Schabram [11].

Accordingly, a systematic search on the topic was conducted in two electronic databases: Scopus [12] and Google Scholar [13], and the main objective was to identify and select research papers related to data-driven disaster management research area. With this in mind, a query was formulated to make the selection of the works carried out in this area. The query is the following: (("Disaster Management" OR "Incident Management") AND ("smart city" OR "data analysis" OR "data mining" OR "big data" OR "machine learning")). Additionally, a ten-year time window was defined (2010–2020), and the research covered areas such as Decision Science, Computer Science, Environmental Science, and Engineering. In terms of document typology, only journal articles, articles, and book chapters were considered. The documents were selected through the abstract and in cases where the information contained in the abstract was not sufficiently complete, the document was consulted in its entirety. The work done in this area covers both natural and man-made disasters.

2.1 Natural Disasters

Natural disasters are events that are characterized by the substantial impact they cause on society, interrupting its normal functioning. Work has been done in this area of data-driven disaster management to provide decision support systems that assist decision-makers in making decisions in a faster and more informed way, that is, based on analytical results. It was with this purpose that Jeong and Kim [14] developed a research where they conducted a statistical analysis of electrical incidents such as fires or failures occurring in Korea caused by climate changes. This study established a relationship between climate change and accidents involving electrical equipment.

Another study [15] conducted in 2017, reflected link between BD systems and disaster management. Big Data Analytics technologies was implemented on a dataset from the National Hydraulic Research Institute of Malaysia in order to analyze the hydroclimate data. The goal was to extract insights on climate change and thus provide information to prepare, mitigate, respond and recover from natural disasters. The application of BD technologies allowed the detection of periods of extreme precipitation and runoff as well as tracing drought episodes.

Through the application of DM techniques, also in 2017 another research was developed by the authors Briones-Estébanez e Ebecken [16] to identify and analyze the patterns in the occurrence of extensive and intensive events, including floods, river overflows, and landslides, related to precipitation intensity in five cities in Ecuador.

In addition to works developed to analyze disasters from a spatial and temporal perspective, other works have been developed to conduct a quantitative analysis of the damage caused by natural disasters. This is the case of the analysis carried out by the authors Alipour et al. [17]. They present a systematic framework that takes into account the different aspects that explain different types of risk (such as vulnerability and exposure) and apply Machine Learning models to predict the damage caused by flash floods in the Southeast, US.

With a similar approach, Park et al. [18] conducted a study aiming to quantify the possible effects or effectively the damage caused by three types of disasters namely typhoons, heavy rain, and earthquakes on water supply systems in Korea.

The work done in the area of data-driven disaster management is diverse as various techniques are adopted to make information available to decision-makers. In the case of the study carried out by Saha, Shekhar, and Sadhukhan [19], they presented the analytical results in more iterative way by developing a dashboard to predict and identify areas vulnerable to flooding in West Bengal, India, using geographic map visualization.

Other studies [20–23] used a combination of DM and GIS techniques to construct disaster susceptibility maps. The central objective of these studies focuses on the identification and classification of vulnerable areas to natural disasters with the difference that different DM models are used in the different research works.

2.2 Man-Made Disasters

Regarding man-made disasters, Smith et al. [24] developed a research that consisted in the implementation of Big Data technologies for disaster management. They used the statistical tool R, as well as its visualization capabilities, to analyze a dataset regarding fires that occurred in Australia.

Still in the context of fire data analysis, Balahadia et al. [25] applied the K-means clustering algorithm to generate patterns and create clusters of fire events based on the recorded data of fires that occurred in the city of Manila, Philippines. In summary, the goal was to obtain characteristics of fire events that can be used for risk assessment and risk management concerning these types of disasters as well as to assist in the development of prevention measures.

In the study of Asgary et al. [26] an attempt was made to use spatiotemporal methods to analyze the spatial and temporal patterns of fire-related incidents in Toronto, Canada. Insights were extracted by analyzing the relationship between the economic, physical, and environmental aspects of various neighborhoods and the total number of fires that occurred in those neighborhoods.

In the study of Liu et al. [27] was proposed a DM method based on using Bayesian Network to model building fires in urban areas. From the historical records of fires in a city in china between 2014 and 2016, they analyzed the potential fire risk according to building construction characteristics and external influences. Another study aiming to analyze fire patterns was conducted by Lee et al. [28] by applying the Support Vector Machine model to analyze the correlation between building characteristics, occupants, and fire incidents in Sydney.

Finally, in a study developed by Wan, Xu, He, and Wang [29] BD technologies were applied to analyze the distribution and influence factors of harmful gases in the urban underground sewage pipe network of Chongqing city, and explore the impact of smart city developments on harmful gases in the urban underground sewage pipe network.

In short, the literature review allowed to verify that most of the researches developed in this area were in China and it was also found that the research in this field covers natural disasters events as well as man-made disasters and that in the case of natural disasters there is a predominance of analysis of flood incidents and in the case of man-made disasters there is a predominance of the analysis of fire-related incidents.

3 Methodology

The analysis carried out in this research has two distinct focuses that serve the same purpose, i.e., spatial-temporal analysis of occurrences recorded in Lisbon to extract knowledge about the circumstances in which they occur. The Cross-Industry Standard Process for Data Mining (CRISP-DM) [30] methodology was applied separately on both datasets namely, the firefighters' dataset and data extracted from the application *"Na Minha Rua Lx"* to extract insights about disasters that affect the city of Lisbon with emphasis on buildings.

The analysis process based on the CRISP-DM methodology began with the business understanding that allows contextualizing and understanding the scope of the project. In this sense, an assessment of the business problem was made through the analysis of the aspects that characterize the city of Lisbon from different perspectives such as demographic, climatic, and edification aspects. After the business understanding step was completed the next phases consisted of data understanding, data preparation, modeling, and evaluation.

It is important to note that these steps of the CRISP-DM methodology, except for the business understanding, were applied to both datasets, separately, since it was not possible to merge the two datasets. The reason for the impossibility of merging the two datasets is due to the fact that there was no point of interest between the datasets, that is, a column that was common to both datasets and that had the exact same values. The join between the datasets could be made through the parish column, which is common to both, however, the datasets did not have a complete correspondence between the parishes and data could be lost when merging. The impossibility of merging the datasets impacted the prediction process since it was only possible to apply the predictive models on the firefighters' dataset, as it is richer in terms of information.

3.1 Firefighters' Dataset

The firefighter's dataset provided by the Lisbon City Hall, is a CSV file that contains information regarding the occurrences registered by the firefighters. Information covers aspects such as the description of the occurrence, date of the occurrence, location of the occurrence, i.e., latitude, longitude and address, and the human (number of persons) and material resources (number of vehicles) allocated to each occurrence. The dataset contains data from 2011 to 2018 consisting of 135 200 records (rows in the CSV file) and 22 attributes (columns in the CSV file). All the columns are of type "object", and 13 columns have some null values.

During the data preparation it was found that the years 2011 and 2012 have significantly less data than the others and, in order to perform an analysis where all years have representative data, those years where eliminated. Also, in this phase, cleansing techniques were applied that included column format conversion: the selection of relevant features/ attributes for the analysis, where attributes that did not add value to the scope of this research were eliminated. The records with null values were eliminated since it was not possible the replacement of the null values by the mean or median, because they are geographic coordinates, parishes, and descriptions of the occurrences.

This phase also included tasks such as the creation of new attributes from existing attributes and the adding of attributes from external sources such as INE [31] and IPMA [32]. External data contains information that characterizes the city of Lisbon in terms of population and building characteristics. In the last case there is information such as the average age of buildings per parish, the proportion of buildings in need of major repairs or very degraded per parish. Characterizing the city of Lisbon there are meteorological conditions such as average air temperature, relative humidity, average wind speed, and precipitation.

Lastly, it was necessary to categorize the types of occurrences that took place in buildings, since they are in a significant amount and a categorization facilitates the visual analysis. The information regarding the types of occurrences is found in the "Occurrence Description" column and this attribute has 25 types of occurrences that were defined by the firefighters' occurrence management system. These 25 types of occurrence were grouped into the following seven categories: Infrastructures – Collapse, Infrastructures – Floods, Infrastructures – Landslide, Fire, Accidents (with equipment or with elevators), Ind. technol. - Gas leak, and Ind. technol. - Suspicious situations (check smoke or check smells).

With the data preparation phase complete, the modeling phase begins. This phase is focused on extracting knowledge that can help decision-makers to manage the city in an efficient way when it comes to disaster situations. The first analysis is focused on understanding the distribution of the data over the years. It was possible to verify that in the period from 2013 to 2018 there was a downward trend in the number of occurrences recorded in the firefighter's occurrence management system, however, this decrease was not linear as there were oscillations over the years. There were 17 176 occurrences registered in the year 2013, 17 607 occurrences in 2014, 16 717 occurrences in 2015, 15 089 occurrences in 2016, 17 582 occurrences in 2017, and 13 368 occurrences in 2018.

Firefighters respond to many different types of occurrences comprising several areas of action. For a better understanding of the activities performed by firefighters, the types of occurrences were analyzed and it was verified that the distribution is not balanced among the nine categories of occurrences recorded in the dataset. There is an over-position of one category, namely the Services category, which represents 45.6% of occurrences recorded in the dataset. This category includes services such as road cleaning services, opening and closing doors, hospital transport, water supply, and prevention services at shows, sports, and patrolling.

The occurrences related to Infrastructures and Communication routes, what includes collapses, floods, landslides, falling trees and structures, and falling electric cables represents, 14.7% of the occurrences recorded in the dataset. While the occurrences related to accidents, what includes railroad accidents, road accidents, and accidents with equipment (elevators, escalators) present a proportion of 10.1%.

The categories that have the smallest representation in the dataset are Activities with 5.9%, Industrial-technological with a proportion of 5.1%, Legal conflicts with 0.5%, and civil protection events that represent 0.004% of the occurrences registered.

After a general analysis of the type of occurrences, the study is focused on the occurrences that took place in the buildings of the city of Lisbon to characterize them spatially and temporally.

As shown in Fig. 1, collapse with 3 742 records and floods with 3 356 records are the types of occurrences that most affect the buildings in the city of Lisbon, followed by occurrences related to suspicious situations that include verification of smells and smoke that count with 3 105 records. Also, with a significant proportion of incidences, but less expressive when compared with the previously mentioned categories, are accidents involving equipment or elevators with a total of 2 399 records, fires with 1 892 records, and gas leaks with 1 259 records.

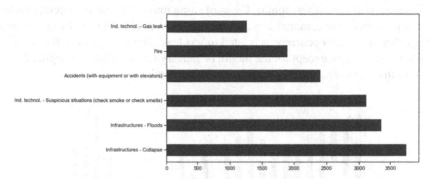

Fig. 1. Distribution of occurrences according to categories

When these occurrences are analyzed over time, i.e., their distribution over the years (Fig. 2), it is verified that there are occurrences that over the years occur in greater proportion, such as collapses, suspicious situations (checking smoke or smells), and accidents with equipment and elevators. The occurrences related to floods had a higher incidence in 2013 and 2014, with a decrease in the following years.

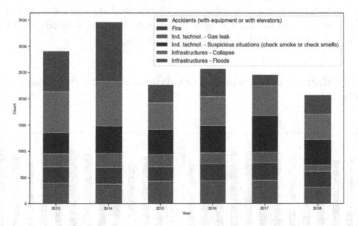

Fig. 2. Distribution of occurrences per year

Focusing the analysis on each occurrence to extract insights about its pattern of occurrence over the 12 months of the year, it is possible to verify that in the case of the occurrences referring to the infrastructure categories, i.e., collapses and floods represented in Fig. 3, that in the case of collapses (A), these occurred more frequently in the autumn and winter months, reaching maximum values (over 400 records) in the months of October and January.

As the spring and summer months approach, the number of records of this type of occurrence decreases, reaching lower values in the summer peak. Regarding floods (B), there is a higher incidence in the winter months with the highest values in the months of October to December, while during the summer months these values are much lower when compared to the winter months. Cases of suspicious situations (C) occur, similar to the types described above, more frequently in the winter months, especially in December. On the other hand, the occurrences related to gas leaks (D) show an oscillation during the months of the year, except for the month of January where values are higher than the other months, exceeding the 140 registered in this month.

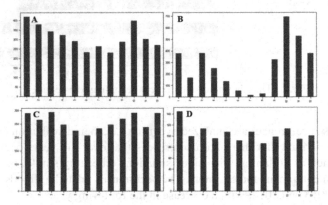

Fig. 3. The bar chart from figure **A** shows the temporal distribution of Collapses, the bar chart from figure **B** shows the temporal distribution of Floods, the bar chart from figure **C** shows the temporal distribution of Suspicious situations (check smoke or check smells), and the bar chart from figure **D** shows the temporal distribution of Gas leaks.

Lastly, the distribution of accidents involving equipment or elevators and fires is shown in Fig. 4.

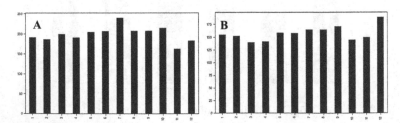

Fig. 4. Temporal distribution of the occurrences. The bar chart from figure **A** shows the temporal distribution of accidents with equipment or elevators and the bar chart from figure **B** shows the temporal distribution of Fires.

Regarding accidents with equipment or elevators (A), this type of occurrence presents an incidence with similar values throughout the months except for the month of July where there is an increase and the month of November where there is a decrease. In the case of fires (B), these occur mainly in the last month of the year, and these observations may be due to the fireplaces and candles that are used in greater density at this time of year.

The first analysis showed that there are types of occurrences that have a higher incidence in certain seasons of the year, such as collapses, floods, suspicious situations (checking for smoke or smells) occurring with a higher incidence in the winter/spring months, the influence of weather conditions on the incidence of different types of events affecting the city of Lisbon has been verified.

With this in mind, the influence of precipitation on the different types of occurrences data was analyzed through four distinct periods, namely when it does not rain, when the rain is low, when the rain is moderate, and when the rain is heavy. The creation of these four levels allows the precipitation to be classified in qualitative terms. For this purpose, an interquartile approach was adopted and from the interquartile ranges it was possible to build 4 datasets with the four precipitation levels previously mentioned.

From the analysis of occurrences according to the four precipitation levels, it was possible to conclude that there are two types of occurrences, namely floods and collapses that increase when precipitation levels increase. In the case of floods, the increase in incidence depending on precipitation levels is outstanding, since in cases where the precipitation was zero its incidence was 4.02%, in situations of low precipitation it was 19.23%, in situations of moderate precipitation it was 47.98%, and finally in situations of heavy precipitation it was 75.81%.

Shifting the focus to an analysis of occurrences from a spatial perspective to verify how occurrences are distributed throughout the city of Lisbon, heatmaps were created for the six types of occurrences that most affect buildings in the city of Lisbon. Figure 5 shows the spatial distribution of collapses and floods.

Fig. 5. Spatial distribution of the occurrences. Figure **A** shows the spatial distribution of Collapses and figure **B** shows spatial distribution of Floods,

From the heatmaps presented above it is possible to infer that the occurrences related to collapses, which is the type of events that most affects the city of Lisbon, have a higher concentration of points in the central zone of the city, which means that collapses affect mainly parishes in the central area of the city, such as *Arroios, Santo António, São Vicente, Misericórdia, Campolide, Avenidas Novas, Penha de França*, and areas of the Historical Center of Lisbon. The occurrences referring to floods, similarly to collapses, have a higher concentration in the downtown area of the city with the difference that this type of occurrence also happens with high incidence in the northwestern part of the city, namely the parishes of *Benfica* and *São Domingos de Benfica*.

Figure 6 refer to the geospatial distribution of occurrence regarding Suspicious situations, Gas Leaks, Accidents with equipment or elevators, and Fires.

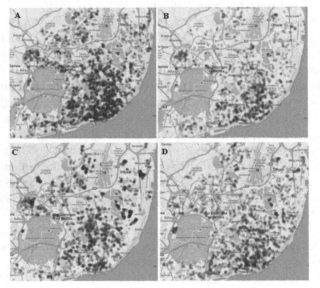

Fig. 6. Spatial distribution of the occurrences. Figure **A** shows the spatial distribution of Suspicious situations (check smoke or check smells), figure **B** shows the spatial distribution of Gas leaks, figure **C** shows the spatial distribution of accidents with equipment or elevators, and figure **D** shows the spatial distribution of Fires.

Suspicious situations present a higher concentration in the central zone of the city of Lisbon, namely the parishes of *Arroios, Santo António, São Vicente, Misericórdia, Campolide, Avenidas Novas, Penha de França* and areas in the Historical Center of Lisbon. On the other hand, situations concerning gas leaks (B) are more concentrated in the Lisbon Historical Center area and the districts of *Penha de França, Arroios*, and *Benfica*.

In terms of accidents involving equipment or elevators (C), this type of occurrence, unlike the types of occurrences already analyzed, does not present a higher concentration in a single Lisbon area, but instead affects the entire Lisbon city area with a similar proportion. On the other hand, although fires (D) are a type of occurrence that in general is registered in the entire Lisbon area, their concentration is slightly higher in the Lisbon historic center area.

Since there is a concentration of occurrences in a specific area of the city of Lisbon, it was sought to deepen the knowledge about Lisbon by analyzing aspects such as the state of conservation of buildings and the average age of buildings in the different parishes. Through the spatial visualization of the buildings that are degraded or in need of repair and through the visualization of the parishes where the oldest buildings are located, it is possible to establish the association between the spatial concentration of occurrences and the condition of the buildings.

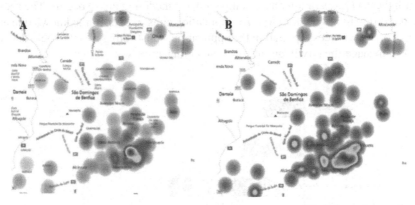

Fig. 7. Figure **A** shows the spatial representation of the proportion of buildings that are degraded or in need of major repairs and figure **B** shows the spatial representation of the average age of the buildings per parish

From the conclusions reiterated from the two heatmaps created (Fig. 7), it is possible to infer that the areas where the older buildings are concentrated and where there is a greater proportion of degraded buildings or with major needs of repair are more affected by the types of occurrences such as collapses, floods, suspicious situations (check smoke or check smells), and gas leaks..

3.2 *Na Minha Rua Lx* **Dataset**

Regarding the dataset containing the data related to the occurrences recorded on *the Na Minha Rua Lx* application, the first analysis showed that the dataset covers the period from 2017 to 2020 and it is composed of 12 866 records and eight attributes that aggregate information about the occurrences reported in the application such as the date on which the occurrence was reported, the type of occurrence, and the location of the occurrence.

It was verified that there was one duplicate value and zero null values in the entire dataset. Furthermore, six of the eight columns that compose the dataset are of type *object*, except the columns "latitude" and "longitude" that are of type *float*.

The data preparation began with the selection of the relevant attributes and after identifying the necessary attributes to conduct this analysis, data processing techniques were applied to adequate the dataset to the analysis intended to be developed. However, no significant problems were identified, besides one attribute that was not in date format and a duplicate value. Also, in the data preparation phase, new columns were created from an existing column since the information that allows locating the occurrences on a temporal level was extracted from the column "Date-Time". In this way, three new attributes were created from the "Date-Time" attribute: "Year", "Month", and "Hour". Lastly, it was found that the year 2020 has significantly less data when compared to the other years and, to conduct an analysis where all years have representative data, it was necessary to eliminate the year 2020. With all the transformations on the dataset completed, the final dataset has seven columns and 12 865 rows.

With the data preparation phase completed, the modeling phase begins. The analysis of the data from the *Na Minha Rua Lx* application aims to deepen the knowledge about the types of occurrences reported in the application, constituting a tool to help decision-makers to manage the city in an informed and efficient way.

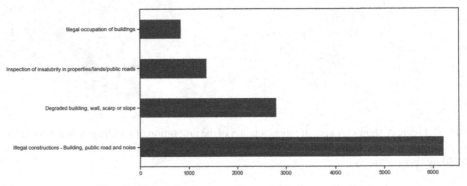

Fig. 8. Types of occurrences reported in the application

From Fig. 8 it is possible to verify that there are four main types of occurrences reported in the application, namely Illegal constructions - building, public roads and noise, Degraded building, wall, scarp or slope, Inspection of insalubrity in properties/lands/public roads, and Illegal occupation of buildings.

In terms of their distribution, it is noted that the occurrences are not equally distributed in the dataset since there is an over-position of the type of occurrence referring to Illegal constructions in relation to the other types of occurrences once, during the period under analysis, 6 217cases of Illegal constructions - Building, public roads, and noise were reported. The other typologies are in lesser proportion with 2 799 cases of Degraded building, wall, scarp or slope, 1 365 cases of Inspection of insalubrity in properties/lands/public roads, and 834 Illegal occupations of buildings.

Analyzing the distribution of these types and occurrences per year, it was concluded that every year there is a large number of reports corresponding to cases of illegal construction, while the other types of occurrences are reported less frequently.

After a general description of the distribution of reports over the years and an analysis of the types of occurrences reported, the analysis focused only on events that took place in the buildings of the city of Lisbon i.e., degraded building, wall, scarp or slope and illegal occupation of buildings.

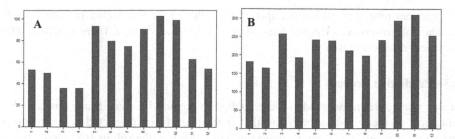

Fig. 9. Temporal distribution of the occurrences. The bar chart from figure **A** shows the temporal distribution of illegal occupation of buildings and the bar chart from figure **B** shows the temporal distribution of degraded buildings, wall, scarp, or slope.

With the purpose of deepening the knowledge about these two types of occurrence, their temporal distribution was analyzed (Fig. 9) and for cases of illegal occupation of buildings are reported in greater expression between the months of September and October, with emphasis on the month of May where there is an increase in this type of occurrence.

On the other hands, cases of degraded buildings, wall, scarp, or slope, there is an increase in reports in the last four months of the year, i.e., from September to October, and then an increase again in March and May.

Shifting the focus to an analysis of occurrences from a spatial perspective, heatmaps were created that present the geospatial distribution of the above-mentioned types of occurrences with the goal of verifying how these occurrences are distributed throughout the city.

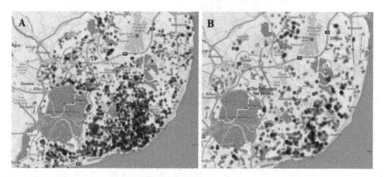

Fig. 10. Spatial distribution of the occurrences. Figure **A** shows the spatial distribution of degraded buildings, wall, scarp, or slope and figure **B** shows the spatial distribution of illegal occupation of buildings.

From the heatmaps presented in Fig. 10, it is possible to verify that in both cases these events are registered with a higher incidence of the downtown area of the city. Cases regarding Degraded building, wall, scarp or slope have higher incidences in the following parishes: *Penha de França, Arrois, Avenidas Novas, Misericórdia, Santo António, São Vicente, Ajuda, São Domindos de Benfica* and *Campolide*. On the other hand, the occurrences related to Illegal occupation of buildings have a higher incidence in the parishes of *Arroios*, *São Vicente*, *Santo António*, *Penha de França*, *Misericórdia*, and the historical downtown area.

3.3 Prediction Process

In this phase, predictive models were applied to predict disasters. Since this is a classification problem and the attribute that is intended to be predicted is a categorical attribute ("Occurrence Type"), supervised classification algorithms [68] were applied and then compared to determine the most efficient classification algorithm for this case. The following predictive models were applied: Random Forest, Decision Tree Classifier, Support Vector Machine, Gaussian Naive Bayes, and Logistic Regression.

Before proceeding to the application of the predictive models it was necessary to make a feature selection, i.e., the selection of relevant attributes for the construction of the predictive models, and the feature selection was conducted using the correlation matrix presented in Fig. 11.

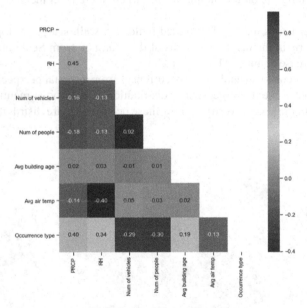

Fig. 11. Correlation matrix

Considering the data presented in the correlation matrix, only the attributes that have greater correlation with the attribute Occurrence Type were selected, since it is the target attribute (independent attribute). Thus, the following attributes were selected as dependent or explanatory attributes (dependent attributes): "PRCP" (precipitation), "RH" (relative humidity), "Num of people", "Num of vehicles", "Avg building age", Avg air temp", "Resident pop", and Avg WS" (average wind speed).

To train the predictive models, it was necessary to split the data to allow not only the training but also the testing of the models. The training set is used to find the relationship between dependent and independent attributes, while the test set evaluates the model's performance. In numerical terms, the division was made so that 70% of the data was for training and the remaining 30% of the data was for model testing.

After defining the X and Y attributes and dividing the data for testing and training, the algorithms were applied, and the predictive results were analyzed. It is important to emphasize that all algorithms were applied twice, wherein a first moment they were applied without hyperparameters and in a second moment, with the purpose of improving the performance of these algorithms, functions that present the best set of hyperparameters were applied and the algorithms were reapplied considering the hyperparameters. The graph in Fig. 12 shows the summary of the predictive results for each model after tuning.

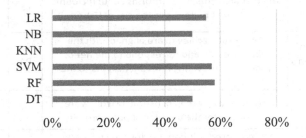

Fig. 12. Summary of the predictive results for each model

The prediction results were not satisfactory (best result 58%), and these results can be explained by the fact that there was no strong correlation between the attributes and also by the fact that the independent attribute (the one predicted) had six possible values: Infrastructures - collapses, Infrastructures - floods, Ind. Technol. -suspicious situations (check smoke or check smells), Ind. - Gas leak, Fires, and Accidents (with equipment or with elevators).

4 Evaluation

The work developed in this research was evaluated through a satisfaction questionnaire. The evaluations were carried out by 3 experts and, regarding the characterization of the panel of evaluators, they hold degrees in territorial engineering, geology and architecture and the average experience of the evaluators is 26 years.

The questionnaire aimed to evaluate five criteria, namely effectiveness, consistency with the organization's objectives, utility, level of detail, clarity, applicability, transferability, and impact. These criteria have four evaluation possibilities: NA (Not Achieved), PA (Partially Achieved), LA (Largely Achieved), and TA (Totally Achieved). The result is shown in Table 1.

The evaluation assigned to the criteria were PA and LA with the exception for the Clarity criterion which was assigned a TA classification by Evaluator 1. The reason why the criteria were classified as PA and LA is due to the fact that the stockholders responsible for this project initially expected this analysis to be conducted at the level of the buildings with a higher level of detail relating the state of conservation of each building with the events that occurred, but it was later concluded that the data did not allow such analysis and therefore the possible analysis would be from a high-level perspective.

Table 1. Results of the evaluation

Project evaluation				
Criterion	**Objective statement**	**#Eva1**	**#Eva2**	**#Eva3**
Efficacy	The research effectively informs about incidents that affect buildings in the city of Lisbon	LA	LA	LA
Consistency with the organization's objectives	The results achieved are aligned with the objectives set and correspond to the needs identified, providing relevant insights to the decision-makers	PA	PA	PA
Utility	Through the research, useful insights were extracted for the decision support process	LA	LA	LA
Detail level	The proposed solution provides the necessary level of detail to assist in the decision support process	LA	PA	PA
Clarity	The research provides clear and easy-to-understand information from the elaborate graphics	TA	LA	LA
Applicability	The solution has practical applicability in the field of disaster management and civil protection	PA	PA	PA
Transferability	The results gathered in this research can be applied to other contexts or areas	PA	LA	LA
Impact	The results achieved positively impact the way disaster situations are managed, thereby increasing the city's resilience	PA	PA	PA

5   Discussion

The analyses performed in this study allowed to verify that disaster management is a multifaceted field which encompasses several aspects. The spatial aspect permitted the analysis of the areas of the city most affected by the occurrences. This information allows the allocation of the intervention teams and placing the resources near the risk locations.

The temporal aspect allowed the verification of the incidence of the different types of occurrences throughout the year. Finally, the analysis of the human and material resources allocated to each type of occurrence allowed to identify the type of event that requires greater resources.

In this way, all this information enables the decision-makers to strategically allocate resources in order to respond to occurrences in a timely manner, since the reduction in response time reduces the impact of the events on the community.

This study allowed to conclude the historical center of the city of Lisbon is the most affected area of the city. Although the other areas are affected by the occurrences, it is the historical center area that has older and more degraded buildings, meaning they are more exposed to risk.

On the other hand, the application of the Random Forest algorithm is an asset in disaster management as it enables prediction of occurrences and helps decision makers to be better prepared to cope with the incidents.

In short, historical data on disasters that have occurred in the past is an important tool for disaster management in the present and in the future since the effective analysis of this data allows not only the extraction of knowledge about the patterns of occurrence, but also their prediction.

This research was based on data from a single city, so the conclusions are only for the city of Lisbon. However, this process can be replicated for other cities, taking into account their specific characteristics.

6   Conclusion

The research carried out shows that the evolution in the IT area has positively impacted the disaster management area since when city management policies are grounded on analytical results resulting from the application of DB technologies to the large amounts of data that have begun to be stored, it allows increasing the authorities' capabilities to cope with disaster situations.

The spatial-temporal analysis conducted in this research is important to understand the types of occurrences to which the city of Lisbon is vulnerable. The extraction of knowledge regarding the patterns of occurrence of these events is useful in the various stages of disaster management as it allows generating an overview of easy understanding among the various stakeholders, which allows the development of appropriate strategies for the various phases of disaster management.

In short, through the application of DM techniques to the firefighters' dataset, it was possible to conclude that the buildings in the city of Lisbon are affected by six types of events namely collapses, floods, suspicious situations (check smoke or check smells), gas leak, fires, accidents (with equipment or with elevators). It was also verified that there is a temporal pattern with regard to these occurrences since in some cases there is a greater predominance of certain occurrences at certain times of the year. In terms of the distribution of the occurrences, it was concluded that the historic center of the city is, in general, the area most affected by these types of occurrences and it is in this area where are concentrated the degraded buildings or with a great need for repair and also the older buildings.

On the other hand, it was verified that in the dataset with data from the application "*Na Minha Rua Lx*", the data reported in the application are not of the same type as the data registered in the firefighters' occurrence management system, since the occurrences involving buildings are Illegal occupation of buildings, Degraded building, wall, scarp, or slope. Furthermore, it was verified that the occurrences of both the firefighters and the application cover the same areas and that in both cases there is a predominance of occurrences in the historic center area of the city.

Additionally, it was expected that the events reported in the *Na Minha Lx application* could complement the firefighters' data, but results showed that the events reported in the application, despite covering the same areas, do not have events of the same extent and weight as the events recorded in the LFBR management system.

Finally, predictive algorithms were applied to the firefighters' data, however the results obtained were not satisfactory and the explanation for these results is due to the poor richness of the data since there were not very strong correlations between the dependent variables and the independent variable had six possible values.

Thus, the fact that it was not possible to join the datasets due to their characteristics, the fact that the data were not rich and consequently did not allow a more detailed analysis (as intended by the stakeholders responsible for this project) and achieve better predictive results, were the main limitations identified during this research.

References

1. Wellington, J.J., Ramesh, P.: Role of Internet of Things in disaster management. In: 2017 International Conference on Innovations in Information, Embedded and Communication Systems (ICIIECS), pp. 1–4 (2017). https://doi.org/10.1109/ICIIECS.2017.8275928
2. Yang, C., Su, G., Chen, J.: Using big data to enhance crisis response and disaster resilience for a smart city. In: 2017 IEEE 2nd International Conference on Big Data Analysis (ICBDA), pp. 504–507 (2017). https://doi.org/10.1109/ICBDA.2017.8078684
3. Zagorecki, A., Johnson, D., Ristvej, J.: Data mining and machine learning in the context of disaster and crisis management. Int. J. Emerg. Manag. **9**, 351–365 (2013). https://doi.org/10.1504/IJEM.2013.059879
4. (PDF) Crowdsourcing Disaster Response. https://www.researchgate.net/publication/268448750_Crowdsourcing_Disaster_Response. Accessed 26 Aug 2021
5. Shah, S.A., Seker, D.Z., Rathore, M.M., Hameed, S., Yahia, S.B., Draheim, D.: Towards disaster resilient smart cities: can internet of things and big data analytics be the game changers? IEEE Access **7**, 91885–91903 (2019). https://doi.org/10.1109/ACCESS.2019.2928233
6. Chaudhari, S., Bhagat, A., Tarbani, N., Pund, M.: Dynamic notifications in smart cities for disaster management. In: Computational Intelligence in Data Mining, Singapore, pp. 177–1902019). https://doi.org/10.1007/978-981-10-8055-5_17
7. Shah, S.A., Seker, D.Z., Hameed, S., Draheim, D.: The rising role of big data analytics and IoT in disaster management: recent advances, taxonomy and prospects. IEEE Access **7**, 54595–54614 (2019). https://doi.org/10.1109/ACCESS.2019.2913340
8. Na Minha Rua LX - Lisboa Inteligente. https://lisboainteligente.cm-lisboa.pt/lxi-iniciativas/na-minha-rua-lx/. Accessed 10 Aug 2021
9. Li, T., et al.: Data-driven techniques in disaster information management. ACM Comput. Surv. **50**(1), 1–45 (2018). https://doi.org/10.1145/3017678
10. Moher, D., Liberati, A., Tetzlaff, J., Altman, D.G.: Preferred reporting items for systematic reviews and meta-analyses: The PRISMA statement. Int. J. Surg. **8**(5), 336–341 (2010). https://doi.org/10.1016/j.ijsu.2010.02.007

11. Okoli, C., Schabram, K.: A guide to conducting a systematic literature review of information systems research. SSRN Electron. J. (2010). https://doi.org/10.2139/ssrn.1954824
12. Scopus - Document search. https://www.scopus.com/search/form.uri?display=basic&edit. scft=1#basic. Accessed 09 Aug 2021
13. About Google Scholar. https://scholar.google.com/intl/en/scholar/about.html. Accessed 09 Aug 2021
14. Jeong, M.-C., Kim, J.: Prediction and analysis of electrical accidents and risk due to climate change. Int. J. Environmental Res. Pub. Health 16(16), 2984 (2019). https://doi.org/10.3390/ijerph16162984
15. Abdullah, M.F., Ibrahim, M., Zulkifli, H.: Big data analytics framework for natural disaster management in Malaysia. In: Proceedings of the 2nd International Conference on Internet of Things, Big Data and Security, Porto, Portugal, pp. 406–411 (2017). https://doi.org/10.5220/0006367204060411
16. Briones-Estébanez, K.M., Ebecken, N.F.F.: Occurrence of emergencies and disaster analysis according to precipitation amount. Nat. Hazards 85(3), 1437–1459 (2016). https://doi.org/10.1007/s11069-016-2635-z
17. Alipour, A., Ahmadalipour, A., Abbaszadeh, P., Moradkhani, H.: Leveraging machine learning for predicting flash flood damage in the Southeast US. Environ. Res. Lett. 15(2), 024011 (2020). https://doi.org/10.1088/1748-9326/ab6edd
18. Park, J., et al.: Ensemble model development for the prediction of a disaster index in water treatment systems. Water Switz. 12(11), 1–19 (2020). https://doi.org/10.3390/w12113195
19. Saha, S., Shekhar, S., Sadhukhan, S., Das, P.: An analytics dashboard visualization for flood decision support system. J. Visual. 21(2), 295–307 (2017). https://doi.org/10.1007/s12650-017-0453-3
20. Célia, R., et al.: Mapping characteristics of at-risk population to disasters in the context of Brazilian early warning system. Int. J. Dis. Risk Reduct. 41, 101326 (2019). https://doi.org/10.1016/j.ijdrr.2019.101326
21. Lee, S., Lee, S., Lee, M.-J., Jung, H.-S.: Spatial assessment of urban flood susceptibility using data mining and geographic information system (GIS) tools. Sustainability 10(3), 648 (2018). https://doi.org/10.3390/su10030648
22. Liu, Y., Li, Z., Wei, B., Li, X., Fu, B.: Seismic vulnerability assessment at urban scale using data mining and GIScience technology: application to Urumqi (China). Geomat. Nat. Hazards Risk 10(1), 958–985 (2019). https://doi.org/10.1080/19475705.2018.1524400
23. Chen, W., Zhang, S., Li, R., Shahabi, H.: Performance evaluation of the GIS-based data mining techniques of best-first decision tree, random forest, and naïve Bayes tree for landslide susceptibility modeling. Sci. Total Environ. 644, 1006–1018 (2018). https://doi.org/10.1016/j.scitotenv.2018.06.389
24. Smith, S., et al.: Adoption of data-driven decision making in fire emergency management. In: Presented at the 24th European Conference on Information Systems, ECIS 2016 (2016)
25. Balahadia, F.F., Dadiz, B.G., Ramirez, R.R., Luvett, M., Lalata, J.P., Lagman, A.C.: Application of data mining approach for profiling fire incidents reports of bureau of fire and protection. In: 2019 International Conference on Computational Intelligence and Knowledge Economy (ICCIKE), pp. 713–717 (2019). https://doi.org/10.1109/ICCIKE47802.2019.9004420
26. Asgary, A., Ghaffari, A., Levy, J.: Spatial and temporal analyses of structural fire incidents and their causes: a case of Toronto, Canada. Fire Saf. J. 45(1), 44–57 (2010). https://doi.org/10.1016/j.firesaf.2009.10.002
27. Liu, X., Lu, Y., Xia, Z, Li, F., Zhang, T.: A data mining method for potential fire hazard analysis of urban buildings based on Bayesian network. In: Proceedings of the 2nd International Conference on Intelligent Information Processing, New York, NY, USA (2017). pp. 1–6. https://doi.org/10.1145/3144789.3144811

28. Lee, E.W., Yeoh, G., Cook, M., Lewis, C.: Data mining on fire records of New South Wales, Sydney. Procedia Eng. **71**, 328–332 (2014). https://doi.org/10.1016/j.proeng.2014.04.047
29. Wang, Z., Xu, J., He, X., Wang, Y.: Analysis of spatiotemporal influence patterns of toxic gas monitoring concentrations in an urban drainage network based on IoT and GIS. Pattern Recognit. Lett. **138**, 237–246 (2020). https://doi.org/10.1016/j.patrec.2020.07.022
30. [PDF] Crisp-dm: towards a standard process modell for data mining|Semantic scholar. https://www.semanticscholar.org/paper/Crisp-dm%3A-towards-a-standard-process-modell-for-Wirth-Hipp/48b9293cfd4297f855867ca278f7069abc6a9c24. Accessed 27 Aug 2021
31. Portal do INE. https://www.ine.pt/xportal/xmain?xpid=INE&xpgid=ine_inst_legislacao&xlang=pt. Accessed 04 May 2021
32. IPMA – Serviços. https://www.ipma.pt/pt/produtoseservicos/index.jsp?page=dados.xml. Accessed 04 May 2021

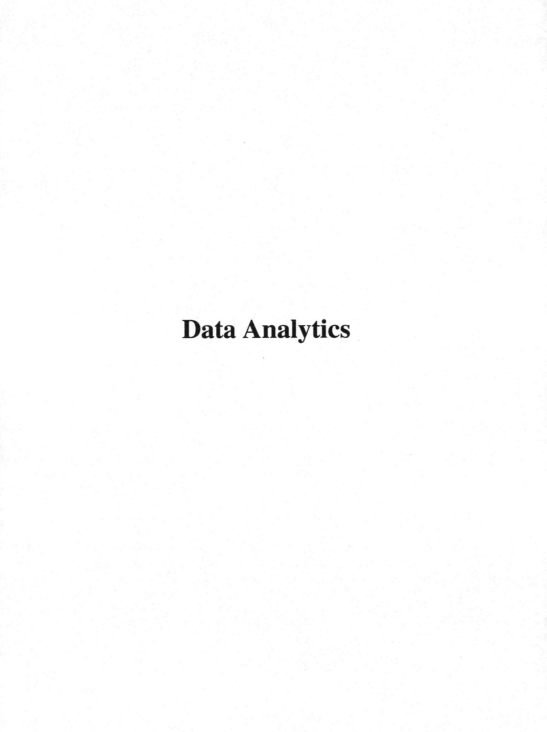

Data Analytics

Cycling Analytics for Urban Environments: From Vertical Models to Horizontal Innovation

Carlos Carvalho[1]([✉]) [iD], Ricardo Pessoa[2] [iD], and Rui José[1] [iD]

[1] Algoritmi Research Centre, University of Minho, Braga, Portugal
{carlos.carvalho,rui}@dsi.uminho.pt
[2] Bosch Car Multimedia, Braga, Portugal
Ricardo.Pessoa@pt.bosch.com

Abstract. The full potential of Intelligent Transport Systems (ITS) can only be achieved by combining the efforts and the knowledge of multiple entities. This is also true for the current efforts towards the application of data, communications and services to improve cycling and its integration into general mobility systems. The currently prevailing paradigm is based on dispersed and self-contained custom processes, which fail to promote distributed and open innovation. These models are hard to reproduce, generalize, recombine or improve outside the context for which they were originally implemented. A digital platform strategy might offer a viable and scalable way to support convergence between multiple models and promote their usage as shared references for cycling ecosystems. In this work, we aim to validate our assumptions about the limitations of current development paradigms and analyse the extent to which a platform strategy could offer a fundamentally different approach to address those limitations. To validate the problem and uncover generalisation opportunities, we study 3 cycling mobility models and make an initial analysis of how the general principles of digital platforms could offer an alternative solution for cycling analytics. The results confirm a high potential for horizontal features and outline a set of key design principles for the development of a digital platform strategy for cycling analytics. This should constitute a contribution to inform the development of a new generation of cycling platforms for urban environments.

Keywords: Cycling analytics · Mobility models · Horizontal innovation · Urban cycling · Smart cycling · ITS for smart cities: sustainable transportation · New trends in ITS

1 Introduction

Cycling, and micro-mobility in general, are increasingly central in urban mobility policies [1]. This change is being driven by a combination of environmental [2], sustainability [3], public health [4], life quality [5] and economic agendas [6, 7], but also by major market trends towards urban, shared, electric and connected bicycles. In this context, the vision of Smart Cycling has been emerging as the shared, real-time, and collaborative

© ICST Institute for Computer Sciences, Social Informatics and Telecommunications Engineering 2022
Published by Springer Nature Switzerland AG 2022. All Rights Reserved
A. L. Martins et al. (Eds.): INTSYS 2021, LNICST 426, pp. 135–148, 2022.
https://doi.org/10.1007/978-3-030-97603-3_10

application of data, communications and services, to help best move people individually, and collectively, across the urban environment [8]. This domain of Intelligent Transport Systems (ITS) can be particularly vital for tackling Europe's growing emissions and congestion problems. ITS can make cycling mobility safer, more efficient, and more integrated into general mobility policies, through the systematic integration of information and communication technologies. Moreover, these technologies should enable new cycling related services with the capability to promote diverse forms of data-driven Innovation, help cyclists with relevant ride information, empower citizens to co-create and inform local mobility policies and allow urban planners to make more informed decisions about cycling infrastructures.

While cycling data is still sparse, recent years have seen considerable interest in the application of mobility models to cycling or even in the development of new models addressing specific cycling needs. Many mobility models have been proposed to represent particular dimensions of the cycling reality of a city or region. These mobility models include compound indexes to assess bikeability [9–11] or bike-friendliness [12–14], custom tools to estimate the potential for cycling [15, 16] or the economic value of cycling [17] and a few commercial services based mostly on data from mobile applications [18]. There is also a very broad range of smaller and more focused models, serving specific perspectives of analysis, such as hilliness [19], pollution [20], route choice [21], comfort [22] or accessibility [23]. These models are often published as open-source projects and, overall, they represent a wide spectrum of analysis of the many dimensions of urban cycling.

However, the full potential of ITS as a transformational force for urban cycling still seems to be unfulfilled. Many of its building blocks may already be there, but they are not connected in ways that allow them to deliver the type of shared, real-time collaborative application of data envisioned by smart cycling. There are many relevant models, but in the end, only a small community of users with strong technical knowledge on how to prepare, process and explore this type of data is able to work with them. This is slowing down the uptake of relevant research results by the market. Common citizens, and even the people that are meant to manage cycling mobility, may not have the expertise, the time or the practices to get value from those models. This is a particularly relevant problem for municipalities and urban planners who miss accurate, comprehensive and actionable data tools to comprehend the cycling reality of their city.

In this work, we hypothesise that the root cause for this problem might be the prevailing development paradigm, mostly based on disperse and self-contained custom processes, which fail to offer the necessary context for distributed and open innovation. A development process for a mobility model normally involves a single entity, which will start from a concrete dataset, develop a custom program, insert a few libraries, generate new data structures, and produce a tailored visualization to represent the new insights. This type of vertical self-contained process is very flexible because there is no need to consider generalization or integration issues, but it leads to monolithic models. Even when source code is shared, it often lacks the level of generalization needed to make it a clear option for other similar cases. Also, even if the model is essentially the same, the diversity of implementations or even just small variations in their assumptions can lead to fragmentation and a reduce capability to build on previous work. As a consequence, each new model becomes a self-contained package of data, specialised expertise, methodological practices, and conclusions that are hard to reproduce, generalize, recombine or improve outside the context of the process for which they were originally implemented.

A digital platform strategy might offer a viable and scalable way to deliver the value of rich mobility analytics to urban cycling ecosystems. Digital platforms are a well-known strategy to optimize the innovation efforts of an ecosystem through combinatorial and distributed innovation across organizational boundaries [24]. They have a unique capability to harness new sources of innovation based on the principles of convergence [24] and generativity [26]. Convergence means that digital technologies can combine what were previously separate components or services. These new convergence spaces enabled by digital technology provide numerous innovation opportunities for products and services, potentially transforming a hugely fragmented space of data sources, mobility models and KPIs into a shared and actionable set of data references for cycling ecosystems. Generativity means that digital technologies can produce unprompted change driven by large, varied, and uncoordinated audiences [25]. They are never complete, as they are inherently dynamic and malleable, continuously evolving and being extended by the actions of users or the contributions of a large community of product and service creators. From the perspective of their communities, digital platforms offer them the possibility to innovate by customizing parts of the digital platform to serve their specific needs.

A platform strategy may also offer the type of continuous service, possibly available for multiple territories and ready to be used, that is needed for real impact. Most models are just conceived as conceptual tools or as a part of specific planning studies. They do not offer any type of service. The few systems supporting the systematic publication of cycling metrics, e.g. Propensity to Cycle Tool [26] or the Bike Friendly Index (www. bikefriendlyindex.com) [14], are focused only on a very specific range of metrics. A properly designed digital platform should be able to provide a systematic, collaborative, and incremental micro-mobility model development paradigm with the capability to support the convergence between multiple models and promote their usage as shared references for cycling ecosystems.

1.1 Objectives

In this work, we aim to validate our basic assumptions about the limitations of current development paradigms for cycling mobility models and analyse the extent to which a platform strategy could be able to offer a fundamentally different approach to address those limitations. As an initial step towards these goals, we conceived a study, mostly based on the analysis of current mobility model implementations, to address the following objectives:

- O1: Validate the prevailing existence of generic functionality across some of those models and characterise the corresponding opportunity for horizontal services that could facilitate their development and convergence

- O2: Make an initial analysis of how a digital platform strategy could provide a more promising approach to address the problem and bring many of those models into a common system with added-value for different cycling stakeholders.

2 Related Work

Researchers, urban planners and decision makers are seeking for new ways to understand cycling and make better decisions on how to promote the adoption of cycling.

Bikeability is a relatively recent concept, derived from walkability, that tries to describe how a city environment contributes to the adoption of cycling [27]. It is related to terms like bike-friendliness [11], bike-attractiveness [28], and bike accessibility [29]. Lowry et al. defined bikeability as the comfort and convenience of a bikeway network for accessing important destinations, and bike-friendliness as a combination of bikeability, laws, policies, and community education [30].

Bikeability and bike-friendliness are composite indexes created from a weighted aggregation of multiple other factors, which can themselves be generated through their own specific models, such as hilliness [10, 19], availability of bikeway infrastructures [31], the number of bikeway lanes or its width and typology [32], the network connectivity [28, 33], the road traffic [34] and the surrounding environment [10, 27, 35]. Data used by these models can be very diverse, including open data sources, such as Gaode [31] or OpenStreetMaps [35], data from specific mobile applications [11, 38], and data obtained from surveys [32].

The Bike Score® index [37] is available for 130 cities across United States, Canada, and Australia. It comprises four equally weighted components, evaluating bike lanes, hilliness, connectivity to destinations and bicycle mode share. Copenhagenize [12] is a biennial index based on 14 different parameters. Parameters are grouped into three main areas: streetscape parameters, culture parameters, and ambition parameters. The Bicycle Cities Index [38] evaluates 16 city indicators related to cycling. This index focuses on six main categories related to weather, percentage of bicycle usage, crime and safety, infrastructure, bike sharing and events. Bike Friendly Index [14] evaluates the city cycling ecosystem using 12 indicators grouped around 5 main areas: hilliness, built environment, infrastructure, politic commitment, and bicycles habits. These components are then weighted to calculate the general index. To ensure replicability, this index is based on open-source data such as Census, Copernicus OSM and BASE Portal.

These indexes are a powerful tool for understanding the cycling reality of a city, possibly acting as a guide for urban planners, designers, and regulators to focus their efforts and investments on the development of a bicycle-friendly transport environment [39]. However, they are complex to generate, especially because only a small part of the metrics involved can actually be generated automatically in a systematic way.

Platforms represent an alternative way to approach cycling analytics. PCT [26] is a web-based tool for estimating cycling potential and corresponding health and CO_2 benefits down to the street level for England and Wales. Using 2011 Census data for commuting and cycle to school, they quantify desire lines and simulate different scenarios. Pedal Heat [40] is a platform that helps cities to visualize cycling traffic. Users can install a mobile application that incentivizes them to ride a bicycle through virtual rewards. Information is then sent to the platform where it can be visualized. The visualization layers include the cycling infrastructure, a heat map of the most demanded street segments and cyclists' flow in real-time. Bike Citizens Analytics [41] is a platform that offers (commercially) cycling analytics and navigation based on data collected by users using the Bike Citizens mobile application. Users are incentivized through challenges, rewards, and badges. Strava Metro [18] is another commercial service that offers analytics services based on data produced by users of the Strava mobile application.

3 Methodology

This work is part of a broader research effort aiming at conceptualizing and developing a new type of cycling analytics platform for urban environments. This broader research is based on the principles of Design Science Research (DSR) [42], with this specific part corresponding to what might be described as first two steps of a DSR process [43]: problem identification and motivation and definition of the objectives for a solution.

In regard to problem identification, our aim is to study the basic premise behind the motivation for this work. This is based on the idea that micro-mobility models are mostly based on custom processes that fail to consider generalization or integration issues, and that it should be possible and advantageous to approach them instead as compositions of shared horizontal services in the context of a common platform. The study of this problem should provide an initial validation of the overall approach, but it should also help to gain a deeper understanding of its multiple opportunities and limitations. To validate the existence of generic functionality across multiple models and identify concrete opportunities for convergence around shared services, we conducted an analysis of 3 commonly used cycling mobility models. The approach is to decompose those models into a set of atomic steps and analyse the existence of shared generic operations. A high-level of shared generic operations should indicate a high potential for the creation of horizontal services that could significantly lower the effort needed to develop those model implementations.

In regard to the definition of the objectives for a solution, our aim is to to make an initial analysis of how digital technology platforms may provide a more promising path for addressing the problem. Our approach is to analyse how the general principles of digital platforms, combined with the results from the study of this concrete problem domain, can be used as a general framework for a new type of solution for cycling analytics. In the process, we also expect to reach an initial perspective on what might be some of the expected properties of such platform.

4 Results

The first step in this study was the selection and analysis of 3 cycling mobility models. We selected a small number because the aim was not to consider the complete range of possibilities, but only to have a diverse sample to assess some of the common operations that compose the algorithms that create those models. To better accomplish these goals, we select 3 models that are relatively simple in their algorithms, but address common, and yet, very diverse data processing goals in the cycling domain. Table 1 enumerates the 3 models used as input for our study.

Table 1. Mobility models analysed in this study.

Model	Description
Hilliness [19]	This model takes a Digital Elevation Model and a set of Street Network Data and classifies network segments according to the respective cycling effort associated with street slope
Accessibility [23]	This model takes an origin-destination matrix with travel costs and classifies city areas according to their accessibility. Connection costs can be very diverse, e.g. travel time, distance, slope or risk,
Route Characterization [Own model]	This model takes a set of cycling tracks and a scope of OSM road network and classifies network segments according to aggregate properties e.g. average speeds, acceleration markers, stops, turns, and volume

The following step was to analyse, in detail, the algorithms of each of these models and decompose them into a set of atomic code blocks. Each of those blocks should correspond to a sequence of related instructions aiming at a common action that would not make sense to execute partially, in this or in other contexts. We then analysed each of these atomic blocks to assess their potential for generalization or integration. Table 2 is a selection of the atomic code blocks, from the 3 models, which we identified as having the potential to be offered to many different models as common horizontal features in a

Table 2. Possible horizontal features identified in the analysis and their dependencies.

Operation	Analysis of possible dependencies
Get street network data from Open Street Map	This requires domain knowledge about the usage of the OSM API. There is an implicit spatial scope that makes this operation specific to the implementation. Output data is generic
Get shapefiles for region boundaries	This requires domain knowledge about the availability and integration of region boundaries. There is an implicit spatial scope embedded in some operations. Output data is generic
Annotate network with slope information	This requires domain knowledge on how to obtain and apply elevation data for a concrete region. There is an implicit spatial scope embedded in some operations. Output data is generic
Classify a route network according to a cycling effort model	This requires domain knowledge on classification models for cycling effort. There is an implicit spatial scope embedded in some operations. Output data is generic
Estimate accessibility from OD matrix and opportunities	This requires domain knowledge on classification models for cycling accessibility. There is an implicit spatial scope embedded in some operations
Map-matching route points to OSM points	This requires domain knowledge on map matching methods
Compute average speed for road network segments	Code can be reused with any compatible route data format, but ability to aggregate multiple routes is essential

digital platform. These algorithms are often created for a specific purpose and, even if they often include many library functions, they also have strong dependencies associated with the concrete assumptions of a particular implementation.

The first observation is the high number of procedures that are not specific to each of these models and could potentially be offered as horizontal features on a digital platform to serve similar needs across multiple cycling models. From the analysis of merely 3 models, we were able to identify 7 atomic blocks corresponding to operations that other models may also need to execute in very similar ways. These results as strongly aligned with our initial hypothesis about the existence of generic functionality across many of these mobility models.

Table 2 also represents the diversity of dependencies that we found in the analysis of these 3 models, and which may prevent their reusage outside their initial implementation context. A very common dependency is the specific domain knowledge embedded across these implementations. This knowledge is often present in the usage of specific enabling services or data sources needed by those models, e.g. MapMatching, application of elevation data, mapping locations to administrative regions and their respective boundaries or working with Open Street Map. None of these is necessarily very complex, per se. However, having to learn about the correct usage of multiple services, all of which are just enablers for the concrete purpose of the model being developed, may represent a huge barrier to the development of new models or the usage of existing ones, even for users with general knowledge on mobility systems.

Another common form of dependency is related with the implicit scope assumptions, and particularly those referring to the spatial context of the work. For example, by focusing the model on a city, the selection of spatial data and the scope of the visualizations created can all be easily aligned. While some of these dependencies may be obvious from the implementation and potentially easy to change, many other are more deeply embedded in the code and severely limit the applicability of the same implementation to other spatial contexts.

There are also implications that can be linked directly to the self-contained nature of these models. An important group of operations involved the association with various type of geographic data, e.g. obtaining OSM road networks, obtaining elevation data to determine segment slope, mapping routes to OSM points or postal codes. These are not only very generic operations, they are also operations that could be done only once to serve the needs of many models. However, since each model is self-contained, it needs to independently obtain all of its data and repeat the process for each execution. In a platform approach, this type of global reference data could be managed as a horizontal feature to be shared across the entire system and made available to multiple models. Likewise, a shared service would also provide a much-needed aggregation context where data from multiple models could be treated in an integrated way and used to generate significant new value from the existing data. In particular, geospatial references are the ultimate convergence mechanism, allowing spatial relationships encoded in source data to support the aggregation of multiple independent data under a common spatial reference, and creating an immediate association between data that refers to the same region, postal code, route or route point.

There are also commonly used functions that operate on a specific dataset. Typical examples may include operations such as: convert between data representation formats, calculate metadata for a given route or the distance between two points in a route network. The existence of these functions saves model creators from additional programming effort, and promotes more robust solutions. While we can expect many of these operations to become part of a digital platform, this form of generalization is already supported by a multitude of code libraries available from multiple sources. Since their execution is self-contained process, similar to a micro-service paradigm, they do not have external dependencies. Still, a coordinated library could play an important role in promoting convergence towards common approaches that improve the transparency of the models that use them and potentiate convergence towards common system approaches and data formats. It should also reduce the complexity involved in selecting and learning how to apply the functions from new libraries.

A final observation refers to the huge diversity of data types and formats that are involved in all of these models. Regardless of the obvious benefits that may emerge from more standard approaches to data publication, a cycling analytics platform should be designed to accommodate this extreme diversity, offering multiple convergence mechanisms to absorb that heterogeneity through various types of data transformations, rather than trying to impose its own data formats.

5   Key Properties for a Platform Strategy for Cycling Analytics

In this section, we make an initial analysis of how a digital platform strategy could provide a more promising approach to address the challenges of urban cycling analytics. Considering that this is still largely an emerging domain, it may be too early yet to fully comprehend the nature of this new opportunity space and the concrete details of what these smart cycling ecosystems will look like. It will take some time, and many cumulative experiments, before we can reach a stage where a more grounded analysis of those properties will become possible.

At this stage, we can build on the results of our study and also on the general principles of platform innovation [24] [26] to make an initial analysis of the key properties that may characterize a platform strategy to uncover the potential of digital innovation in urban cycling analytics.

Cycling specific. The platform should be focused specifically on the needs of micro-mobility. While obviously sharing many principles with more mature forms of mobility analysis, e.g. public transportation or automotive, cycling is nevertheless substantially different in regard to the nature of the data sources, the nature of route classifications, the key performance indicators or the role of real-time data. This focus on the specifics of micro-mobility means placing those core needs at the forefront of the analytics systems. Still, cycling should not be seen as an isolated reality in urban mobility and the platform should always consider its own integration with broader mobility systems, particularly in a MaaS perspective [44].

A Multi-sided Platform for the Cycling Ecosystem. A basic premise for any Digital Platform is the ability to congregate many users and very different types of stakeholders.

Cycling communities should find in this platform the ideal environment for a broad range of collective activities that will significantly expand the cycling experience. However, this form of convergence should also bring together many other types of stakeholders, such as bike sharing operators, bike shops, city authorities, mobility authorities, bike-friendly businesses, citizens in general, public parking facilities, bike manufactures or digital cycling technology companies. By significantly lowering the barriers for interaction, a platform should help to blur the boundaries between these many separate domains and unlock new forms of value exchange that will benefit all the stakeholders involved.

A Global Service for Many Local Contexts. The need for cycling services is a global need. Therefore, the proposed platform should offer a broad set of tools, services, data and algorithms to address the cycling challenges of any city in the world, regardless of its characteristics or its level of cycling readiness. Also, the scale associated with a global service is essential for reaching the critical mass that is needed for the platform to be perceived by others as a catalyst for convergence. However, this global perspective should be counterbalanced by the need to connect to local cycling ecosystems, which constitute a major source for locativeness and generativity-based innovation. This may involve the promotion of local cycling promotion groups, access to detailed information about the local infrastructures and regulations, the opportunity to participate in the co-creation of local mobility policies or specific MaaS integrations.

Collective Intelligence. The platform should have the capability to observe and learn about cycling mobility in a way that supports optimizations and informs decision-making at multiple levels of the system. Under a smart cycling paradigm, the bike should no longer be a single isolated entity. Instead, it should become a vehicle that can sense and share data, that can interact with other vehicles on the road, that can learn from its environment and from the way it is used. This capability to observe reality, learn from the initiatives undertaken, and continually adjust its services to incrementally and measurably improve the overall performance of the system should result in safer, more efficient or more enjoyable rides. Moreover, the significant volumes of digital traces generated from those rides should become a huge driver for new innovations, many of which will not even have been anticipated by the platform creators. Rather than a centralized data collector, the system should explore forms of situated intelligence that begin directly on the bike, e.g. to characterise the riding context, detect near miss situations or even send accident notifications, and go all the way up to the broader understanding of urban mobility.

Horizontal Innovation. A normal consequence of generativity is that innovation activities increasingly become horizontal as efficiencies are gained by applying the same innovation activities and knowledge across multiple products or platforms [24]. A platform should thus provide a horizontal technical foundation upon which many complementary products and services can easily be combined, each offering its own set of knowledge-intensive features. This should lower the barrier for new innovations, as they can more easily emerge from simpler new models or from the multiple recombination possibilities that can emerge from repurposing existing models across many usage contexts. The horizontal innovation involved would also enable the expertise associated with data models to become readily available across domains and usage contexts. This would help to bring together what are now separate experiences and domains, such as Urban planning, Urban KPIs, Mobility models development, cycling activism and cycling itself. Finally, generativity innovation would mean that many more and more advanced models could quickly emerge from the concrete learning resulting from the wide availability and usage of those models.

Progressive Decomposition and Convergence. From the results of the study with mobility models, we can identify the need to promote convergence between many independently developed analytics models. This should go beyond the use of a shared set of horizontal services or libraries and lead to a mesh of multiple interconnected models that may depend on each other as different layers of data processing. Given the inherent diversity of mobility models and data sources, any convergence strategy should be very minimalist, avoiding constraints on how those models are executed, on what programming language they are developed or on the types of input data they might use.

Regarding data, a platform may promote some convergence by facilitating the use of canonical data formats for representing the most common types of data. While totally optional, a few well-known data formats for common data types, promoted by an extensive collection of conversion and aggregation functions may offer a shared resource that makes data convergence simpler, whenever suitable.

Regarding the algorithms of the models, the convergence process should promote their decomposition into basic steps. Each model needs to be described in a way that formally defines the model generation process as dataflows, with specific data sources, data transformations, concrete parameterizations of the algorithms used and concrete and publishable outputs. This could then be used to promote the progressive mapping of some of those parts into horizontal features offered directly by the platform. The explicit description of the transformation processes would thus constitute a key enabler for convergence. Even a simple description process, when made in a coherent way for multiple dataflows, can help to blur differences between various processes and emphasize any existing similarities. This should be a fundamental first step to decouple some of those elements from specific processes and make them available as horizontal features readily available for composing new models.

This should have a major impact in the development of cycling mobility models, reducing the development effort and potentially improving their overall quality, as most of their code would now be based on mature services with greater development quality, better performance and simplified programming models. It should also make more explicit the overlap between different models. Very similar models can be described in different ways and using diverse terminology. While it may not be possible to define absolute boundaries between model concepts, this analytics platform may help to promote convergence towards recognizable model categories with similar goals and offering similar properties. This should facilitate comparative analysis that place side-by-side alternative ways to produce similar outputs and assess their relative performance. This progressive abstraction and decomposition should ultimately lead to a many-to-many relationship between data sources and models, with common data types being explored in multiple ways by many complementary models and some models supporting the ability to be generated from alternative sources, and in this way be able to adjust themselves to the data reality of different cycling ecosystems.

6 Conclusions

Achieving the full potential of ITS requires the convergence of the efforts and the knowledge of multiple entities. This is also true for cycling mobility and for the many models that aim to provide particular perspectives on the cycling reality of cities. Currently, their prevailing development paradigm is based on dispersed, vertical, self-contained and custom processes, which fail to offer the necessary context for distributed and open innovation. As a consequence, each new effort results in a new package of data, expertise and methodologies that are hard to reproduce, generalize, recombine or improve outside their original context.

We have shown that despite their current dispersion, commonly used cycling models are composed of basic processes with a high potential to be used as horizontal features in the context of a digital platform approach. This represents an initial validation of the problem and highlights an opportunity for a new type of solution based on a platform strategy. We have also identified some of the dependencies that are often embedded in the implementation of those models and prevent them from being widely repurposed by people outside their initial development context. These are fundamental hints for understanding how they can be redesigned around horizontal features shared among multiple model implementations.

Building on those results, and also on the more general principles of digital innovation associated with digital platforms, we have also outlined a set of key design principles for the development of a digital platform strategy for cycling analytics. This should constitute a valuable contribution to inform the development of a new generation of cycling platforms for urban environments.

6.1 Future Work

We are currently working on an initial prototype of a digital technology platform that can deliver the knowledge from micro-mobility models in ways that professional urban planners, policymakers and citizens can use to create solutions for their own specific micro-mobility problems. This should include data processing capabilities, an analytics database with aggregated data, an API for supporting the creation of public services, collective intelligence services and a web portal with ready to consume data and services. This platform will be a major output of this work, but also one of its most fundamental research tools. As a generative platform, the platform will also be continuously challenged and continuously evolving with the progressive integration of new models and also more data, particularly data obtained from cyclists. We expect it might serve a powerful collaborative tool for engaging with other researchers and experts, especially in the field of urban mobility, who will have the opportunity to deploy their own models and explore their own research or planning goals.

Acknowledgements. This work is supported by: European Structural and Investment Funds in the FEDER component, through the Operational Competitiveness and Internationalization Programme (COMPETE 2020) [Project n° 039334; Funding Reference: POCI-01-0247-FEDER-039334].

References

1. Bulc, V.: Cycling: green and efficient transport for the future, European Commission. (2016). https://ec.europa.eu/commission/commissioners/2014-2019/bulc/blog/cycling-green-and-efficient-transport-future_en. Accessed 31 Oct 2019
2. Fishman, E., Washington, S., Haworth, N.: Bike share: a synthesis of the literature. Transp. Rev. **33**(2) (2013)
3. Neves, A., Brand, C.: Assessing the potential for carbon emissions savings from replacing short car trips with walking and cycling using a mixed GPS-travel diary approach. Trans. Res. Part A: Policy Pract. **123**, 130–146 (2019)
4. Oja, P., et al.: Health benefits of cycling: a systematic review. Scand. J. Med. Sci. Sports **21**(4), 496–509 (2011)
5. Penedo, F.J., Dahn, J.R.: Exercise and well-being: a review of mental and physical health benefits associated with physical activity. Curr. Opin. Psychiat. **18**(2), 189–193 (2005)
6. Blondiau, T., van Zeebroeck, B., Haubold, H.: Economic benefits of increased cycling. In: Transportation Research Procedia. pp. 2306–2313 (2016)
7. Arancibia, D., Savan, B., Ledsham, T., Bennington, M.: Economic impacts of cycling in dense urban areas: literature review. In: Transportation Research Board 94th Annual Meeting (2015)
8. Stratta, P.: Towards a Smarter Cycling. On the brink of a Smart (R)evolution, European Cyclists' Federation. https://ecf.com/what-we-do/cycling-new-technologies/towards-smarter-cycling, Accessed 30 June 2020
9. Gholamialam, A., Matisziw, T.C.: Modeling bikeability of urban systems. Geogr. Anal. **51**(2), 73–89 (2019)
10. Grigore, E., Garrick, N., Fuhrer, R., Axhausen, I.K.W.: Bikeability in basel. Trans. Res. Record J. Trans. Res. Board. **2673**(6), 607–617 (2019)
11. de Matos, F.L., Fernandes, J.M., Sampaio, C., Macedo, J., Coelho, M.C., Bandeira, J.: Development of an information system for cycling navigation. Trans. Res. Procedia. **52**(2020), 107–114 (2021)
12. Copenhagenize: 2019 Copenhagenize Index - Copenhagenize, Copenhagenize index. https://copenhagenizeindex.eu/, Accessed 28 July 2020 (2019)
13. WalkScore: Bike Score Methodology. https://www.walkscore.com/bike-score-methodology.shtml. Accessed 18 May 2021 (2018)
14. Figueiredo, A.P. e Vale, D.S.: BikeFriendlyIndex – Um indíce para avaliação da amigabilidade de um concelho para a utilização da bicicleta enquanto modo de transporte urbano. www.bikefriendlyindex.com (2018)
15. PCT.BIKE: Welcome to the Propensity to Cycle Tool (PCT). https://www.pct.bike/. Accessed May 04 2021
16. Silva, C., S. Marques, J., Lopes, M., M. Dias, A.: The gross potential for cycling: planning for human scale urban mobility. In: Mladenović, M.N., Toivonen, T., Willberg, E., Geurs, K.T. (eds.) Transport in Human Scale Cities. pp. 157–168. Edward Elgar Publishing, United Kingdom (2021)
17. Ferreira, J.P., Isidoro, C., Moura Sá, F., Baptista Da Mota, J.C.: The economic value for cycling – a methodological assessment for Starter Cities. Hábitat y Sociedad. **13**, (2020)https://doi.org/10.12795/HabitatySociedad.2020.i13.03
18. Lee, K., Sener, I.N.: Strava Metro data for bicycle monitoring: a literature review. Transp. Rev. **41**(1), 27–47 (2021)
19. U-Shift lab: Declives-RedeViaria. https://github.com/U-Shift/Declives-RedeViaria. Accessed 28 May 2021 (2020)
20. Tran, P.T.M., Zhao, M., Yamamoto, K., Minet, L., Nguyen, T., Balasubramanian, R.: Cyclists' personal exposure to traffic-related air pollution and its influence on bikeability. Transp. Res. Part D Transp. Environ. **88**, 102563 (2020). https://doi.org/10.1016/j.trd.2020.102563

21. Alattar, M.A., Cottrill, C., Beecroft, M.: Modelling cyclists' route choice using Strava and OSMnx: A case study of the city of Glasgow. Trans. Res. Inter. Persp. **9** (March), 100301 (2021)
22. Berger, M., Dörrzapf, L.: Sensing comfort in bicycling in addition to travel data. Trans. Res. Proc. **32**, 524–534 (2018)
23. David Vale: Calculate accessibility from an OD matrix on python (version 2.0). https://github.com/davidsvale/calculate-accessibility. Accessed 24 June 2021 (2020)
24. Ciriello, R.F., Richter, A., Schwabe, G.: Digital innovation. Bus. Inf. Syst. Eng. **60**(6), 563–569 (2018). https://doi.org/10.1007/s12599-018-0559-8
25. Zittrain, J.L.: The generative Internet (2006)
26. Lovelace, R., Goodman, A., Aldred, R., Berkoff, N., Abbas, A., Woodcock, J.: The propensity to cycle tool: An open source online system for sustainable transport planning. J. Trans. Land Use. **10**(1), 505–528 (2017)
27. Porter, A.K., Kohl, H.W., Pérez, A., Reininger, B., Pettee Gabriel, K., Salvo, D.: Bikeability: assessing the objectively measured environment in relation to recreation and transportation bicycling. Environ. Behav. **52**(8), 861–894 (2020)
28. Kamel, M.B., Sayed, T., Bigazzi, A.: A composite zonal index for biking attractiveness and safety. Accid. Anal. Prevent. **137**(October 2019), 105439 (2020)
29. Saghapour, T., Moridpour, S., Thompson, R.G.: Measuring cycling accessibility in metropolitan areas. Int. J. Sustain. Transp. (2017)
30. Lowry, M., Callister, D., Gresham, M., Moore, B.: Assessment of communitywide bikeability with bicycle level of service. Transp. Res. Rec. **2314**(2314), 41–48 (2012)
31. Gu, P., Han, Z., Cao, Z., Chen, Y., Jiang, Y.: Using open source data to measure street walkability and bikeability in China: a case of four cities. Transp. Res. Rec. **2672**(31), 63–75 (2018)
32. Schmid-Querg, J., Keler, A., Grigoropoulos, G.: The munich bikeability index: A practical approach for measuring urban bikeability. Sustainability **13**(1), 428 (2021). https://doi.org/10.3390/su13010428
33. Lin, J.J., Wei, Y.H.: Assessing area-wide bikeability: a grey analytic network process. Transp. Res. Part A: Policy Pract. **113**(1), 381–396 (2018)
34. Arellana, J., Saltarín, M., Larrañaga, A.M., González, V.I., Henao, C.A.: Developing an urban bikeability index for different types of cyclists as a tool to prioritise bicycle infrastructure investments. Trans. Res. Part A Policy Pract. **139**, 310–334 (2020)
35. Tran, P.T.M., Zhao, M., Yamamoto, K., Minet, L., Nguyen, T., Balasubramanian, R.: Cyclists' personal exposure to traffic-related air pollution and its influence on bikeability. Trans. Res. Part D Trans. Environ. **88** (November), 102563 (2020)
36. Resch, B., Puetz, I., Bluemke, M., Kyriakou, K., Miksch, J.: An interdisciplinary mixed-methods approach to analyzing urban spaces: the case of urban walkability and bikeability. Int. J. Environ. Res. Public Health **17**(19), 6994 (2020). https://doi.org/10.3390/ijerph17196994
37. Walk Score: Bike Score Methodology. https://www.walkscore.com/bike-score-methodology.shtml. Accessed 10 May, 2021 (2018)
38. Coya: Global Bicycle Cities Index 2019 | Coya. https://www.coya.com/bike/index-2019. Accessed 18 May 2021 (2019)
39. Krenn, P.J., Oja, P., Titze, S.: Development of a bikeability index to assess the bicycle-friendliness of urban environments. Open J. Civil Eng. **05**(04), 451–459 (2015)
40. KAPPO: Ciclistas - KAPPO Bike. https://www.kappo.bike/web/app.php. Accessed 05 May 2021
41. Bike Citizens: The GPS cycling data analysis tool - for evidence based transport planning. https://cyclingdata.net/. Accessed 18 May 2021 (2017)

42. Hevner, M., Park, R.: Design science in information systems research. MIS Quart. **28**(1), 75–105 (2004)
43. Peffers, K., et al.: Design science research process: a model for producing and presenting information systems research. ArXiv (2020)
44. Jittrapirom, P., Caiati, V., Feneri, A.-M., Ebrahimigharehbaghi, S., Alonso-González, M.J., Narayan, J.: Mobility as a service: a critical review of definitions, assessments of schemes, and key challenges. Urban Planning. **2**(2), 13–25 (2017)

Mobisuite: A User-Friendly Tool to Exploit E-Ticketing Data and Support Public Transport Planning

Alexander Fazari, Maurizio Arnone$^{(\boxtimes)}$, Cristiana Botta, Brunella Caroleo, and Stefano Pensa

Links Foundation, Via Pier Carlo Boggio, 61, 10138 Torino, Italy
{maurizio.arnone,cristiana.botta,brunella.caroleo,
stefano.pensa}@linksfoundation.com
https://linksfoundation.com/

Abstract. Smart cards for public transportation have become a significant source of information for analyzing mobility trends and assisting public authorities and transportation organizations in making decisions. This article describes a visualization tool developed by LINKS Foundation that exhibits spatial and temporal characteristics, with the goal of demonstrating the potential of analysing and visualising smart card validation and transit data towards better decision making. The Piedmont region's transit data was used as a case study. The developed public transport visualization tool (called Mobisuite) represents the transit system supply, the mobility demand, and the ticketing system through three primary visualization modules. The tool employs a virtual check out algorithm, which estimates the users' travel diary and aids in the calculation of various transit indicators, e.g. passenger kilometers, maximum load, number of on-boarding passengers, average load. Mobisuite can be a helpful tool for displaying the public transport system for the whole transport network at a glance, and it can be used to simplify communication between transit operators and public agencies regarding the public transport planning, operation and fares.

Keywords: Smart-card ticket · Decision support systems · Fare collection · E-ticketing data · Transit planning · Public transportation · Transportation demand · Intelligent transportation systems

1 Introduction

In the last decade, Public transportation authorities are increasingly relying on smart card electronic fare collection systems [1]. In urban public transport, smart cards collect data of millions of users boarding vehicles over the network every day.

The large amount of daily collected data from smart card validations has created an opportunity to feature data engineering in order to better understand the complexities of urban mobility, which is a challenge for transportation researchers and stakeholders. The term "big data" emerged to describe the

A. L. Martins et al. (Eds.): INTSYS 2021, LNICST 426, pp. 149–161, 2022.
https://doi.org/10.1007/978-3-030-97603-3_11

massive amount of data generated, which exposes a significant new age transformation and reflects a significant change in how people live, act, and think [2]. Although the big data is varying in terms of source and type, it remains data. Thus, data processing and analysis are required including data acquisition, data harmonization, data storage and management, data processing (including data mining and smart analysis) and data presentation [3].

The big data on human mobility has been used to study human behaviors [4], allowing the discovery of new complex mobility patterns in the form of insightful indicators, that can be useful to manage and improve mobility in cities and in urban areas. In essence, these big data sources may help respond to the needs of planners and decision makers. In fact, planning is a decision process that needs to mine rich information to serve plan development, decision making and plan implementation evaluation [3].

Surveys have usually been used to determine demand and supply in the transportation industry. However, since surveying entails primarily in-person interviews and a heavy workload, it is an expensive and restricted form of data collection [5], as more datasets related to the use of transportation systems and human mobility have been created and made available, new opportunities beyond survey towards data-driven research has been emerged, especially data visualization tools. Data visualization converts these datasets into appropriate digital representations, which can lead to improvements in transportation system design, administration, and operations [6]. Bridging the demand-supply gap in transit service is critical for public transportation management, as planning steps can be taken to increase supply in high-demand areas or boost inadequate transit service deployment in low-demand areas [7].

Demand in transport systems can be very sensitive to sudden disruptive events. For example, during COVID-19 pandemic, public transport was one of the most disruptive sectors with early estimates suggesting that the drop in ridership during lockdown periods has been as much as 80%–90% in major cities in China, Iran, Italy and the United States, and as much as 70% for some operators in the United Kingdom [8]. Different measures have been taken into consideration by service providers, which include the reduction of service frequencies, the change of timetables and vehicle schedules, and the reduction of the total duration of the daily operations. All of these measures translate into the dimensioning of service capacity. Several transport operators have reduced their service frequencies to less than one-third of the pre pandemic time. Nonetheless, such decisions are rarely made based on a system-wide analysis [9]. In consequence, public transportation providers and local authorities have an urge for tools to help them make decisions on how to use their existing services more efficiently.

In recent years, many researchers approached the issue of visualizing information coming from public transport data in order to support public transport providers' decisions. For example, Prommaharaj et al. (2020) [10] developed a visualization tool for public transport data, but this tool was related only to the supply side (i.e. GTFS data) and not on the demand side (i.e. user validations).

Other research approached the problem of data fusion of APC (Automated Passenger Counting), Smart Cards and GTFS to visualize public transit use (Giraud et al., 2016) [11], but the resulting web interface was mainly aimed at supporting transit planners to see the movements of the users within the network. Also other studies developed open architecture platforms for transit data demonstration, analysis and visualization. For example, Kurkcu et al. (2017) [12] applied a bus trajectory data to develop a web-based tool to acquire, store, process and visualize bus trajectory data. Palomo et al. (2016) [13] proposed an online visualization tool, Trips Explorer (TR-EX), for analyzing reliability of transportation schedules. The tool allows users to compare planned timetables against real service, to analyze speed profile at route segments level, and to assess delay, wait time and reliability at station level. The AFC (Automated Fare Collection) data have been also explored by Anwar et al. (2016) [14] to develop a web-based application to monitor and visualize the performance of bus fleets.

Mobisuite fits into this line of research, seeking to combine - in addition to the analysis and visualisation of supply and demand - an analysis of ticketing fares related to the use of public transport, so that planners and transport operators can have a complete and integrated perspective of their services.

In this work Mobisuite is presented as a tool aimed to support transport planning to analyse and visualise transit data towards better decision making for the enhancement of the services of transport operators. Mobisuite is not a simulation or optimization tool. It analyzes and compares current supply and demand data. Moreover, it evaluates the impact of new integrated fare models on users and transport operator systems. Mobisuite reflects various transit system characteristics through three different interfaces: (1) users' demand: visualizes the current service usage (also enabling for temporal comparisons in terms of historical data), provides how much, when, where, and by whom the public transport (PT) services are used; (2) public transport supply: illustrates the structure of the PT service network (e.g. how many rides are provided, when and where); (3) ticketing: shows how different sorts of smart card titles are utilized (in terms of how much, when, where, and by whom). Thanks to Mobisuite, the PT planners and the transport operators will be able to have a full perspective of the system of services and their utilization. The insights they get from Mobisuite will help them fulfill the demands of transportation customers, allowing them to modify the services they offer and so provide a high-quality and tailored service.

The article is structured as follows: the data definition, architecture specifications and analysis indicators of Mobisuite are described in Sect. 2; the functioning of the tool and the results are discussed in Sect. 3; finally, Sect. 4 provides conclusions and future research directions.

2 Methodology

2.1 Business Understanding

BIP [15] - Biglietto Integrato Piemonte is the integrated electronic ticketing system of the Piedmont Region, located in the northwest of Italy, that allows, thanks to a contactless smart card, access to any public transport in any area of the regional territory. BIPEX [16] is the protocol for data exchange between transport companies, organizations and governments. BIPEX was developed using European and international open standards (TransModel, NeTEx, and SIRI) with the aim of enabling electronic ticketing systems to communicate with each other as widely as possible and harmonize data collection. BIP and BIPEX were created by 5T [17] (i.e. Telematic Technologies for Transport and Traffic in Turin) on behalf of the Piedmont Region and it is in use at PT companies (road and rail) operating in the Piedmont BIP electronic ticketing system. The contactless smart card based on BIP can be used to load both pay per use credit and travel passes to cover all possible trips and types of PT tickets available in the Piedmont Region, regardless of route, mode of transportation, or the PT company involved, as well as to use bike-sharing.

The Piedmont Region is used as a case study to show the development of a tool to help transportation planning by analyzing and visualizing transit data in order to make better decisions for the expansion of transportation operators' services.

2.2 Data Understanding

The data was provided by 5T which contains the metadata based on NeTEx standard. NeTEx [18] is a CEN "European Committee for Standardization" Technical Standard for exchanging Public Transport schedules and related data. It is divided into three parts, each covering a functional subset of the CEN Transmodel [19] for Public Transport Information:

1. Part 1 describes the Public Transport Network topology (CEN/TS 16614-1:2014);
2. Part 2 describes Scheduled Timetables (CEN/TS 16614-2:2014);
3. Part 3 covers Fare information (CEN/TS 16614-3:2015);

The metadata is based on a complete and flexible XML schema, the XML is further flattened and relevant fields are selected to create the input data for Mobisuite tool. Along with the Public Transport Network topology, Scheduled Timetables and Fare information, the passenger validation data and sales data were also provided for the months of January and February 2018, which Mobisuite used in the development phase.

2.3   Data Preparation

Extract and Harmonized Module. Mobisuite is a tool which makes use of BIP data to build various fundamental infrastructure modules shown in Fig. 1; the first module was created to extract and harmonize BIP raw data.

Fig. 1. Flow of the elaborations and analysis process of BIP data, from raw data to visualization within the Mobisuite tool.

Extract and harmonized module transforms the raw data collected with electronic smart cards into 8 unstructured data categories listed in Table 1 in a dictionary serialization using Python programming language, where each object has a key and a corresponding value represented as a pair (key: value). Python libraries such as Pandas, Numpy, and Geopy were utilized to elaborate and analyze the data.

2.4   Data Modeling

Virtual Check-Out Module: All the previous data extracted from the extract and harmonization module acts as an input to the virtual_check-out module which was created based on the trip-chaining model for estimation of the check out of the passengers[20]. The majority of passengers are travel pass holders (who just need to check-in), and there aren't enough pay-per-use credit transactions to allow for model training. The virtual check-out module was used to create the "travel diary," which is a list of all the trips carried out by a user on a given day, organized chronologically and with all essential information (recorded or calculated), such as: date, service, line, vehicle, operator, boarding bus stop (recognized by GPS system at check-in), boarding time (check-in time), alighting bus stop (estimated for travel pass users), alighting time (calculated for travel pass users based on the estimated bus stop alighting location and travel duration between boarding and alighting), kilometers traveled (the distance between the boarding and alighting bus stops) and time on board (the difference between the boarding and alighting times).

Virtual check-out trip chaining models are based on few key assumptions [20]:

1. A passenger's most likely alighting stop is the boarding stop of his next trip (or one close by);
2. Passengers do not use private cars between two consecutive public transportation trip legs;
3. Passengers do not move over a long distance;

Table 1. BIP data harmonization

Extract and Harmonized Module Output	Descriptions
Trip	Contains nested data described by a key of the Trip_id and data for Route_id, Line_id as values: (Trip_id: Trip_ id,Route_id, Line_id)
Calendar	Contains the dates where the trip is active, formatted in a dictionary with the Trip_id as key and a list of days with this format DD/MM/YYYY as the values: (Trip_id: [Date])
Stop code	Contains the stop number as key and the corresponding Stop_id as value: (Stop_number: Stop_id)
Trip_stops	Contains nested data identified by Trip_id as key, and the list of the stops_id in this trip as values. Then each stop_id has nested data describing the stop: (Trip_id:[Stop_id:[Stop_id, Trip_id, Date, Direction, Route_id, Line_id, Arrival_time, Stop_sequence]
Arch	Is a data structure, with a a couple of consequent Stops_id as key: (departure and arrival stops) and nested data related to the distance between the two stops, as a value: (Stop_departure, Stop_arrival, Arch_Km, Arch_id)
Programmed and definitive trip	Stores the trip_id in the definitive version (executed trip) and its corresponding programmed trip. It is used as a validator in the virtual check-out algorithm
Validation	A relational database containing the validation information for each smart card, including the card's Id, the time of validation, the validation procedure, the stop_id of the validation, the line_id, the trip_id and the route_id. The validation procedure differs between travel pass holders (who just need to check-in) and pay-per-use passengers (required to both check-in and check-out)
Sales data	Includes smart card title sales and passenger renewals, which were utilized in ticketing analyses

Virtual check-out algorithm follows several steps:

1. For each BIP smart card ID, a list of the validations and boarding stops sorted by time of check-in is created. Each check-in is associated with the corresponding service so that it is possible to identify the sequence of services used and boarding stops for each trip chain ("travel diary");
2. Services are matched with their route;
3. The BIP smart card ID corresponding to "single trips", whose destination cannot be estimated, are identified and eliminated from the starting database;
4. for each BIP smart card ID corresponding to a normal trip and for each consecutive couple of boarding stop and previous route used, the entry of the boarding stop of the next route and the previous route is the estimated alighting stop of user transferring from the route in day based on the fulfillment of the algorithm assumptions;
5. the alighting stops estimated represent the virtual check-outs and are inserted in the travel diary associated to each BIP smart card ID;

Data Processing Module: The last module is data processing, which does additional analysis and computation of various transport indicators before feeding it to the last mile visualization tools. The analyses are based on the output of the Virtual check-out trip chaining model and sales data.

2.5 Evaluation

The Virtual check-out trip chaining models has been tested and validated using the travelling data collected in the province of Cuneo, located within the Piedmont Region, at the end of 2017 where the algorithm was able to estimate the alighting bus stop of 94% of the valid travel pass holder validations[20]:. The model's reliability was assessed in particular by using the same technique to a data sample of the pay-per-use credit (where both check-in and check-out are necessary) and comparing estimated alighting bus stops with those recorded automatically. More than 70% of the estimated alighting bus stops in the case study matched the one reported or was at a maximum distance of 500 m from it.

As a result of the accuracy and reliability achieved by the algorithm, the trip-chaining model was chosen to estimate the pass holder passengers' travel diary for Mobisuite.

Mobisuite has revealed that, for various reasons, the data collected do not allow to trace 100% of the trip legs. In the case study it was possible to estimate 95% and 94% of the total travel pass holder validations, equal to 97880 and 98830 validations respectively, in January and February 2018. With the use of the virtual checkout algorithm it was possible to reconstruct from the correct validations 94% and 93% of the trip legs (sequence of check-in and check-out). In particular, 84% and 83% respectively in January and February 2018 did not require any elaboration whereas 10% in both months showed errors that were corrected with algorithms developed ad hoc (e.g. single trips and trips where the distance between consecutive stops is higher than 1 km), it was necessary to use another estimation method (i.e. OD matrix expansion using the matrix obtained through the check-out algorithm as base matrix). Only 6% and 7% from the correct validations could not be reconstructed, respectively in January and February 2018.

2.6 Deployment

The visualization interface was created using Microsoft PowerBI, which is designed with three main modules that depict several variables related to user demand, public transit supply, and ticketing.

3   Results and Discussion

Mobisuite visualizes transit system indicators from the viewpoints of public transportation lines, routes, journeys and stops. Figure 2 depicts Mobisuite, which has four main display tabs: home, users demand, public transport supply and ticketing, based on data retrieved and prepared for each module. The interface has been developed in Italian to facilitate the interpretation by the end user; the interested reader will find the English translation of the main terms in the glossary at the end of this article.

Microsoft PowerBI was used as a visualization tool, where it was designed with four main displays: home display, user's demand module display, supply display and finally the ticketing display. The home displays in Fig. 2 provides an overview of all the lines and routes, including a set of indicators such as bus-km, passenger-km, maximum load, number of on-boarding passengers, average load, and commercial km, the results of which may be shown based on the transport agency, year, month, line, and route.

Average load can be filtered monthly and daily with hour reference, which is an essential indication for determining the efficacy of lines, routes, and trips. Moreover, it determines the temporal and spatial characteristics of transportation demand, which leads to improved transportation service planning [21]. Understanding the average load, can be used to reduce the gap between supply and demand by adapting the fleets to the actual demand, resulting in a reduction in overall CO2 emissions pro capite [22].

In Fig. 3, the user's demand module display shows several indications for the selected line and route, as well as the number of trips carried out by each user categorised by smart card title. Other information, such as the distribution of km range vs. number of trips traveled, and the number of people going between zones, are also provided. The insights from Mobisuite user's demand module will assist in meeting the needs of transportation users, allowing the PT planner and transport operator to adjust the services they provide and so provide a higher-quality service that is suited to their customers' needs.

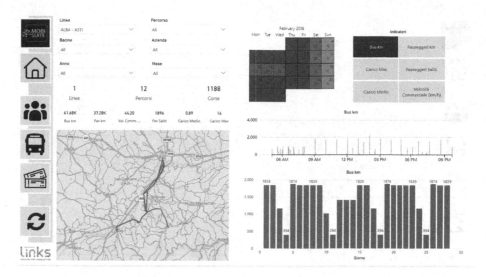

Fig. 2. Mobisuite interface - Screenshot of the home page of the tool.

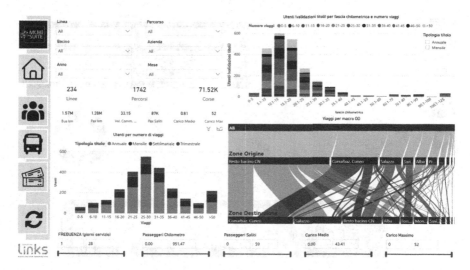

Fig. 3. Mobisuite interface - Screenshot of the user demand analysis page of the tool

The supply display Fig. 4, contains all accessible service statistics, such as frequency of service and number of stops, as well as bus km, passenger km, maximum load, number of on-boarding passengers, average load, and commercial km. Through the supply display, the PT planner and transport operator can get a comprehensive view of the whole PT system features.

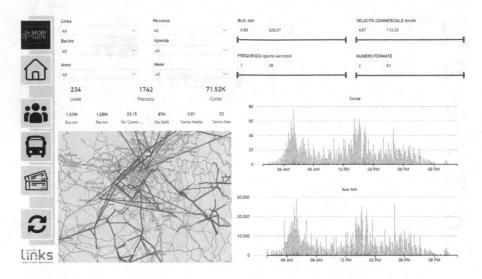

Fig. 4. Mobisuite interface - Screenshot of the supply analysis page of the tool

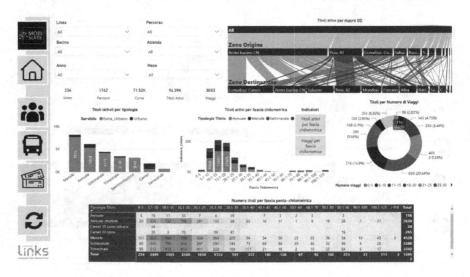

Fig. 5. Mobisuite interface - Screenshot of the ticketing analysis page of the tool

Finally, the ticketing display Fig. 5 shows statistics related to the active smart card titles in urban and extra-urban services, such as the active smart card titles for trip ranges traveled, and the active smart card titles for the macro Origin/Destinations pairs (OD).

The ticketing display not only categorizes different types of travel pass holders, but also shows how a subset of passengers used them in terms of number of trips, kilometers traveled, and cost, particularly across distinct urban and extra-urban zones, with the goal of evaluating the impact of new integrated fare models on the user and on the PT system.

4   Conclusion

Mobisuite is a tool that allows to compare the supply of public transport services (i.e. routes, number of rides, daily frequency) with the related demand (i.e. passengers per route, passenger*km) and to assess how different types of tickets or transport credit are used (i.e. number of trips, kilometers traveled, cost) by different subsets of users (i.e. students and employees) across urban and extra-urban zones.

Thanks to Mobisuite, the public transport planners and the transport operators will be able to have a full perspective of the system of services and their utilization.

The insights that can be gained from interpreting the Mobisuite calculations help planners to better meet the needs of public transport customers, as the ability to clearly analyze the relationship between supply and demand, allows to redesign services in order to offer quality, tailor-made services. Reducing the gaps between supply and demand allow to limit the CO_2 emissions pro capite and the operational costs in the face of limited travel demand.

Mobisuite user-friendly interface and easy-to-read elaborations (charts, maps, tables) ensure easy use, even by less experienced users. Moreover, the data and elaboration visualization helps to improve communication between transit operators and local authorities regarding public transportation planning and operation.

The tool is still under improvement with the integration of a module that focuses on analyzing specific stops and trips. Another area that might be improved in the future is the use of static data paired with real-time data to create additional visual analytics modules that can conduct a range of real-time strategies and actual system performance.

Glossary

Linea. Name of the Bus Line

Percorso. Name of the Line Path. Each line could have different path according, for instance, to time of the day in which the service is operated

Bacino. Basin, the geographical area in which services are operated

Azienda. Company that provide the services

Anno. Year

Mese. Month

Linee. Lines, number of lines that match the filtered search

Percorsi. Paths, number of line paths that match the filtered search

Corse. Trips, number of trips that match the filtered search

Pax km, Passeggeri km. Passengers - km, total distance in kilometres traveled by all passengers on board on a trip or a set of trips

Vel. Comm.Velocita Commerciale (km/h). Commercial Speed

Pax Saliti, Passeggeri Saliti. Boarded Passengers, total number of passengers boarded on a trip or a set of trips

Carico Medio. Average Load, average number of passengers aboard a trip or a set of trips

Carico Max. Maximum load, maximum number of passengers on board on a trip or a set of trips

Indicatori. Indicators, indexes

Utenti per numero di viaggi. Users per numbers of trips

Utenti (validazioni titoli) per fascia chilometrica e numero viaggi. Users (validated tickets) per distance range and number of trips

Viaggi per macro OD. Number of trips per aggregated OD

Frequenza (giorni servizio). Frequency, number of days per month in which the service is operated

Numero fermate. Stops, number of stops per trip

Titoli Attivi. Active Tickets, tickets validated at least once in the reference period

Viaggi. Trips

Titoli (attivi) per tipologia. Active Tickets, per typology of subscription

Titoli attivi per fascia chilometrica. Active Tickets, per distance range

Viaggi per fascia chilometrica. Trips, per distance range

Titoli per Numero di Viaggi. Tickets/Subscriptions per numbers of trips

Annuale. Annual Subscription

Annuale Studenti. Annual Subscription for students

Carnet 10 corse urban. 10 Urban Ticket Carnet

Carnet 20 corse. 20 Ticket Carnet

Mensile. Monthly Subscription

Settimanale. Weekly Subscription

Trimestrale. Quarterly Subscription

Totale. Total

References

1. Pelletier, M.P., Trépanier, M., Morency, C.: Smart card data use in public transit: a literature review. Transp. Res. Part C Emerg. Technol. **19**(4), 557–568 (2011)
2. Mayer-Schonberger, V., Cukier, K.: Big Data: A Revolution that Will Transform How We Live, Work and Think. Houghton Mifflin Harcourt Publishing Company, Boston (2013)
3. Yu, W., Mao, M., Wang, B., Liu, X.: Implementation evaluation of beijing urban master plan based on subway transit smart card data. In: 22nd International Conference on Geoinformatics (2014)
4. Chen, C., Ma, J., Susilo, Y., Liu, Y., Wang, M.: The promises of big data and small data for travel behavior (aka human mobility) analysis. Transp. Res. Part C Emerg. Tech. **68**, 285–299 (2016)
5. Ferreira, N., Poco, J., Vo, H.T., Freire, J., Silva, C.T.: Visual exploration of big spatio-temporal urban data: a study of New York city taxi trips. IEEE Trans. Visual Comput. Graph. **19**(12), 2149–2158 (2013)
6. Chen, W., Guo, F., Wang, F.Y.: A survey of traffic data visualization. IEEE Trans. Intell. Transp. Syst. **16**(6), 2970–2984 (2015)

7. Kaeoruean, K., Phithakkitnukoon, S., Demissie, M.G., Kattan, L., Ratti, C.: Analysis of demand-supply gaps in public transit systems based on census and GTFS data: a case study of Calgary, Canada. Publ. Transp. **12**(3), 483–516 (2020)
8. Batsas, M.: Public transport authorities and COVID-19, impact and response to a pandemic. International Association of Public Transport, Australia/New Zealand. https://australia-newzealand.uitp.org/sites/default/files/V1_COVID-19 %20impacts_AJ_v03.pdf. Accessed 17 May 17 2020
9. Gkiotsalitis, K., Cats, O.: Public transport planning adaption under the COVID-19 pandemic crisis: literature review of research needs and directions. Transp. Rev. **41**(3), 374–392 (2021)
10. Prommaharaj, P., Phithakkitnukoon, S., Demissie, M.G., Kattan, L., Ratti, C.: Visualizing public transit system operation with GTFS data: a case study of Calgary, Canada. Heliyon **6**(4), e03729 (2020)
11. Giraud, A., Trépanier, M., Morency, C., Légaré, F.: Data fusion of APC, smart card and GTFS to visualize public transit use. Centre interuniversitaire de recherche sur les réseaux d'entreprise Ldots, Technical report, CIRRELT (2016)
12. Kurkcu, A., Miranda, F., Ozbay, K., Silva, C.T.: Data visualization tool for monitoring transit operation and performance. In: 2017 5th IEEE International Conference on Models and Technologies for Intelligent Transportation Systems (MT-ITS), pp. 598–603. IEEE (2017)
13. Palomo, C., Guo, Z., Silva, C.T., Freire, J.: Visually exploring transportation schedules. IEEE Trans. Visual Comput. Graph. **22**(1), 170–179 (2015)
14. Anwar, A., Odoni, A., Toh, N.: Busviz: big data for bus fleets. Transp. Res. Rec. **2544**(1), 102–109 (2016)
15. BIP: BIP Piedmont. http://www.5t.torino.it/progetti/bip-piemonte/. Accessed 19 May 2021
16. BIPEX: BIPEX Piedmont. http://www.5t.torino.it/progetti/bipex/. Accessed 26 Oct 2021
17. 5T: 5T. http://www.5t.torino.it/. Accessed 22 May 2021
18. NeTEx: Netex. http://www.netex-cen.eu/. Accessed 26 Oct 2021
19. Transmodel: Transmodel. http://www.transmodel-cen.eu/. Accessed 26 Oct 2021
20. Arnone, M., Delmastro, T., Giacosa, G., Paoletti, M., Villata, P.: The potential of e-ticketing for public transport planning: the piedmont region case study. Transp. Res. Proc. **18**, 3–10 (2016)
21. Gettleman, J., Schultz, K.: Modi orders 3-week total lockdown for all 1.3 billion Indians. New York Times **24** (2020)
22. Fong, W.K., Matsumoto, H., Lun, Y.F.: Application of system dynamics model as decision making tool in urban planning process toward stabilizing carbon dioxide emissions from cities. Build. Environ. **44**(7), 1528–1537 (2009)

Improved Bus Service on Ten Times Less Energy

Tyler C. Folsom[✉] iD

University of Washington, Bothell, WA, USA
tfolsom@uw.edu

Abstract. We have designed the MilliPod™, a platoon of electric, fully automated two-person microvehicles following a professionally operated lead vehicle. The MilliPod picks up passengers without stopping and uses an order of magnitude less energy than the transit buses it replaces. To reduce congestion, the pods physically couple to each other, but are all individually powered and steered creating an agile all-wheel drive vehicle.

The MilliPod is designed to move people in the city with minimal energy. It is expected to cost less than a bus but provides faster trips A major technical contribution is a control system that will let the pods drive bumper-to-bumper smoothly.

The MilliPod achieves its efficiency by applying automated vehicle technology to microvehicles weighing less than the riders. It takes advantage of the high energy efficiency required for human-powered vehicles that can break highway speed limits. The passenger pods are fully automated, but are restricted to a limited operational driving domain, and depend on a professional operator to ensure safety. This level of automation can be done with today's technology.

Because of its high energy efficiency, each pod can be powered by a 20 kg battery, enabling refueling by battery swap and eliminating range anxiety. A bank of discharged batteries can be recharged whenever local renewable energy is available.

Keywords: Automated vehicles · Microvehicles · Micromobility · Buses · Public transportation · Sustainable energy

1 Introduction

It is feasible to electrify all land transportation [1]. Is it possible to generate the required electricity sustainably? A 1500 kg car carrying an 80 kg person is not sustainable, even if it is electric. Neither is a 17,300 kg bus, which in the U.S. averages 56 l/100 km and carries on average 9 people [2, 3]. On a weight basis, gasoline packs much more energy than batteries, making electric cars heavier. This paper proposes a method to move people in the city using an order of magnitude less energy.

Reducing the required amount of energy used in transportation is critical to mitigate global warming. Energy growth has been greatest in Asia, Africa and the Middle East, with Europe and North America stable [4]. China and India are projected to experience the largest increase in electricity usage through 2050 [5]. It is thus important that the proposed solution can be deployed in developing countries.

© ICST Institute for Computer Sciences, Social Informatics and Telecommunications Engineering 2022
Published by Springer Nature Switzerland AG 2022. All Rights Reserved
A. L. Martins et al. (Eds.): INTSYS 2021, LNICST 426, pp. 162–176, 2022.
https://doi.org/10.1007/978-3-030-97603-3_12

1.1 Energy Overview

Neither electricity nor hydrogen constitutes primary energy; either must be produced from coal, petroleum, natural gas, nuclear, or renewable sources. The main uses of energy are to power buildings, industry and transportation. There are feasible methods to use renewable energy for buildings and industry [6]. Transportation is more problematic. In the U.S., 66% of petroleum goes to transportation [7]. Figure 1 shows that the main consumers are cars and light trucks (gasoline), heavy trucks and buses (diesel) and aviation (jet fuel) [8].

U.S. transportation energy sources/fuels, 2020 [1]

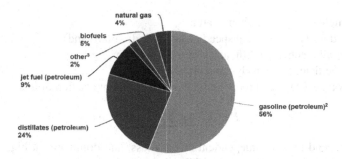

natural gas
4%

biofuels
5%

other[3]
2%

jet fuel (petroleum)
9%

distillates (petroleum)
24%

gasoline (petroleum)[2]
56%

Fig. 1. Most U.S. petroleum goes to gasoline, diesel and jet fuel.

Transportation reform is critical to eliminating liquid fossil fuels. In the Netherlands, 27% of all trips are by bicycle [9]. However, this model seems to have limited transferability elsewhere. In the U.S., bicycle commuting accounts for less than 1% [10]. Asian countries used to have extensive bicycle usage, but the usual pattern is to trade the bike for a motorcycle, and then a car as prosperity improves.

Like a battery, hydrogen offers a method to store energy. Most hydrogen is produced by refactoring natural gas, and has an environmental footprint that is worse than using the gas directly [11]. It is theoretically possible to produce sustainable hydrogen by using renewable energy to electrolyze water, but it is not clear that the process is commercially feasible.

1.2 Energy to Move a Land Vehicle

The power required to move a land vehicle is the sum of energy change to overcome rolling resistance (W_R) plus energy change to overcome aerodynamic drag (W_D) [12]

$$\frac{dW_R}{dt} = \frac{v \sum m}{\eta} g \left[C_R + \frac{s}{100} + \frac{a}{g}\left(1 + \frac{m_W}{\sum m}\right)\right] \tag{1}$$

$$\frac{dW_R}{dt} = k_1 v \sum m \tag{2}$$

v: vehicle speed m: masses of vehicle, riders and baggage

s: % up-slope m_W: effective rotational mass of wheels
a: acceleration   *g*: gravitational acceleration
η: overall mechanical efficiency of transmission
C_R: coefficient of rolling resistance
k_1 is not really a constant, but it includes things over which there is little control or variance.

The equation for overcoming aerodynamic drag is

$$\frac{dW_D}{dt} = \frac{v}{2\eta} A\rho C_D (v + w)^2 \tag{3}$$

$$= k_2 v^3 A\ C_D \tag{4}$$

v: vehicle speed   *A*: frontal area
ρ: air density   *w*: wind speed (+ headwind; − tailwind)
η: overall mechanical efficiency of transmission
C_D: coefficient of aerodynamic drag
The total energy required when there is no slope or acceleration is

$$E = k_1 v C_R \sum m + k_2 v^3 A C_D \tag{5}$$

The second term is independent of the mass, and dominates at higher speeds. For heavier vehicles, such as an automobile, the two terms are equal at about 55 km/h; for light vehicles aerodynamic forces dominate above 20 km/h [13]. Thus, streamlining is important for light vehicles, even at slow speeds.

Figure 2 gives the total energy to move a vehicle, showing that a bicycle is vastly more energy efficient than a car [14]. When the bike is converted to a streamlined human-powered vehicle (HPV), the efficiencies are even greater. The figures shown are for a practical commuting HPV, not for a racing HPV.

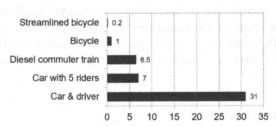

Fig. 2. Total energy consumption at 50 km/h (kW per person)[1]

For 2018, ratings from the U.S. Environmental Protection Agency (EPA) for the efficiency of electric cars varies from 15.5 to 29 kWh/100 km [15]. By contrast, a HPV can achieve 0.69 kWh/100 km [16]. Electrification of transportation is a missed

---

[1] The bottom three numbers in Fig. 2 are taken from the table on p. 166 of Wilson, converting kcal/km to kilowatts at 50 km/h. The bicycle energies are taken from the figure on p. 140, reading the power for commuting HPV and utility bicycles at 13.8 m/s.

opportunity if 90% to 99% of the energy is wasted in moving the vehicle instead of the person. Electrifying the entire present vehicle fleet would place demands on the electric grid that would require generation from coal or natural gas. Radical weight reduction of the vehicle fleet will reduce the demand for electricity and eliminate the need for new generating capacity.

Vehicle energy consumption is the same, regardless of whether the energy is generated by human power, gasoline or a battery. Using radical vehicle design, fuel efficiencies equivalent to 0.25 l/100 km (1000 mpg) are feasible.

1.3 Transit Efficiency

Transit's claimed efficiency is based not on fuel consumption, but on other factors. It is argued that transit avoids the infrastructure required to support a large number of single occupancy vehicles. This is modeled as Land Use Efficiency, and also includes avoided automobile trips. The formula used is

$$TransitMultiplier = \frac{T_{eff} + L_{eff}}{T_{eff}} \tag{6}$$

T_{eff}: Transportation efficiency, or reduction of vehicle kilometers travelled from transit passengers

L_{eff}: Land Use Efficiency, or indirect reductions in vehicle kilometers traveled.

The study introducing this methodology claims a Transit Multiplier ranging from 5.97 to 13.04 [17]. This approach is valid for European cities with good public transit where it is feasible to live car-free. It is more questionable for U.S. cities with poor public transportation. It is much easier to live without a car in New York City than in Los Angeles. Some American communities discourage public transit in the belief that it keeps out poor people [18].

Walking, bicycling, and remote work have even better Land Use Efficiency than transit, as illustrated in Fig. 3, which is based on the seldom-achieved ideal of packing 66 people into a bus [19].

Fig. 3. Street usage for cars, buses and bicycles

1.4 Speeds and the City

Automobile manufacturers would like us to believe that their vehicles operate at over 100 km/h and provide an exhilarating driving experience. In the city, this is rarely the case. The U.S. EPA test for city fuel efficiency is based on an average speed of 34 km/h and 23 stops in an 18 km trip [20]. The Japanese test is based on an average speed of 25 km/h. The New European Driving Cycle includes an Urban Driving Cycle with an average speed of 19 km/h.

Transit doesn't do much better. Proponents of U.S. light rail cite average scheduled speeds of 31 to 42 km/h, with some lines reaching 61 km/h [21]. They concede that bus speeds are 19 to 21 km/h. Seattle's new Link Light Rail system serves a 25 km route from downtown to the airport in 38 min, for an average speed of 39 km/h [22]. Scheduled speeds for Washington D.C. are 48 km/h, but for New York City, it is only 28 km/h [23]. Older lines where the stops are closer together tend to be slower, and newer lines with longer spacing between stops go faster.

Stops for transit passenger pickup and drop-off are unpredictable and delay bus schedules. Loading a wheelchair or bicycle produces even larger delays. Scheduling must deal with time estimates for stops [24].

$$t_d = P_a t_a + P_b + t_{oc} \tag{7}$$

where:
t_d = dwell time (time spent on passenger load and unload);
P_a = number of alighting passengers per bus through the busiest door;
t_a = alighting time per passenger;
P_b = number of boarding passengers per bus through the busiest door;
t_b = passenger boarding time;
t_{oc} = door opening and closing time.

Typical boarding time per passenger is 2 to 3 s, with a minimum of 6 s per stop. It takes 2 to 5 s to open and close the doors. Delay for a wheelchair runs between 60 and 200 s; a bicycle delay is 20 to 30 s. In addition to the dwell time, schedulers must allow 10 to 15 s for the bus to start and travel its own length. The unknowns of whether the bus needs to stop and how many riders will board or exit makes robust scheduling challenging.

1.5 Automated Vehicles

Many of today's systems are hyped as more than they offer, since a fully automated vehicle does not need a driver or safety rider. Two advantages expected from automated vehicles are improved safety and increased road capacity. Fully automated vehicles will never be deployed unless they can demonstrate improved safety. Safety may be achieved by partial automation through Advanced Driver Assistance Systems (ADAS). Connected vehicles provide vehicle to vehicle (V2V), vehicle to infrastructure (V2I), or anything else (V2X) and may be enough to halt the carnage on the roads. The most dangerous transportation mode is the motorcycle, with a fatality rate of 15.92 per 100 M vehicle kilometers travelled compared to 0.58 for a passenger car, a factor of 27 [25]. If traffic accidents become rare, and the car sees the motorcycle even when the driver does not, microvehicles can become nearly as safe as SUVs, especially at city speeds.

Europe and North America have lower traffic accident rates; Africa and Asia higher [26]. The U.N. has projected that by 2025, traffic accidents could be the fifth largest health problem globally. From a humanitarian viewpoint, it may be better to deploy automated vehicles in Asian and African middle and low-income countries as soon as they are demonstrated to be safe. These countries also tend to have lower regulatory barriers.

Automated Vehicles can be choreographed to efficiently operate in platoons, increasing road capacity by two to three times. Close platooning saves fuel, which is one of the main factors behind automation of long-haul trucks. A standard adaptive cruise control (ACC) system has been shown to be inadequate for platoons [27]. A cooperative ACC is needed where vehicle positions and intentions are shared [28]. Existing platooning control systems have difficulties when the inter-vehicle gap becomes small, leading to a jerky and uncomfortable ride. Producing a smooth ride requires increasing the gap, incurring a penalty in road capacity and energy savings.

2 Moving People with Minimal Energy

Based on the considerations of the previous section, the next step is to design a system for moving people in the city with minimum energy. It is necessary to design an entire system, not just a vehicle.

2.1 Design Considerations

Equation (1) dictates that the mass must be kept small. The ideal vehicle has an empty weight less than its riders. An electric bicycle passes this criterion, but Eq. (3) requires an aerodynamic shell when the speed exceeds 20 km/h. The shell also provides protection from weather, extending the conditions under which the vehicle will be used.

The acceleration term in Eq. (1) is a penalty for stop-and-go. The system should be designed so that the vehicle rarely needs to change its velocity. A vehicle that can travel at a constant 50 km/h uses less energy than one that hits 100 km/h but only averages 50 km/h. Vehicle efficiency depends on its operating environment and the two should be designed simultaneously.

Energy consumption is minimized by reducing mass, reducing frontal area, streamlining, minimizing accelerations, and avoiding uphills. Energy is reduced when vehicles travel in platoons with the smallest possible gap between them.

The smallest possible gap is zero, when vehicles travel bumper-to-bumper. There are at least three ways to achieve a gap of zero:

1. Electronic virtual coupling: vehicles are close but not touching.
2. Rigid coupling: vehicles merge to form a single non-articulated vehicle.
3. Articulated coupling: as for railroad cars.

All these methods have been tried, but the problems with the first two make them unsuitable Suppose that a 12-m transit bus seating 40 people were replaced by a road train of 2.4-m-long pods seating two people each. If the bus were carrying 10 people (average U.S. bus occupancy) and the pods had no gaps between them, the platoon would be the same length as the transit bus. If the platoon carried 40 people, it would be four times as long as the transit bus. Virtual coupling of automated vehicles may be done with a headway between vehicles of only 0.5 s, though regulators may insist on more [29]. At 50 km/h, a 0.5-s gap is a spacing of 6.7 m, stretching the platoon to a problematic nine bus lengths. Physical coupling is required to avoid congestion.

Next Future Transportation has a Modular Bus concept with pods carrying 10 passengers and rigidly coupling. This vehicle is about the same size as a transit bus, but does not allow social distancing.

Articulated coupling permits a 48-m bus to move like a snake to negotiate tight turns. However, the mechanical forces on a couple can be large. The French company Modulowatt tried a similar concept in which vehicles mechanically coupled and the lead vehicle towed the others. The system failed because the articulated couples broke [30]. For the concept to succeed, all vehicles must be independently powered and controlled so that there is close to zero force on the couples at all times.

2.2 MilliPod Concept and Operation

The MilliPod™ (patent pending) offers cities a tool to mitigate climate change and improve social justice [31]. It provides faster service, costs less, and uses ten times less energy. It is a train of 2-person, fully-automated electric microvehicles following the bus driver's pod. The MilliPod never needs to stop; it picks up passenger pods on the fly.

A rider would come to a bus stop, then select a destination and pay the fare using a kiosk or smart phone. They would then be assigned to a pod parked at the bus stop, which would unlock for them. The rider has exclusive use of the pod, which may optionally be shared with a companion. A group of riders or a person with extra baggage may rent more than one pod, which will travel together to the selected destination.

As the MilliPod approaches, the passenger pods pull out into the street and begin accelerating to match the speed of the main train. When it passes them, the passenger pods change lanes and gently couple onto the MilliPod. It then continues until the destination, when the passenger pod uncouples, opens a gap between vehicles, then changes lanes and decelerates, parking at the destination bus stop.

The main MilliPod never needs to stop to pick up or discharge passengers, letting it service bus routes faster. The MilliPod carries people, wheelchairs and bikes, but loading is off-line and does not slow the ride. Thus, drivers can cover more distance during their shifts and provide more frequent bus service. Without the uncertainty of passenger load/unload times, schedules can be more reliable. If individual pods break down, they can be taken out of service without affecting the system.

The passenger pods use technology derived from both bicycles and cars, but they have no pedals, no handlebars or steering wheel and no controls operatable by a driver.

COVID-19 has decimated bus ridership [32]. The MilliPod eliminates the need to share space with a stranger, which may help transit agencies recover ridership.

Typical dimensions for the pods are 1.2 m wide and 2.4 m long. This allows the MilliPod to split a standard lane in two, using the outer half-lane as a through lane and the inner half-lane as an acceleration/deceleration lane.

The lead pod is professionally driven. The passenger pods are fully autonomous but only in a limited Operational Driving Domain. Autonomy consists of accelerating to dock with the MilliPod, maintaining position in the train, and uncoupling and decelerating to the destination.

If there are multiple MilliPod routes, the passenger pods will drive themselves to the transfer bus station and then connect with the next MilliPod on that line. If the connection is to a standard bus or train line, the passengers will walk to the transfer point. A MilliPod may provide off-peak service on a route with a standard bus handling high-demand times.

2.3 Energy Efficiency

The target weight for the pod loaded with two male riders is 330 kg. The pods will automatically weigh their loads and an overloaded pod will refuse to operate. A transit bus typically weighs 17,300 kg, a factor of 52 [33]. Rolling resistance is directly proportional to vehicle mass. If the MilliPod consists of 26 pods, it still weighs only half as much as the bus. On a lightly used route serviced by 10 pods, the bus weighs 5 times as much.

A standard bus must stop and start to pick up riders. For the MilliPod, only a few pods need to start or stop. Acceleration is addressed inside the brackets of Eq. (1). On a level road with the mass of the wheels much less than the total mass, the acceleration term is approximately $[C_R + a/g]$. A typical value of C_R for bicycle wheels on asphalt is 0.004; for car tires it is about 0.010 [34]. With no acceleration, a microvehicle uses 2.5 times less energy from this term.

Rolling energy is proportional to mass. At a constant speed, 26 MilliPod units use 5 times less rolling energy than a bus; a 13-unit MilliPod uses 10 times less. If there is acceleration, it dominates the unitless term in the brackets and is multiplied by the weight of the vehicle. If three pods need to decelerate or accelerate at a stop at 0.1 g, the required power is proportional to $3*330*(0.004 + 0.1) = 103$ kg. For a conventional bus, the number is $17,300*(0.01 + 0.1) = 1900$ kg, a factor of 18.

Typical drag coefficients are 0.12 for a streamlined velomobile, 0.25 for a modern car or 0.6 to 0.8 for a bus [35]. We expect that the microvehicles would have a drag coefficient of about 0.25 and have four times less frontal area than a bus; thus, energy to overcome drag is about 12 times less for microvehicles. A typical bus has frontal area of 2.5 m wide and 3 m high [36]. The pods will be approximately 1.2 m wide and 1.5 m high. Typical traffic lanes are 3 to 3.7 m wide, and automated vehicles perform better in narrow lanes than do manually driven vehicles, which enables splitting a lane in two.

Equation (5) compares MilliPod efficiency to the bus. For rolling resistance, there is a factor of 2 to 5 for mass and 2.5 times for C_R for a total of 5 to 12.5 times less energy with no acceleration. When the bus needs to stop, the factor can reach 90. Overcoming aerodynamic drag involves a factor of 12, which is relatively more important for the MilliPod because of its reduced weight. These numbers justify the claims of an order of magnitude improvement in energy efficiency.

The MilliPod is designed to operate at a constant 50 km/h without stopping. If it operates in lanes where transit has priority and signals are synchronized with it, it provides the fastest way to move in the city.

2.4 MilliPod Localization and Control System

The lead pod of the MilliPod is generously endowed with Level 2 ADAS to let the driver devote their full attention to safe operation of the system. If any obstacles are observed that would impede operation of the passenger pods, a warning is transmitted and the MilliPod may stop or take other actions to ensure safe operation.

The passenger pods operate at Level 4 automation in a limited Operational Driving Domain. Their control system is illustrated in Fig. 4. The vehicle state minimally consists of position, attitude, velocity, acceleration, weight and the fixed vehicle-specific quantities from Eqs. (1) and (3). At start-up the vehicle state is initialized with its last values, including position and attitude, with velocity and acceleration set to zero. A sensor measures the loaded vehicle mass.

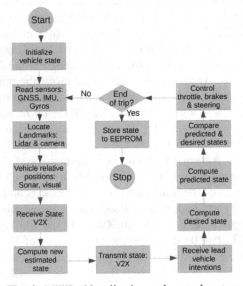

Fig. 4. MilliPod localization and control system

As the vehicle operates, its estimated state is updated by sensors such as Global Network Satellite System (GNSS), Inertial Measurement Units (IMU) and Gyroscopes. These will produce an approximate absolute position, which is made more precise by landmark recognition. Each bus stop will have a distinctive landmark, such as a 5-m-tall orange column. The absolute position of each landmark on the route is known. From the approximate vehicle position, the expected location and size of the landmark in the camera focal plane can be computed. The pod will use visual or Lidar sensors to establish the distance and bearing to the landmark, thus establishing a more accurate absolute position for itself.

As the MilliPod approaches the bus stop, it broadcasts the absolute positions and velocities of the first and last vehicles. The joining pods will then compute the relative distances between themselves and the end of the MilliPod, and accelerate to match its speed and position. When the joining vehicle is in range of the target vehicle, it then uses relative position sensors to dock to the end of the MilliPod. Relative docking sensors can take the form of a known pattern of LEDs on the rear of the target vehicle, which are processed by a position sensing diode, bypassing the complicated computations of machine vision [37]. The algorithm was originally designed for spacecraft docking where there is little interference from ambient light, but we have calculated how to remove that effect. The precise docking information lets the joining vehicle change lanes and smoothly couple to the end of the MilliPod.

If several pods are joining the MilliPod at the same time, they will couple before joining and act as a single vehicle. Once all pods have coupled, they each know their relative positions and can use this information to reconcile the states of all vehicles in the MilliPod.

The passenger pods need to control throttle, brakes and steering so that the MilliPod moves as a single unit but with little or no force on the couples. The couple/bumper assembly contains dampers so that any minor mismatch in force is mechanically absorbed. The couples may contain strain gauges to measure force. Intervehicle force is a damped harmonic oscillator:

$$f = m\ddot{x} + c\dot{x} + kx \tag{8}$$

where m is mass, c is the damping coefficient and k is the spring force. Since mechanical and electrical power are equivalent, force can be sensed from

$$f = \frac{Voltage \times current}{velocity} \tag{9}$$

Variants of Eqs. (1) and (3) are used to predict the expected state changes of each vehicle and the forces on the couples. Equation (9) predicts the required motor current. The lead pod will broadcast any pending application of brakes, throttle or steering before the actions happen; other pods will synchronize with the overall behavior of the MilliPod. The slopes on the route can be accessed from a table indexed by position, filling in one of the variable terms of Eq. (1).

As a pod approaches its destination, it uncouples from the pods ahead and behind it. The pods then open a gap, so that the leaving pod can change to the deceleration lane, and come to a stop at the bus stop. Meanwhile, the uncoupled pods fill the gap and recouple.

2.5 Work Done

In 2011, Dr. Folsom started the open-source Elcano Project to demonstrate that low-cost electronics were sufficient to automate an electric recumbent tricycle (Fig. 5) [38]. His lab at the University of Washington received a grant from Amazon for taking bicycles to automated vehicles [39]. Organic Transit donated an ELF vehicle to the project, shown in

Fig. 5. Automated recumbent Catrike   **Fig. 6.** Automated organic transit ELF

Fig. 6 [40]. Three full-scale electric tricycles have been converted to automatic operation, with the throttle, brakes and steering controlled by an Arduino 8-bit microcontroller.

Another lab at the University of Washington has converted a 1/10 scale radio control (RC) car into an autonomous robot for indoor use [41]. It is equipped with a more powerful Jetson Nano microprocessor, an Intel RealSense depth camera, and a rotating laser range finder. Dr. Folsom and students are converting the platform for outdoor use, incorporating GNSS, IMU, and vision processing for navigation from landmark detection. The scale models carry the same sensors and electrons as the full-scale prototypes, which have been updated for the Jetson Nano and accessories.

2.6 Future Work

Six 1/10 model cars have been configured to mimic MilliPod operations. It is intended to show that the control system can perform the maneuvers for joining and leaving a platoon and driving bumper-to-bumper. The full-scale trikes will be fitted with the same electronics used in the scale demonstration and put through a similar demonstration. When the feasibility of the operation has been demonstrated, custom vehicles will be designed and constructed. We are looking for partners to demonstrate these vehicles in a transit pilot program.

Including electronics and sensors, the expected price of a passenger pod is $15,000 ± $3,000. Our two recumbent prototype vehicles were built for $3,875 and $4,370. The driver's pod could cost $25,000. About 20 pods would provide the service of a bus. As shown in Table 1, The MilliPod price of $310,000 compares favorably to $550,000 for a diesel bus or $800,000 for electric. The main bus operating costs are driver salary and fuel. The former is the same for the MilliPod and traditional buses. The MilliPod costs much less to fuel than a diesel bus and uses ten times less electricity than an electric bus. Each pod could be powered by a 20 kg battery, enabling battery swap, with the depleted batteries charged from renewable energy.

Table 1. Comparison of buses and the MilliPod

	Diesel bus	Electric bus	8 vehicle MilliPod	31 vehicle MilliPod
Passenger capacity	60	60	14	60
Average ridership	9	9	9	45
kWh/Passenger km	0.600 [42]	0.148 [43]	0.014	0.014
Vehicle cost	$550,000	$800,000	$135,000	$480,000

3 Sustainability and Automated Microvehicles

3.1 MilliPod Extension to First and Last Kilometer

The MilliPod covers bus routes; it is not a solution for the first or last kilometer. The first and last kilometer could be covered by allowing the pods to operate either in automatic mode or be manually driven, with the addition of manual controls for throttle, brakes and steering. A dual mode pod could be operated as a dockless bike or car share. It would be manually driven to the final destination or to a bus stop, where it could join the MilliPod for automatic transportation.

Pods could be privately-owned. They would need to be qualified to be able to fulfill all requirements for the MilliPod and electronically verified when attempting to enter automatic mode.

3.2 Renewable Energy

Ten times less energy requires ten times less battery. The MilliPod has a 20 kg battery, in contrast to the 100 to 544 kg batteries needed for automobiles [44]. The 20 kg battery is expected to provide 30 km of range, which is sufficient for a city trip. Refueling can be done by battery swap. The batteries would be interchangeable and not a permanent part of the vehicle. Batteries can be swapped in less time than it takes to fill a gas tank.

When a MilliPod passenger vehicle senses low charge, it will take itself to a bus stop accommodating battery swap. Batteries take about four hours to charge from standard 110 V circuits. They can be recharged at off-peak hours when grid demand is low. Eventually, recharging bus stops would install wind or solar generators and the batteries can be recharged at any time that renewable energy is available. By contrast, much of the energy to charge cars or buses will often need to be generated from fossil fuels.

The limited battery range is an advantage. It keeps vehicle weight low and energy efficiency high. It is sufficient for the pod to handle one or two trips and take itself to a recharging station. At the recharging station, the pod will be thoroughly cleaned. Any damage or vandalism will be noted and the last riders will be billed for it.

3.3 Self-Driving Micro-Taxis

Eventually, automated vehicle technology will mature to the point that the driver and safety rider are no longer needed. The MilliPod lead pod could then be eliminated.

Automation is an enabler for ultra-light vehicles. If full or partial automation can fulfill its promise of reduced traffic accidents, microvehicles become a safe way to move people around the city at speeds that cars and transit rarely reach. Automation choreographs microvehicles, which could otherwise produce chaotic traffic.

With full automation, pods will no longer need manual controls to handle the first and last kilometers. The pods will evolve into self-driving micro-taxis that can go anywhere in the city without schedules. These will operate on an order of magnitude less energy than automobile taxis and will not require a charging infrastructure. The pods can couple to form platoons with no gaps between vehicles, increasing street capacity.

3.4 Impact

Americans drive five trillion kilometers a year, with 65% classified as urban. The average urban trip is 19 km, making 1.6 trillion kilometers of shorter trips that could be handled by micromobility. Assuming that the micromobility trips use ten times less energy than the trips that they displace, the result is a 32% energy savings. For the United States, this would represent a reduction of 3.8 million barrels of petroleum per day [7]. This translates to 1.6 million metric tons of CO_2 daily [45]. This much CO_2 is equivalent to 43 coal trains [46]. Similar results are expected across the globe.

4   Conclusion

The MilliPod provides faster rides since it never needs to stop. The MilliPod is always the right size for its passenger load and vastly more energy-efficient. It runs entirely on renewable energy and does not pollute. It is expected to cost less than the buses it replaces and is a step to self-driving micro-taxis. It avoids exposure to Covid-19.

Microvehicles traveling at 50 km/h in the city without stopping are faster than cars or buses and use much less energy. Technology can form microvehicles into orderly platoons and lower the cost of city transportation.

In a post-automotive age, automated micro-taxis can become the urban vehicle of choice. Electric automobiles can provide rural and intercity service, but they are too energy hungry to deserve a place in the city.

References

1. Gilbert, R., Perl, A.: Transportation Revolutions: Moving People and Freight without Oil. New Society Publishers, Gabriola Island (2010)
2. National Renewable Energy Lab. https://www.nrel.gov/news/program/2016/nrel-fuel-cell-bus-analysis-finds-fuel-economy-to-be-14-times-higher-than-diesel.html. Accessed 28 Aug 2021
3. National Transit Database. 2018 National Transit Summaries and Trends, p. 16. https://www.transit.dot.gov/sites/fta.dot.gov/files/docs/ntd/data-product/134401/2018-ntst_1.pdf. Accessed 28 Aug 2021
4. U.S. Energy Information Administration. Today in Energy. https://www.eia.gov/todayinenergy/detail.php?id=37932. Accessed 28 Aug 2021

5. U.S. Energy Information Administration's International Energy Outlook 2020. https://www.eia.gov/outlooks/ieo/pdf/ieo2020.pdf. Accessed 28 Aug 2021
6. Lovins, A.B.: Reinventing Fire. Chelsea Green, White River (2011)
7. Use of Oil. https://www.eia.gov/energyexplained/oil-and-petroleum-products/use-of-oil.php. Accessed 28 Aug 2021
8. Energy Use for Transportation. https://www.eia.gov/energyexplained/use-of-energy/transportation.php. Accessed 28 Aug 2021
9. Harms, L., Kansen, M.: Cycling Facts, Netherlands Institute for Transportation Policy Analysis, The Hague (2018). https://www.government.nl/binaries/government/documents/reports/2018/04/01/cycling-facts-2018/Cycling+facts+2018.pdf. Accessed 28 Aug 2021
10. Schneider, R.J., Hu, L., Stefanich, J.: Development of a neighborhood commute share mode using nationally-available data. Transportation **46**, 909–929 (2019). https://doi.org/10.1007/s11116-017-9813-z,lastaccessed2021/11/1
11. Friedlander, B.: Touted as clean, 'blue' hydrogen may be worse than gas or coal (2021). https://news.cornell.edu/stories/2021/08/touted-clean-blue-hydrogen-may-be-worse-gas-or-coal. Accessed 28 Aug 2021
12. Whitt, F.R., Wilson, D.G.: Bicycling Science, 2nd edn., p. 157. MIT Press, Cambridge (1983)
13. Ibid. pp. 171–175
14. Wilson, D.G.: Bicycling Science, 3rd edn, p. 140, 166. MIT Press, Cambridge (2004)
15. Fuel Economy of 2018 All-Electric Vehicles. https://fueleconomy.gov/feg/byfuel/EV2018.shtml. Accessed 28 Aug 2021
16. Velomobiles. http://www.velomobiles.co.uk/tag/bluevelo/. Accessed 28 Aug 2021
17. National Academies of Sciences, Engineering, and Medicine. An Update on Public Transportation's Impacts on Greenhouse Gas Emissions. The National Academies Press, Washington (2021). https://doi.org/10.17226/26103. Accessed 29 Aug 2021
18. Taylor, B.D., Breiland, K.: Transit's Dirty Little Secret: Divergence of Public Policy and Transit Use by the Poor. Transportation Research Board 90th Annual Meeting, Washington (2011). https://trid.trb.org/view/1091861. Accessed 29 Aug 2021
19. Seattle Bike Blog. https://www.seattlebikeblog.com/2013/12/05/why-seattle-must-invest-in-protected-bike-lanes-and-transit-in-one-moving-gif/. Accessed 29 Aug 2021
20. Davis, S.C., Boundy, R.G.: Transportation Energy Data Book, 39th edn. Oak Ridge National Laboratory, Oak Ridge (2021). Tables 4.35 and 4.36. https://tedb.ornl.gov/wp-content/uploads/2021/02/TEDB_Ed_39.pdf. Accessed 28 Aug 2021
21. Light Rail Schedule Speed. https://www.lightrailnow.org/myths/m_lrt012.htm. Accessed 28 Aug 2021
22. Sea-Tac Airport. https://www.soundtransit.org/ride-with-us/popular-destinations/sea-tac-airport. Accessed 28 Aug 2021
23. Average Scheduled Speed (2010). https://ggwash.org/view/4524/average-schedule-speed-how-does-metro-compare. Accessed 28 Aug 2021
24. Transit Capacity and Quality of Service Manual. http://onlinepubs.trb.org/onlinepubs/tcrp/tcrp_webdoc_6-b.pdf. Accessed 28 Aug 2021
25. WHO. Global Status Report on Road Safety, Geneva (2009). https://apps.who.int/iris/bitstream/handle/10665/44122/9789241563840_eng.pdf?sequence=1. Accessed 30 Aug 2021
26. Car vs. Motorcycle Accidents. https://www.autoinsurance.org/motorcycle-vs-car-accidents/. Accessed 29 Aug 2021
27. Swaroop, D., Hedrick, J.K., Choi, S.B.: Direct adaptive longitudinal control of vehicle platoons. IEEE Trans. Vehicul. Technol. **50**(1), 150–161 (2001)
28. Shladover, S.E.: Automated driving: real-world feasibility and benefits. In: 90th Annual Meeting of the Transportation Research Board, Washington, DC, 26 January 2011 (2011)
29. Anderson, J.E.: The Capacity of a Personal Rapid Transit System (1997). https://faculty.washington.edu/jbs/itrans/cap2.htm. Accessed 29 Aug 2021

30. Parent M, INRIA, France. Personal Communication. 22 Jan 2013
31. https://millipod.xyz/. Accessed 29 Oct 2021
32. Liu, L., Miller, H.J., Scheff, J.: The impacts of COVID-19 pandemic on public transit demand in the United States. PLoS ONE **15**(11) (2020). https://doi.org/10.1371/journal.pone.024 2476. Accessed 29 Aug 2021
33. Bus   Weight.   https://www.reference.com/world-view/weight-bus-dee41e459d38318f. Accessed 29 Aug 2021
34. Rolling   Friction.   http://www.energiazero.org/risparmio_energetico/rolling%20friction% 20and%20rolling%20resistance.pdf. Accessed 29 Aug 2021
35. Drag   Coefficient.   https://www.engineeringtoolbox.com/drag-coefficient-d_627.html. Accessed 29 Aug 2021
36. Transit Buses. https://www.dimensions.com/element/city-transit-buses. Accessed 29 Aug 2021
37. Morris, J.C.: Automated Spacecraft Docking Using a Vision-Based Relative Navigation Sensor, Thesis. Texas A&M University, College Station (2009). https://oaktrust.library. tamu.edu/bitstream/handle/1969.1/ETD-TAMU-2009-08-2820/MORRIS-THESIS.pdf?seq uence=1&isAllowed=y. Accessed 29 Aug 2021
38. Elcano Project. http://www.elcanoproject.org/. Accessed 29 Aug 2021
39. Larson, S.: Don't look now, but they've invented self-driving bikes, Crosscut, Seattle (2016). https://crosscut.com/2016/12/dont-look-now-but-theyve-invented-self-driving-bikes. Accessed 29 Aug 2021
40. Organic Transit ELF. https://organictransit.com/product/elf-2fr/. Accessed 29 Aug 2021
41. MuSHR: The UW Open Racecar Project. https://mushr.io/. Accessed 29 Aug 2021
42. Bureau of Transportation Statistics. https://www.bts.gov/content/energy-intensity-passenger-modes. Accessed 30 Aug 2021
43. EV   Obsession.   https://evobsession.com/nrel-proterra-ev-buses-possess-average-fuel-eco nomy-roughly-4-times-higher-than-that-of-cng-baseline-buses/. Accessed 30 Aug 2021
44. Berjoza, D., Jurgena, I.: Influence of batteries weight on electric automobile performance. Engineering for Rural Development (2017). http://tf.llu.lv/conference/proceedings2017/Pap ers/N316.pdf. Accessed 31 Aug 2021
45. EPA Greenhouse Gases Equivalencies. https://www.epa.gov/energy/greenhouse-gases-equ ivalencies-calculator-calculations-and-references. Accessed 30 Aug 2021
46. CO_2 weight is divided by 3.667 for the weight of carbon. Assume 100 tons per car and 100 cars per train

EV Battery Degradation: A Data Mining Approach

Rui Rodrigues[1]([✉]) [iD], Vitória Albuquerque[2] [iD], Joao C Ferreira[1] [iD],
and Miguel Sales Dias[1] [iD]

[1] ISCTE - University Institute of Lisbon, 1649-026 Lisbon, Portugal
{rui_simao_rodrigues,joao.carlos.ferreira,
miguel.dias}@iscte-iul.pt
[2] NOVA Information Management School (NOVA IMS), Campus de Campolide,
Universidade Nova de Lisboa, 1070-312 Lisbon, Portugal
d20190115@novaims.unl.pt

Abstract. The increase in greenhouse gas emissions into the atmosphere, and their adverse effects on the environment, has prompted the search for alternative energy sources to fossil fuels. One of the solutions gaining ground is the electrification of various human activities, such as the transport sector. This trend has fueled a growing need for electrical energy storage in lithium-ion batteries. Precisely knowing the degree of degradation that this type of battery accumulates over its useful life is necessary to bring economic benefits, both for companies and citizens. This paper aims to answer the current need by proposing a research question about electric motor vehicles. It focuses on habits EV owners practice, which could harm the battery life. This paper seeks to answer this question using a data science methodology. The results allowed us to conclude that all other factors had a marginal effect on the vehicles' autonomy decrease except for the car year. The biggest obstacle encountered in adopting electric vehicles was the insufficient coverage of the charging stations network.

Keywords: Electric vehicles · Charging process · Behavior

1 Introduction

The electrification of most human activities is nowadays a necessity. It is crucial to reduce greenhouse gas emissions – targeting the larger goal of decarbonizing human society. The application of energy storage technology in the transportation sector, mainly adopted in electric passenger vehicles, is a strategic step towards the widespread adoption of this type of mobile technology towards the mentioned decarbonization of society. This research on lithium-ion (Li-ion) batteries aims to know more about a subject still requiring broader understanding. Also, it aims to collect and obtain insights into the state-of-the-art on the topic and extract information from data relinquished by EV owners. This information is expected to discuss the degree of satisfaction EV users have with

A. L. Martins et al. (Eds.): INTSYS 2021, LNICST 426, pp. 177–191, 2022.
https://doi.org/10.1007/978-3-030-97603-3_13

the current solutions available in Portugal, potentially repel consumers from purchasing this type of vehicle.

In recent decades, the increased occurrence of manifestations of intense and erratic climatic change has made it crucial to find alternative forms of energy consumption and conservation to conventional methods such as fossil fuel that significantly contribute to greenhouse gas emissions. Therefore, it is of particular importance to adopt these alternatives with the utmost celerity.

Battery aging is currently a problem that cuts across all sectors of activity that depend on them now or may depend on it soon, such as the transport sector in general and specifically in private vehicles. For example, electric mobility is an emerging, ever-growing mode of transport that causes an increased demand for Li-ion batteries in vehicles. However, these batteries have a limited useful life and are usually grouped in packs that make them difficult to replace. In addition, the recycling of batteries' toxic components has proven to be a hazard to the environment. Thankfully, there is a growing need to find methods that can extend the life of these battery packs to reduce their environmental footprint [1] and instead find non-toxic elements to their manufacturing process.

In the automotive industry, this premature aging of batteries is adverse in two ways: firstly, it limits the autonomy range of the private vehicle, and it also affects its general acceptance and adoption by the public. Therefore, the need to know the exact pace of battery degradation often motivates information campaigns for technology adoption, academic research, and industrial research and development to improve its performance and longevity [1].

Future potential owners of vehicles powered by Li-ion batteries are starting to require accurate information on how long their vehicle batteries will last [1]. Hence, consumers are interested in determining whether it is advantageous to invest in this new technology and pay extra fees for its early adoption.

Our study focuses on EV owners driving habits. Data for this study were retrieved from a public inquiry to Tesla vehicles owners. The Tesla dataset was published [2], an electrical news website, on Apr. 14, 2018. It depicted a downward trend curve for vehicle degradation that stabilized at a deficit of 10% of battery total capacity after one hundred and sixty thousand miles, which was promising news. Furthermore, confirming the Tesla findings, in early 2020, Tesla Inc. published a report stating their batteries would retain 90% of their original capacity after 200,000 miles of usage [3].

We applied the Cross-Industry Standard Process for Data Mining (CRISP-DM) methodology to the Tesla dataset by creating a classification model based on the variables available in the raw file obtained by the Tesla article [2]. The end goal was to answer the following research question "Which factors have the most impact on the battery degradation?".

2 Literature Review

Actions [4–7] to reduce greenhouse gases (GHG) emissions have been implemented, even before the covid-19 pandemic, resulting in CO_2 emissions decreasing by 1.8% from 2018 to 2019. The USA Environmental Protection Agency (EPA) [5] as well as the European Green Deal [6] explain that this was primarily due to a drop in total energy used and improved energy efficiency in 2019 compared to 2018, brought down by fossil fuel emissions reduction [5]. In tandem with CO_2 emissions reduction, an ongoing shift from coal to natural gas (the least harmful greenhouse gas-emitting fossil fuel) occurs in the energy sector.

One alternative solution to the burning of fossil fuels in the transportation sector is adopting Li-ion batteries. This type of battery is currently empowering EVs. Technological improvements have been implemented in the last ten years to increase these batteries' energy capacity and efficiency [8]. However, because its capacity is finite, any factor that decreases its energy retention ability is crucial. The degradation of the energy capacity of this type of battery, which is observed, for instance, in cell phones, is one of the main problems faced by energy experts.

Battery early aging often depends on the Li-ion battery materials' chemical composition, namely its anode, cathode, and electrolyte. In addition, external factors, such as voltage, discharge intensity, temperature, and the number of charging-discharging cycles performed, are also considered important factors. However, the reference literature does not quantify how relevant these factors are to the overall battery longevity. For instance, the Tesla manufacturer applies solutions to mitigate premature battery aging; all its vehicles have a management system whose primary function is to control the battery's temperature to remain below 55 °C [1].

However, behavioral factors associated with the operation and charging of electric cars and their storage are significantly considered to impact the degradation of batteries [1]. As already observed with mobile phones, car batteries are subjected to premature aging if left unused. This concern regards that both cases use the same technology and materials. On the other hand, their continued use also leads to progressively shorter service life. May [9] suggest that both technologies' similarities would not stop at that point, and the EV would be as prevalent as the mobile phone. May also envisions that one day, everyone would be able to have one.

The evaluation of Li-ion batteries' performance is still an ongoing process. This technology continues to be studied and matured iteratively by the scientific community that seeks different methods to measure its capacity, internal resistance, and voltages and its influence in charge and discharge cycles [10–12].

According to Yun, [11] the high complexity of practical solutions brings difficulty in measuring the variables mentioned above, especially in controlling the internal variables related to the consistency of the manufacturing quality of the various components of the batteries. Thus, it becomes necessary to assess batteries' health status or State of Health (SoH).

The SoH of the battery, expressed as a percentage, represents its current capacity in Watts, concerning its original capacity. This value weighs various parameters of Li-ion batteries, such as their voltage, current, and capacity. Currently, few articles [13–18] can accurately predict the actual value of SoH.

There are two types of battery capacity forecasting methods to determine the SoH: model-based methods and data-based methods. Model-based methods were always related to the chemical composition of batteries, and there is plenty of reference literature available on this subject. However, most authors did not focus on this area of scientific knowledge.

There are two types of battery capacity forecasting methods to determine the SoH: model-based methods and data-based methods. Model-based methods were always related to the chemical composition of batteries, and there is plenty of reference literature available on this subject.

Regarding data-based prediction models, these sometimes use the parameters referred to earlier [18–23] to monitor the SoH and forecast the state of the RUL [19, 20]. Compared to prediction methods based on chemical models, these data-based methods [21] are faster, more convenient, and less complex [22]. Moreover, Machine Learning (ML) methods can be used, resulting in the accuracy improvement of these models. These prediction methods have raised a growing interest in verifying the SoH of batteries [23].

3 Data Analytics

CRISP-DM [24] is a methodology widely used by data science specialists to develop solutions for business problems based on data [24]. CRISP-DM can be understood as a cross-industry standard process for data mining and envisages transforming the company's data into knowledge and helpful information for management and decision-making.

Data Mining is part of Data Science, which uses statistics, mathematics, and ML approaches as a basis for crossing data, using induction techniques to propose hypotheses and solve business issues.

The CRISP-DM approach gathers the best practices so that the DM is as productive and efficient as possible, analyzing financial data, human resources, production, customer habits, and other data sources to propose data-based models for improvement or problem-solving. It defines a Data Mining project's life cycle, dividing it into the six phases, shown below in Fig. 1, and following a linear progression.

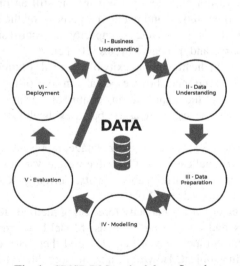

Fig. 1. CRISP-DM methodology flowchart.

It is essential to emphasize the theoretical character of this research. The application of the CRISP-DM phases to our case is therefore limited. For this reason, there are phases of this methodology that are less explored than others.

3.1 Business Understanding

The first phase of CRISP-DM aims to understand the entity's primary needs and business requirements where the methodology will be implemented. It looks for all the details about its internal organization, terminology, marketing strategies, target audience, and available products. The conclusion of this step defines guidelines for the steps that follow, such as the selection, cleaning, and interpretation of the information retrieved for the implemented data mining project. In the case of this study, the final client is an individual electric car driver. For example, a potential EV car buyer needs estimates of what an EV car's range would be. The EV car buyer would be interested in predicting the range of a car on a full charge based on its attributes. More precisely, the EV car buyer would need to answer the business question related to our research question: "Which factors have the most impact on battery degradation?".

3.2 Data Understanding

The second step of CRISP-DM consists of organizing and documenting all the available data sources relevant to the institution or client. This documentation implies the identification of a target audience and the selection of sources of data. This stage is an iterative process that includes searching for data sources and data essential for its selection. It is expected to obtain an extensive dataset with the potential of obtaining meaningful information about EV users and their vehicles. Ideally, it would reach a diversity of responses high enough to ensure a comprehensive analysis of the problem in focus.

However, in this paper, the original dataset was obtained through a single source. It came from an international news blog called Elektrek [2]. This blog shares a dataset compiling answers to a survey from a forum of Tesla users, who registered their range entries and other data in an excel spreadsheet, collecting a total of 1425 observations, structured in 43 variables.

3.3 Data Preparation

The data preparation phase aims to transform the information collected into clean, structured, and integrated data. It comprised procedures performed with the Python programming language [25], using the Jupyter Notebook tool [26]. Our data preparation included four steps: first, removal of out-of-scope variables, followed by the elimination of blank records, elimination of outliers and finally the matching of variable formats. These four steps are described as follows:

Removal of Out-of-Scope Variables: the original dataset (with 43 variables) had out-of-scope variables for this study. Table 2 below lists all the variables present in the Tesla dataset, as collected, before any data cleaning operations, their data type, exclusion status from the study, and the reason behind the exclusion.

Table 1. Tesla dataset variable list by type.

Variable name	Data type
Location	String
Model	String
Mileage in Miles	Float
Mileage per day	Float
EPA rated range	Float
RNG Mode On/Off	Float
EPA range Mode off	Float
Battery Replacement Y/N	Boolean
Battery mileage after replacement	Float
Battery days after replacement	Float
Total Average Energy Consumption	Float
Rated range when new	Float
Remaining original range	Float
Wh capacity until range is zero	Float
Freq. SCHG	String
Freq. 100%	String
Freq. empty	String
Daily charge level	Float
Daily charge power in Watts	Float
100% range when new	Float
Range mode on/off previous reading	Float
Vehicle age (days)	Float
Cycles	Float
Total Km	Float
Wh/mi to Wh/km	Float
Avg. Cap. All cars at this mileage	Float
Cap below trendline	Float

Elimination of Blank Records: some of the observations from the dataset had missing fields. A visual representation of each variable's number of null values was created (see Fig. 2). The higher the bars, the more complete the variable was. Given that these missing values can lead to bias, leading to wrong conclusions, all missing responses had to be excluded from the dataset for further analysis.

Elimination of Outliers: when existing variable values were too far from the remaining observations, they were considered outliers and needed to be removed. The method used to detect outliers was based on percentiles. With the percentile's method, all data variables outside an interval formed by the 5th and 95th percentiles were considered potential outliers and removed (see Fig. 3).

Matching of Variable Formats: the normalization of the dataset variables with formats (e.g., dates, distance units in the Imperial system). Some of the variables were in object format (mostly text ones), which had to be transformed from their original format to a numerical form. Variable encoding was performed as follows: for the location variable, integers were attributed to the name of the countries; for the model variable, each car model was given a distinct integer; for the Freq. SCHG, Freq. 100%, and Freq. empty, their values were encoded by employing a Likert scale, whose values ranged from 1 to 8. This step processed the variables across all observations (see Table 1).

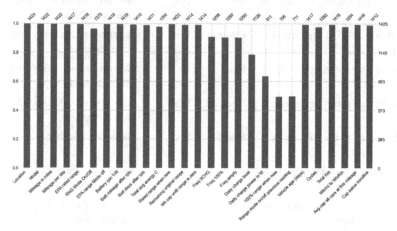

Fig. 2. Visual representation of null values by each variable.

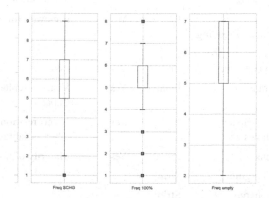

Fig. 3. Example of outliers' identification of the three Frequency variables.

Most vehicles from the sample traveled a few kilometers because the vast majority have a range below 100,000 km. This occurrence aligns with the fact that most vehicles in the sample are less than ten years old.

Table 2. Exclusion of the Tesla dataset variables.

Variable	Type	Excluded	Reason
Username	String	Yes	Irrelevant
Location	String		
Vehicle manufacture date	Date		
Date of range reading	Date	Yes	No insights were found
Model	String		
Mileage in miles	Int		
Mileage per day	Float	Yes	Duplicate variable
EPA rated range at 100% charge in miles	Int	Yes	No correlations were found with other variables
Range mode on/off at the time of reading?	Boolean	Yes	No correlations were found with other variables
EPA range after correction if range mode was off	Float	Yes	No correlations were found with other variables
Did you have a battery replacement?	Boolean	Yes	Very few vehicles had their battery replaced
What happened to the EPA range after replacement?	String	Yes	Excessive number of null values
At what miles did you replace the battery?	Int	Yes	Excessive number of null values
Mileage in mi after correction if the battery was replaced	Int	Yes	Dependent on battery replacement
Battery age (days) after correction if the battery was replaced	Int	Yes	Dependent on battery replacement
Lifetime average energy consumption at the time of reading Wh/mi	Int	Yes	Irrelevant for this study
Rated range of this model when new	Int	Yes	Like variable mileage in miles
Remaining original range	Float	Yes	Variable replaced by Average Capacity
Remaining usable Wh capacity until typical range shows zero		Yes	No correlations were found with other variables
Unanswered questions	Int	Yes	Majority of no answers
Frequency of supercharging	String		
Frequency of 100% charge	String		
Frequency of almost empty (5 mi or less)	String		

(*continued*)

Table 2. (*continued*)

Variable	Type	Excluded	Reason
Daily charge level	Float	Yes	Excessive number of null values
Daily charge power in watts	Float	Yes	Excessive number of null values
What was the 100% rated range when the car was new?	Int	Yes	Excessive number of null values
Range mode on/off at the time of reading the previous column?	Boolean	Yes	Excessive number of null values
Rated range at the beginning of the trip	Int	Yes	Excessive number of null values
Rated range at the end of the trip	Int	Yes	Excessive number of null values
Consumption for this trip	Float	Yes	Excessive number of null values
Range mode on/off when reading these trip numbers?	Boolean	Yes	Excessive number of null values
Typical range consumption for the trip	Float	Yes	Excessive number of null values
Typical range after correction if range mode was off	Int	Yes	Excessive number of null values
Remaining usable capacity until typical range shows zero according to trip data	Float	Yes	Excessive number of null values
Remaining original capacity	Float	Yes	Excessive number of null values
Trip based battery capacity calculation explained	Float	Yes	Excessive number of null values
100% range when the car was new after range mode adjustment	Int	Yes	Dependent on range mode
Vehicle age (days)	Int		
Cycles	Int		
Mileage in miles	Int		
Wh/mi to wh/km	Float	Yes	Unit conversions made in Python and SPSS
Average capacity of all cars at this mileage according to chart trendline	Float	Yes	Irrelevant for this study
Your capacity minus chart trendline at this mileage	Float	Yes	Irrelevant for this study

3.4 Modeling

In this phase, ML techniques were applied to the Tesla dataset to understand how several factors affected the range of the EVs present in the dataset, as stated in our research question. Therefore, it was necessary to take the following steps to know which variables affect a car maximum range with a full charge:

Classification Analysis: Several ML supervised classification algorithms from the Scykit-learn package [27] were exploited to classify which variables influenced the cars' maximum range on a full charge, addressing the research question. The objective of these classifiers was to label the current range that each car had in comparison to the original range value announced by their respective manufacturers. We created a new discrete variable called "Degradation," containing two labels: "Normal" and "Abnormal." These two labels represented the batteries' degree of energy capacity loss in a percentage of the original maximum range. Degradation levels lower than 10% were labeled "Normal" and higher than 10% as "Abnormal." The 10% threshold was used based on the Elektrek article claiming that 10% was the average capacity degradation of EVs after 160,000 miles [2]. The following ML classification models were chosen and assessed to perform the labeling task:

- K-Nearest Neighbours (KNN) [28]
- Logistic Regression [29]
- Naïve-Bayes [30]
- Support Vector Machine – Linear (L-SVM) [31]
- Support Vector Machine – Radial (R-SVM) [32]

These models were selected because they are of low complexity, and as such, they should generalize better when dealing with small datasets. Since the Tesla dataset is a small dataset with just 1,425 observations, the decision boundary of complex models such as Decision Trees or the Random Forest would change wildly and, therefore, be inappropriate to tackle our problem. As a result, the results from those more complex models would have high degrees of variance. Simpler models such as those chosen above were believed to perform better as they have more minor degrees of freedom.

Following best practices from the literature, each classification model was preceded by a split of the original dataset into a training set and a test set, the split chosen was 80–20%, respectively, [33, 34], so that fitted models would be evaluated regarding their performance and compared using a confusion matrix.

Cross-Validation: We employed a standard iterative cross-validation technique [35] to compare model performance, obtain the best model, and avoid overfitting [36]. Overfitting happens when a model obtains near-perfect scores after being trained with known training and testing sets but cannot make accurate predictions when using new data. In our case, the training set was split into ten smaller equal sets. A model was trained using nine sets as training data and judged its results against the tenth set. Then, a loop was created to switch the testing set between all ten sets. The average of the values computed in the loop reports the global performance of the model.

3.5 Evaluation

The evaluation phase aims to assess the validity of the results of our automatic labeling process. First, the cars' current range was checked to see if the vehicles retained more or less than 10% of the initial total battery capacity. Subsequently, the classification models and the cross-validation technique labeled the vehicles with an abnormal or regular decline of energy capacity. Finally, the factors that had the most negative impact on the batteries were pinpointed, answering our research question. Generally, the models' performance presented accuracy results ranging between 57.18% and 62.84%, as seen in Table 3.

3.6 Modeling Results

Table 3 shows test accuracy models by median and standard deviation. The median accuracy was calculated by using the accuracy formula shown in Eq. 1.

Table 3. Test accuracy results from the cross-validation.

Classifiers	Median	Standard deviation
K-Nearest Neighbours	0.5718	0.0682
Logistic Regression	**0.6284**	**0.1068**
Naïve-Bayes	0.5872	0.0847
L-SVM	0.5921	0.1109
R-SVM	**0.6175**	**0.1058**

$$Accuracy = \frac{TP + TN}{TP + TN + FP + FN} \qquad (1)$$

Equation 1 – Accuracy formula used for determining the classifiers' performance. TP-True Positive, TN-True Negative, FP -False positives, FN-False Negatives.

The two best-fitted models identified using cross-validation are highlighted in bold. The key takeaway from the cross-validation evaluation results was the Logistic Regression and the Radial Support Vector Machine (Radial SVM). These were the two best performing models from the group, reaching 62.84% and 61.75% of median accuracy, respectively, for the labeling task. Moreover, it shows that from the 500 observations (vehicles), the best classification model, the Logistic Regression, correctly guessed 62.84% of the degradation labels.

At this point in the analysis, each independent variable's weight over the *Degradation* dependent variable remains unknown to answer the research question. However, t below depicts just that, showing both the weight and significance of each variable.

Table 4. Degradation - coefficients of the independent variables

Degradation	Regression coefficient	Chi-squared	p-Value
Country	0.384	4.52	0.052
Year	2.191	12.62	0.037
Maker	0.137	0.03	0.184
Model	0.012	0.01	0.982
Freq. Fast	−0.02	0.90	0.814
Freq. Full	0.09	0.55	0.555
Freq. Empty	0.027	0.28	0.370
Mileage	0.059	0.10	0.627
Max Range	0.061	0.88	0.837

From Table 4, it is possible to conclude that there were two predominant independent variables: the *Year* and *Country*. Furthermore, these two predictors seem to have positive and strong correlations with the *Degradation* dependent variable. Lower values for the *Year* variable correspond to older vehicles, and an "Abnormal" value of the *Degradation* variable means a higher than usual degrading of the battery.

There is a correlation regarding the variable Country, possibly due to a large volume of vehicles from Asia and the Pacific regions, causing a dataset imbalance. However, it would be necessary to have more data to draw more elaborated conclusions to explain this phenomenon. As for the remaining variables listed, there seems to be no relationship between them and *Degradation*.

In conclusion, the variable *Year* was the most impactful factor on the rate of degradation. However, none of the behavioral factors were significant, which would aid in answering the research question *Which factors have the most impact on battery degradation?*

3.7 Deployment

In the deployment phase, knowledge extracted from the data is delivered and applied. From this moment, the processes within the organization might be changed or new products created. Our Logistic Regression ML classification algorithm is, in essence, our final prototype. It aims to determine which behavioral habits from the EV drivers negatively impact the Li-ion battery capacity of the cars, answering the research question.

The chosen model allowed us to gather and label the degree of battery degradation in two categories and get a general sense of the degradation trend of all vehicles. For the personas to whom this study is aimed, i.e., the owners of EVs, this information can be crucial. It sheds light on the current rate of degradation of the car batteries and anticipates the need for future maintenance events, such as a complete battery replacement.

4 Conclusions

This paper aimed to investigate the effect of capacity degradation on electric vehicles' batteries by following a data science and analytics approach. The objective was attained by answering the research question *"Which factors have the most impact on the battery degradation"?*

As shown in Table 4, charging and parking habits were negligible at best and almost irrelevant to the decay of the cars' Li-ion batteries. EVs regularly charged at fast-charging stations did not display significantly lower values from the *Max Range* variable than those that avoided that practice. Additionally, the results have revealed that the cars' model year (expressed by the *Year* variable) was the only variable that significantly impacted the batteries' capacity. In short, the CRISP-DM methodology answered the research question by identifying the vehicle's year of release as the determining factor for battery degradation, without any of the identified behavioural factors having a meaningful part in the decay effect.

Our work relied on a dataset made public by a forum of EV users, limited to its participants. This approach can be improved by reaching more platforms of EV users, obtaining more responses, and a larger dataset. This could improve the model's accuracy score. In addition, future work could include other factors that affect battery performance, such as battery replacements and data extracted from the vehicles' Battery Management Systems, such as voltage, temperature, and current going in and out of the batteries.

Acknowledgments. This study was performed in the scope of ISCTE collaboration with Santos e Vale, who financed the research.

References

1. Saldaña, G., Martín, J.I.S., Zamora, I., Asensio, F.J., Oñederra, O., González, M.: Empirical electrical and degradation model for electric vehicle batteries. IEEE Access **8**, 155576–155589 (2020)
2. Lambert, F.: Tesla battery degradation at less than 10% after over 160,000 miles, according to latest data. Elektrek (2018). https://electrek.co/2018/04/14/tesla-battery-degradation-data/. Accessed 04 May 2021
3. Tesla, I.: 2020 Tesla Impact Report (2020). https://www.tesla.com/ns_videos/2020-tesla-impact-report.pdf. Accessed 16 Aug 2021
4. Masson-Delmotte, V., et al.: Climate Change 2021: The Physical Science Basis. Contribution of Working Group I to the Sixth Assessment Report of the Intergovernmental Panel on Climate Change, Cambridge (2021). https://www.ipcc.ch/report/ar6/wg1/downloads/report/IPCC_AR6_WGI_Full_Report.pdf
5. EPA. "United States Environmental Protection Agency. Inventory of US Greenhouse Gas Emissions and Sinks: 1990–2019," Report No. EPA 430-R-15-004 (2019). https://www.epa.gov/ghgemissions/inventory-us-greenhouse-gas-emissions-and-sinks. Accessed 19 Feb 2021
6. European Commission. European Green Deal (2021). https://ec.europa.eu/info/strategy/priorities-2019-2024/european-green-deal_en. Accessed 18 Aug 2021
7. Plano Nacional de Energia e Clima 2021–2030 (2019). https://www.portugalenergia.pt/setor-energetico/bloco-3/. Accessed 16 Aug 2021

8. Chan, C.C.: The state of the art of electric, hybrid, and fuel cell vehicles. Proc. IEEE **95**(4), 704–718 (2007)
9. May, G., El-Shahat, A.: Battery-degradation model based on the ANN regression function for EV applications. In: Proceedings of the IEEE Global Humanitarian Technology Conference (GHTC 2017), January 2017, pp. 1–3 (2017)
10. Singh Ceng, M., Janardhan Reddy, K.: Predicting Life-Cycle Estimation of Electric Vehicle Battery Pack through Degradation by Self Discharge and Fast Charging. SAE Technical Paper No. 2020 (2020)
11. Yun, Z., Qin, W.: Remaining useful life estimation of lithium-ion batteries based on optimal time series health indicator. IEEE Access **8**, 55447–55461 (2020)
12. Tan, X., et al.: Real-time state-of-health estimation of lithium-ion batteries based on the equivalent internal resistance. IEEE Access **8**, 56811–56822 (2020)
13. Hu, X.S., Yuan, H., Zou, C.F., Li, Z., Zhang, L.: Co-estimation of state of charge and state of health for lithium-ion batteries based on fractional-order calculus. IEEE Trans. Veh. Technol. **67**(11), 10319–10329 (2018)
14. Jiang, Y., Zhang, J., Xia, L., Liu, Y.: State of health estimation for lithium-ion battery using empirical degradation and error compensation models. IEEE Access **8**, 123858–123868 (2020)
15. Aaboud, M., et al.: Search for long-lived, massive particles in events with displaced vertices and missing transverse momentum in root S = 13 TeV pp collisions with the ATLAS detector. Phys. Rev. D **97**(5) (2018)
16. Kim, J., et al.: Data-driven state of health estimation of Li-ion batteries with RPT-reduced experimental data. IEEE Access **7**, 106987–106997 (2019)
17. Li, K., Wei, F., Tseng, K.J., Soong, B.-H.: A practical lithium-ion battery model for state of energy and voltage responses prediction incorporating temperature and ageing effects. IEEE Trans. Ind. Electron. **65**(8), 6696–6708 (2018)
18. Liu, D., Yin, X., Song, Y., Liu, W., Peng, Y.: An on-line state of health estimation of lithium-ion battery using unscented particle filter. IEEE Access **6**, 40990–41001 (2018)
19. El Mejdoubi, A., Chaoui, H., Gualous, H., Van Den Bossche, P., Omar, N., Van Mierlo, J.: Lithium-ion batteries health prognosis considering aging conditions. IEEE Trans. Power Electron. **34**(7), 6834–6844 (2019)
20. Wei, J.W., Dong, G.Z., Chen, Z.H.: Remaining useful life prediction and state of health diagnosis for lithium-ion batteries using particle filter and support vector regression. IEEE Trans. Ind. Electron. **65**(7), 5634–5643 (2018)
21. Vidal, C., et al.: Hybrid energy storage system state-of-charge estimation using artificial neural network for micro-hybrid applications. In: 2018 IEEE Transportation and Electrification Conference and Expo, ITEC 2018, pp. 868–873 (2018)
22. Qu, J., Liu, F., Ma, Y., Fan, J.: A neural-network-based method for RUL prediction and SoH monitoring of lithium-ion battery. IEEE Access **7**, 87178–87191 (2019)
23. Vidal, C., Malysz, P., Kollmeyer, P., Emadi, A.: Machine learning applied to electrified vehicle battery state of charge and state of health estimation: state-of-the-art. IEEE Access **8**, 52796–52814 (2020)
24. Cross Industry Standard Process for Data Mining (CRISP-DM) (1996). https://www.datascience-pm.com/crisp-dm-2/. Accessed 18 Aug 2021
25. Python.org. https://www.python.org/. Accessed 24 Aug 2021
26. Project Jupyter. https://jupyter.org/. Accessed 24 Aug 2021
27. Pedregosa, F., Varoquaux, G., Gramfort, A.: Scikit-learn: machine learning in python. J. Mach. Learn. Res. **12**, 2825–2830 (2011)
28. Altman, N.S.: An introduction to kernel and nearest-neighbor nonparametric regression. Am. Statist. **46**(3), 175 (1992)

29. Walker, S.H., Duncan, D.B.: Estimation of the probability of an event as a function of several independent variables. Biometrika **54**(1/2), 167 (1967)
30. John, G.H., Langley, P.: Estimating Continuous Distributions in Bayesian Classifiers. http:// robotics. Accessed 20 Aug 2021
31. sklearn.svm.LinearSVC — scikit-learn 0.24.2 documentation. https://scikit-learn.org/sta ble/modules/generated/sklearn.svm.LinearSVC.html#sklearn.svm.LinearSVC. Accessed 20 Aug 2021
32. RBF SVM parameters — scikit-learn 0.24.2 documentation. https://scikit-learn.org/stable/ auto_examples/svm/plot_rbf_parameters.html. Accessed 20 Aug 2021
33. Petersen, P., Thorgeirsson, A.T., Scheubner, S., Otten, S., Gauterin, F., Sax, E.: Training and validation methodology for range estimation algorithms. In: Proceedings of the 5th International Conference on Vehicle Technology Intelligent Transport System (VEHITS 2019), pp. 434–443 (2019)
34. Pokharel, S., Sah, P., Ganta, D.: Improved prediction of total energy consumption and feature analysis in electric vehicles using machine learning and Shapley additive explanations method. World Electr. Veh. J. **12**(3), 94 (2021). https://www.mdpi.com/2032-6653/12/3/94/ htm. Accessed 28 Oct 2021
35. 3.1. Cross-validation: evaluating estimator performance — scikit-learn 0.24.2 documentation. https://scikit-learn.org/stable/modules/cross_validation.html. Accessed 19 Aug 2021
36. The Danger of Overfitting Regression Models. https://blog.minitab.com/en/adventures-in-sta tistics-2/the-danger-of-overfitting-regression-models. Accessed 20 Aug 2021

Real-Time Detection of Vehicle-Based Logistics Operations

Joel Ribeiro[1]([✉]), Jorge Tavares[1,2], and Tânia Fontes[1]

[1] INESC TEC, Rua Dr. Roberto Frias, 4200-465 Porto, Portugal
{joel.ribeiro,tania.d.fontes}@inesctec.pt
[2] Faculty of Engineering, University of Porto,
Rua Dr. Roberto Frias, 4200-465 Porto, Portugal

Abstract. Geolocation data is fundamental to businesses relying on vehicles such as logistics and transportation. With the advance of the technology, collecting geolocation data become increasingly accessible and affordable, which raised new opportunities for business intelligence. This paper addresses the application of geolocation data for monitoring logistics processes, namely for detecting vehicle-based operations in real time. A stream of geolocation entries is used for inferring stationary events. Data from an international logistics company is used as a case study, in which operations of loading/unloading of goods are not only identified but also quantified. The results of the case study demonstrate the effectiveness of the solution, showing that logistics operations can be inferred from geolocation data. Further meaningful information may be extracted from these inferred operations using process mining techniques.

Keywords: Geolocation data · Event detection · Logistics operations

1 Introduction

Specific areas of the transportation sector such as fleet management, are being revolutionised by data and digital transformation. The use of telematics in fleets increased significantly in last years, from 48% in 2017 to 86% in 2019 [1]. As just 23% of fleets used big data analytics to guide strategic decision-making, new opportunities arise for the businesses to improve their fleets' operations.

Geolocation data rely on a geographic coordinate system such as the GPS (Global Positioning System), which define the positions on Earth. The inference of events using geolocation data can provide a valuable insight into business processes, especially in transportation and logistics, for example for the analysis of routes, vehicles and drivers [11]. The identification of travel events and motivations has been studied over the last few decades [14].

Focusing on public transportation, Pinelli et al. [9] proposed a methodology to detect the location of the scheduled and unscheduled bus stops using

© ICST Institute for Computer Sciences, Social Informatics and Telecommunications Engineering 2022
Published by Springer Nature Switzerland AG 2022. All Rights Reserved
A. L. Martins et al. (Eds.): INTSYS 2021, LNICST 426, pp. 192–205, 2022.
https://doi.org/10.1007/978-3-030-97603-3_14

the speed and acceleration variation, distinguishing then the type of stop relying on density-based clustering. Biagioni et al. [5] also identifies the location of bus stops with an automatic system which uses GPS traces collected from smartphones, identifying the routes and inferring schedules afterwards. Gong et al. [6] developed a methodology to identify activity stops in continuous GPS trajectories collected using mobile phones and combining clustering techniques with Support Vector Machines (SVM). Tavares et al. [13] defined and evaluated diverse approaches for identifying – from geolocation data – relevant locations where vehicles stopped.

Focusing on logistics, Pluvinet et al. [10] defined a GPS-based data collection technique and data processing algorithm to identify the delivery stops and route characterization, and Holguín-Veras et al. [7] developed a procedure to identify urban freight activity stops from raw GPS data using three parameters: GPS data points, the value of the cutoff acceleration (typically between 25 and 40 km.h^{-2}), and the cutoff speed parameter (typically between 0 and 10 km.h^{-1}). Yang et al. [15] proposed an algorithm to identify the delivery stops using second-by-second GPS data of different delivery tours according to the top speed and time between stops. Since a great number of stops are generated due to high road traffic, the delivery stops are distinguished from the remaining ones according to their features. Kinjarapu et al. [8] developed a heuristic-based model to identify and classify truck stops. These authors found that a combination of trucks' dwelling times and their entropy can be used to classify truck stops by purpose. Aziz et al. [4] analyzed GPS data of truck movement, identifying the truck stops, clustering the several stoppages, and characterizing the truck stops according to their arrival time and duration distributions. In order to overcome the limitations of the existing clustering practices in freight studies, Taghavi et al. [12] use a Hidden Markov Model to identify truck trip segments and extract activity and non-activity stops from GPS data while accounting for the spatio-temporal properties of GPS points.

The analysis of the literature allowed to identify some gaps and limitations. First, even though procedures to identify freight activity stops from raw GPS data are already defined (e.g., [7,13,15]), such procedures use a set of variables as geolocation data, vehicle speed and acceleration. Second, to the best of our knowledge, such procedures were designed to work offline, which limit the use of the collected data for operational monitoring of vehicles and cargos or management of resources (e.g., work re-planing). Third, previous studies use an average cadence of geolocation entries lower than 60 s (e.g., [7,15]).

This paper addresses the application of geolocation data for monitoring logistics processes, namely for detecting vehicle-based operations in real time. This work includes the development of a methodology based on *stationary events* [11], which is designed to work simply on a stream of geolocation entries with arbitrary cadences, in real time and in an incremental fashion. A real-life logistics process is used as a case study to demonstrate the effectiveness of the methodology, namely the automatic detection of operations like the load/unload of goods.

The remainder of this paper is organized as follows. The context of the work is described in the next section. Then, the methodology for automatic detection of vehicle-based operations is defined. Next, a preliminary evaluation of the application of the methodology is presented, as well as a discussion of the results. Finally, the main conclusions and future work are outlined in the last section.

2   Context

This work is conducted to provide insight into the business processes of an international logistics company that operates mainly in the European market. The company relies on over 2000 vehicles, transporting – each year – 7 million *ton* of goods across 200 million *kms*. Each month, over 25000 distribution routes are performed to pick and transport about 4.5 million packages.

Generated by fleet tracking technologies, geolocation data is currently used for monitoring the state of vehicles in terms of positioning and navigation. Information about the execution of operations such as the start and conclusion of load/unload operations is generated by human resources, which has proven to be ineffective due to delayed, imprecise or missing inputs. As a consequence, not only the management of the logistics processes becomes more difficult but also the operations scheduling. Therefore, the exploitation of geolocation data for the detection of vehicle-based logistics operations in real time is an opportunity for improving the monitoring and management of logistics operations, namely the load/unload of goods. Also, this solution can be used to enhance the customer service, by providing means to negotiate more adjusted contracts to reality, and by enabling on-the-fly notifications to customers about their packages.

3   Automatic Detection of Vehicle-Based Operations

This section is structured in four main topics. First, the definition of geolocation entry and stationary event is presented (Sect. 3.1). Then, the operations detection (Sect. 3.2) and operations inference (Sect. 3.3) are described. The detection of vehicle-based operations consists of finding stationary events in a sequence of geolocation entries. Since a stationary event represents some abstract operation that occurred in some geolocation, the inference of logistics operations is necessary to assign a meaning to these events. The last section explains how vehicle-based logistics operations can be detected in real time (Sect. 3.4).

3.1   Geospatial Event Data

In the scope of this work, events consist of vehicle-based operations with a geospatial component. Geospatial events can be categorized as *stationary* and *non-stationary* events, depending on whether the location where the operation took place changed or not during its execution [11]. In a logistics process, operations like the load/unload of goods are stationary events, which can be automatically detected by analyzing the sequences of geolocation entries generated using the vehicle's GPS tracking device. For that, let us consider the following definition [11,13].

Definition 1 (Geolocation entry and stationary event). *Let the geolocation of a vehicle (v) at a specific time instant (t) be defined as the entry* $l = (v, t, lat, lon)$, *where lat and lon identifies the latitude and longitude of the vehicle's position on Earth. Given two geolocations* $l_1 = (lat_1, lon_1)$ *at time instant* t_1 *and* $l_2 = (lat_2, lon_2)$ *at time instant* t_2:

- *the function* **distance**(l_1, l_2) *computes the orthodromic distance between the position of* l_1 *and* l_2.
- *the function* **speed**(l_1, t_1, l_2, t_2) *computes the average speed of the movement from the position of* l_1 *to* l_2.

Let $L = [l_1, l_2, ..., l_n]$ *be a sequence (time series) of geolocation entries of the same vehicle. A stationary event E is a subsequence of L with at least two elements, in which all elements must be within a given range of distance, time, and/or average speed values. The following functions are defined for a given stationary event E:*

- *the function* **location**(E) *identifies the centroid* $c = (lat_c, lon_c)$ *defined by the elements of the subsequence, which represents the geolocation of E.*
- *the function* **duration**(E) *computes the duration of E, which consists of the time difference between the first and last entries of the subsequence.*
- *the functions* **start**(E) *and* **end**(E) *identifies the time instants of the first and last entries of E.*

$\square$

3.2 Operations Detection

Algorithm 1 describes how stationary events can be identified, in an incremental fashion. This algorithm assumes that, for each vehicle, there is a data structure that holds the history of stationary events as well as the current stationary event candidate.

In this work, a stationary event is defined by a sequence of geolocation entries such that every element must be less than 15 m from the elements' centroid (δ threshold), the movement from an element to another consecutive must be less than 1 km.h^{-1} (v threshold), and the time difference between two consecutive elements must be less than 2 h (Γ threshold). These threshold values are the same as the ones considered in [13]. Since no logistics operation shorter than 1 min is expected to occur, $\theta = 1$ min is used as the minimum event duration in order to filter some noise in the data.

3.3 Operations Inference

The operations inference consists of linking stationary events to logistics operations. In the scope of this work, the execution of the logistics processes rely on some *work plan*, which is composed by an ordered list of *planned operations*.

Algorithm 1: Identification of stationary events

Input   : A geolocation entry (v, t, lat, lon) as defined in Definition 1. As
             thresholds, δ is the maximum distance (default 30 m), ψ the
             maximum speed (default 1 $km.h^{-1}$), Γ the maximum time (default
             2 h), and θ the minimum event duration (default 1 min).

Output: A stationary event, if identified.

Method
1    $S \leftarrow$ null;   // the stationary event to be returned
2    $E \leftarrow$ retrieve the current stationary event candidate of vehicle v;
3   **if** $E \neq null$ **and** end$(E) = t$ **then**   // equal timestamps, discard entry
     | **return** S;
     end
4   **if** $E \neq null$ **and** distance$(\text{location}(E),(lat, lon)) \leq \delta$ **and**
         speed$(\text{location}(E),\text{end}(E),(lat, lon),t) \leq \psi$ **and** $(t - \text{end}(E)) \leq \Gamma$ **then**
     | // update E with geolocation (lat, lon) at time instant t
5 | append (v, t, lat, lon) to E;
     else
     | // the stationary event candidate is over
6 | **if** $E \neq null$ **and** duration$(E) \geq \theta$ **then**
7 | | add E as an executed event of vehicle v;
8 | | $S \leftarrow E$;
     | **end**
     | // create a new stationary event candidate
9 | $E \leftarrow$ new stationary event located in (lat, lon) with t as start time;
10 | set E as the current stationary event candidate of vehicle v;
     end
11   **return** S;

Definition 2 (Planned operation and work plan). *Let v be a vehicle with
a GPS tracking device.*

*A planned operation p describes a future load/unload operation of a logistics
process using vehicle v, which is expected to occur at a specific location. The
function* **location(p)** *identifies the geolocation where p is supposed to occur. No
time information (start time) is directly associated with planned operations.*

*A work plan $W = [p_1, p_2, ..., p_m]$ is an ordered list of planned operations for
vehicle v, which consists of a trip in which each event represents the trip's check-
points. The function* **start(W)** *identifies the time instant when W is supposed to
start. Only one work plan can be executed at a time, even though there are cases
for which it is not possible to determine when a work plan ends and another
starts. These cases happen when the first event of a work plan is at the same
location of the last event of the previous work plan.*

                                                                                            □

An overview of the real-time monitoring of work plans (and the corresponding
operations) is presented in Fig. 1. Comparing to the traditional definition of a

business process [2], the work plans are process instances, while the operations are process events.

Work plan	State	Vehicle	Start time	Operation 1	Operation 2	Operation 3	Operation 4
Work plan 1	Active	V04	08:15	Location A 08:19 - 09:10	Location B non-executed	-	-
Work plan 2	Finished	V10	07:30	Location C 07:15 - 7:50	Location D 09:22 - 09:57	Location E non-executed	Location F 10:22 - 11:30
Work plan 3	Planned	V04	14:00	Location A non-executed	Location B non-executed	-	-
Work plan 4	Finished	V07	07:30	Location E 07:23 - 7:38	Location F 08:19 - 08:40	Location B 09:51 - 12:13	-

Fig. 1. Overview of the real-time monitoring of work plans.

Since a planned operation is geolocated, the operations inference is achieved by checking whether a stationary event occurred nearby to that planned operation. In this work is considered that, if the orthodromic distance between a stationary event E and a planned operation O is no farther than 1000 m then E should represent the execution of O. If no planned operation satisfies the aforementioned condition for E, then it can be assumed that E represents a *negligible* operation (e.g., vehicle refueling or driver's resting). In the scope of this work, these unmatched stationary events are discarded.

Given a stationary event E and the list of work plans for some vehicle, Algorithm 2 describes how to identify the current active work plan (or plans, if one is ending in the same location as another starts). This algorithm assumes that there is a function that describes whether a planned operation was already executed or not. The *Radius* threshold defines the maximum orthodromic distance between E and the planned operations, which is set to 1000 m as explained before. The *minT* and *maxT* thresholds define the allowed time offset range for starting a new work plan, which are set to −5 h and +12 h of the planned starting time.

3.4   Real-Time Computation

Given a stream of geolocation entries and a list of work plans, vehicle-based logistics operations can be detected in real time using Algorithm 3. The geolocation entries are considered to compute stationary events by applying Algorithm 1. The stationary events are considered to identify the active work plans and planned operations by applying Algorithm 2. The non-executed planned operations of the active work plans are matched with the non-reported stationary events for checking the execution of operations. It is important to mention that the execution of a planned operations may be supported by more than one stationary event. A good example of this case is when a vehicle performs some check-in operation in one location prior to the load/unload of goods in another location a few hundred

---

Algorithm 2: Identification of active work plans and operations

---

Input : For a specific vehicle v, a list of work plans ($W = [w_1, w_2, ..., w_n]$) and a stationary event (E). [minT; maxT] is the allowed time offset range for starting a work plan (default $[-5\ h; 12\ h]$). Radius defines the area where operations must be performed (default $1000\ m$).

Output: The work plans and planned operations activated by E, if exist.

Method

    // Current and past work plans

1    $B \leftarrow \{w$ in $W \mid w$ contains at least one planned operation that was executed already$\}$;

    // Future work plans that can be activated

2    $C \leftarrow \{w$ in $W \mid w$ not in $B\ \wedge\ $minT $\leq$ start$(E) -$ start$(w) \leq$ maxT$\}$;

    // Current work plan

3    $A \leftarrow \{w$ in $B \mid \forall_{x\ \neq\ w\ in\ W}[x$ not contains a planned operation which was executed after any executed event in $w]\}$;

    // Check whether the current work plan is still active

4   **if** $\exists_{w\ in\ A}[\nexists_{p\ in\ w}[\ p\ is\ not\ executed\ \wedge$ distance(location (E),location $(p)) <$ Radius$]]\ \wedge$ $\exists_{w'\ in\ C}[\exists_{p'_x\ in\ w'}[\ p'_x\ is\ not\ executed\ \wedge\ x \leq 3\ \wedge$ distance(location (E),location $(p')) <$ Radius$]]$ **then** $A \leftarrow \emptyset$;

    // Find the work plan and planned operation activated by E

5   **if** $A = \emptyset$ **then**

      // Current work plan is not active, find a new one

6      $X \leftarrow \{(w, p_1) \mid w \in C\ \wedge\ p_1\ in\ w\ \wedge$ distance$(\alpha, \beta) <$ Radius $\wedge$ $\forall_{w'\ \neq\ w\ \in\ C}[p'_1\ in\ w'\ \wedge$ distance$(\alpha, \gamma) \geq$ distance$(\alpha, \beta)]\}$, where $\alpha =$ location(E), $\beta =$ location(p_1), and $\gamma =$ location(p'_1);

7   **return** $(X, \emptyset)$;

    else

      // Current work plan is active, find the activated operation

8      $X \leftarrow \{(w, p) \mid w \in A\ \wedge\ p\ in\ w\ \wedge\ p$ is not executed$\}$;

9      $Y \leftarrow \{(w, p) \in X \mid \forall_{(w', p')\ \neq\ (w, p) \in X}[$distance$(\alpha, \gamma) \geq$ distance$(\alpha, \beta)]\}$, where $\alpha =$ location(E), $\beta =$ location(p_1), and $\gamma =$ location(p'_1);

      // Find a next work plan for which the first event is at the same location of the current operation of the active plan

10      $Z \leftarrow \{(w, p_1) \mid w \in C \wedge p_1\ in\ w \wedge \exists_{(w', p') \in Y}[$location$(p')=$location$(p_1)]\}$;

11   **return** (Y, Z);

    end

---

meters away. In the scope of this work, all stationary events that represent the execution of a specific planned operation are aggregated. This means that, the logistics company is interested to simply know the time a vehicle remains at the location of some planned operation. Hence, the results consist of messages notifying and quantifying – in real time – the execution of planned operations.

Algorithm 3: Real-time detection of logistics operations

Input : A stream of geolocation entries (Input) and the list of work plans (WPs). Radius defines the area where planned operations must be performed (default 1000 m).

Output: A stream of detected logistics operations.

Method

1 Open Output as the stream of detected logistics operations;
2 $O \leftarrow \emptyset$, the stack of events associated with some unreported planned operations ;   // Activated planned operations to be reported
3 **while** *stream* Input *is open* **do**
4 | $(v, t, lat, lon) \leftarrow$ wait/get geolocation entry from Input;
5 | $W \leftarrow$ get list of work plans of vehicle v from WPs;
6 | **foreach** $(A, B, C) \in O$ **do**
7 | | $(w, p) \leftarrow$ the only element in A;
| | // Check whether the vehicle left the operation area, so no more events can occur in there
8 | | **if** distance(location(p), (lat, lon)) $>$ Radius $\times$ 2 **then**
| | | // Report the execution of the matched planned operations
9 | | | change the state of operation p to *executed*;
10 | | | change the state of every event $e \in C$ to *reported*;
11 | | | $start \leftarrow$ earliest start time of the events in C;
12 | | | $end \leftarrow$ latest end time of the events in C;
13 | | | **if** $B \neq \emptyset$ **then**
14 | | | | $(w', p') \leftarrow$ the only element in B;
15 | | | | $middle \leftarrow$ time instant that is equidistant to $start$ and end;
16 | | | | change the state of p' to *executed*;
17 | | | | add $(v, w, p, start, middle)$ and $(v, w', p', middle, end)$ to Output;
| | | **end**
18 | | | **else** add $(v, w, p, start, end)$ to Output;
19 | | | $O \leftarrow O \setminus (A, B, C)$;   // remove from the stack
| | **end**
| **end**
| // Check whether there is a new stationary event for vehicle v
20 | $e \leftarrow$ apply Algorithm 1 with (v, t, lat, lon);
21 | **if** $e = null$ **then** break iteration (go to line 3);
| // Find the work plans and planned operations activated by e
22 | $(X, Y) \leftarrow$ apply Algorithm 2 with W and e;
23 | **if** $X \neq \emptyset$ **then**
| | // Add e to the stack of events, associated to the activated work plans and operations
24 | | **if** $\exists_{(A,B,C)} \in o[A = X \wedge B = Y]$ **then** $O \leftarrow (X, Y, C \cup e) \cup O \setminus (A, B, C)$
25 | | **else** $O \leftarrow (X, Y, \{e\}) \cup O$;
| **end**
end

---

4   Evaluation and Discussion

A preliminary evaluation of the application of the methodology presented in the previous section was conducted using real-life data from the logistics company. In this section, the characterization of the data used for the performed evaluation is presented. Also, the results of the Algorithms 1, 2 and 3 (implemented in Python) are assessed in terms of conformance and performance. The general limitations and impacts of the methodology are discussed in the end.

4.1   Data Characterization

The data used in this work consists of one month of geolocation data for three vehicles, as well as the corresponding work plans (routes). A total of 82000 geolocation entries and 95 work plans were collected from the operational systems. This data captures a combination of urban and sub-urban operations between distribution centers and delivery points. The vehicles usually travel long distances (hundreds of kms per route) through highways to reach urban areas. The average cadence of data used is around 100 s. Vehicle V1 has the highest number of geolocation entries ($N = 29238$), but the lowest number of work plans ($N = 18$). Vehicles V2 and V3 have a similar number of geolocation entries ($N \approx 26000$). However, the volume of work plans is higher for vehicle V3 ($N = 56$) than for vehicle V2 ($N = 21$). On the other hand, vehicle V2 has the triple of stationary events ($N = 1676$), than the vehicle V3 ($N = 658$). This may be related with the level of complexity of work plans as vehicle V2 has, proportionally, more planned operations ($N = 67$) than vehicle V3 ($N = 113$). The input and output data characterization is presented in Table 1.

Table 1. Input and output data characterization.

Indicator	Vehicle		
	V1	V2	V3
Geolocation entries	29328	26329	26335
in stationary event	15722 (53.6%)	17162 (65.2%)	21067 (80.0%)
(average cadence)	92 s	102 s	102 s
Stationary events	589	1676	658
with known location	155 (26.3%)	225 (13.4%)	368 (55.9%)
in work plan	210 (35.7%)	804 (48.0%)	431 (65.5%)
Work plans	18	21	56
fully fulfilled	17 (94.4%)	18 (85.7%)	52 (92.9%)
partially fulfilled	1 (5.6%)	2 (9.5%)	4 (7.1%)
Planned operations	36	67	113
with detected execution	35 (97.2%)	63 (94.0%)	108 (95.6%)

4.2   Conformance Checking

Conformance checking was performed to evaluate whether the work plans were executed according to the expected. On the one hand, start times were analyzed to identify and quantify delays. On the other hand, the detected operations were *parsed* in order to identify deviations to the work plan. These deviations can be either missing or swapped operations, such as the *alignment steps* for replaying event logs on process models [3]. The results of the conformance checking analysis are presented in Table 1.

4.3   Performance Analysis

The performance of the execution of the logistics processes provides insight into the efficiency of the company. The performance analysis can be conducted taking into account different perspectives such as work plans, planned operations and vehicles. At the work plan level, we analyzed the throughput time, the start time, and the delay, while at the planned operations level we computed the execution time. Table 2 provides an overview of some process performance indicators obtained in this evaluation.

Table 2. Overview of the process performance analysis.

Indicator	Vehicle		
	V1	V2	V3
Work plans			
Average throughput time	12:14:33	05:14:19	03:20:02
Average start time (executed vs planned)	−03:14:16	00:12:55	−00:52:28
Average delay	00:07:38	02:47:23	00:39:48
Started on time	16 (88.9%)	15 (78.9%)	41 (74.5%)
Planned operations			
Average execution time	04:48:18	01:01:44	01:18:23

As can be observed, the throughput times range from 3 h to 12 h and the delays between a few minutes to a few hours. Vehicle V1 has the highest throughput time, but the lower delay. These results suggest that the work plans were performed quite efficiently.

A common work plan is given as an example for exploiting the spatial aspect of the results. The work plan, which is executed in a regular basis, consists on just two operations: (1) the loading (of goods) in location A and (2) the unloading in location B. The road distance between A and B is around 200 km, which can be driven in 3 h. Figure 2 depicts – on a map – the history of stationary events associated with these operations. Details about the operations' performance are provided in Table 3. Note that the high time variations described by the standard deviations (event duration and operation execution time) are due to the drivers' resting nearby the location of the operation.

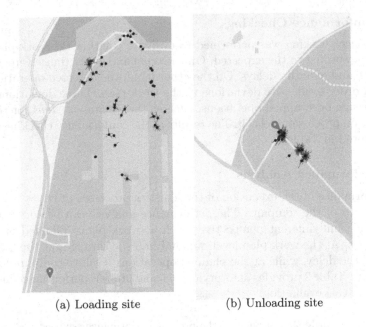

(a) Loading site   (b) Unloading site

Fig. 2. History of stationary events of two logistics operations. The blue markers represent the operations' expected geolocation, while the black circles represent the detected stationary events.

Table 3. Performance analysis of a specific work plan.

Indicator	Loading of goods avg (std)	Unloading of goods avg (std)
Stationary events		
Location offset (distance)	396 m (63 m)	35 m (28 m)
Location offset (azimuth)	117.6° (9.6°)	61.0° (31.4°)
Duration	00:19:41 (00:30:47)	01:26:27 (01:29:27)
Logistics operations		
Aggregated events	6.9 (1.5)	4.6 (4.5)
Execution time	02:00:25 (01:11:34)	08:11:30 (09:17:23)

Note: *avg* and *std* stand for average and standard deviation.

4.4   Discussion

The logistics processes considered in this work can be considered rather structured. This means that, there is neither a high variability in the workflow nor too much unexpected behavior in the execution of the processes. So, once that the focus of this work is simply the load/unload of goods, the application of process discovery techniques would not provide much new knowledge about the logistics processes. The application of conformance checking, however, is useful to verify the correct and complete execution of the work plans. Non-conforming cases may be due to either data issues (e.g., noise or missing data) or work performed in an unexpected manner (e.g., unfulfilled operations).

The real-time computation poses a challenge to the detection of logistics operations. In this work, the execution of an operation is assumed to be completed if the vehicle exits the area where the operation is supposed to be performed. If, for some reason, the vehicle has not exited the area permanently, then the detection would be erroneous. The methodology applied in this work addresses this issue, being able to correctly detect the execution of around 95% of the logistics operations (load/unload of goods).

The accuracy of the geolocation of the logistics operations is also a critical factor for the application of the methodology. The geolocation reference is often computed either using the postal address or the street entrance, which may be several hundred meters away of the location of the logistics operations. This issue is even worse when two or more distinct sites are located close by. In this work, a constant distance value (1000 m) is used to check whether a stationary event represents a logistics operation. However, a dynamic approach would be more adequate, especially because the layout and dimension of the sites where logistics operations occur vary enormously. The location offset, as presented in Table 3, can be used to adjust the location of the logistics operations.

5 Conclusions

This paper addresses the application of geolocation data for monitoring operations of an international logistics company, namely the load/unload of goods. The implementation of the methodology as well as the main issues for its application are described and discussed throughout the paper. The effectiveness of the solution was demonstrated using real-life geolocation data.

The exploitation of geolocation data for the detection of vehicle-based logistics operations in real time is an opportunity for improving the monitoring and management of logistics operations. The scope of this work is primarily to enhance the customer service of the logistics company, by providing means to negotiate more adjusted contracts to reality, and by enabling on-the-fly notifications to customers about their packages. It is acknowledged, however, that this solution has potential to provide new insight into the execution of the existing logistics processes. Process mining techniques should be a valuable complement for that.

As a future work, we envision the extension of the methodology in order to detect all kinds of vehicle-based operations instead of simply the load/unload of goods. This extension will require the classification of events that occur at unknown locations, which might be driven by the points of interest (POIs) in the surroundings of the events' location.

Acknowledgements. This work is financed by the European Regional Development Fund through the Operational Programme for Competitiveness and Internationalisation - COMPETE 2020 Programme and by National Funds through the

Portuguese funding agency, FCT - Fundação para a Ciência e a Tecnologia within project PTDC/ECI-TRA/32053/2017 - POCI-01-0145-FEDER-032053. Tânia Fontes also thanks FCT for the Post-Doctoral scholarship SFRH/BPD/109426/2015.

References

1. Telematics Benchmark Report 2019 - US Edition, Teletrac Navman. https://www.teletracnavman.com/resources/resource-library/articles/telematics-benchmark-report. Accessed 01 Sept 2021
2. van der Aalst, W.: Process Mining: Discovery, Conformance and Enhancement of Business Processes. Springer, Berlin (2011). https://doi.org/10.1007/978-3-642-19345-3
3. van der Aalst, W., Adriansyah, A., van Dongen, B.: Replaying history on process models for conformance checking and performance analysis. Wiley Interdiscip. Rev. Data Min. Knowl. Discov. 2(2), 182–192 (2012). https://doi.org/10.1002/widm.1045
4. Aziz, R., et al.: Identifying and characterizing truck stops from GPS data. In: Perner, P. (ed.) ICDM 2016. LNCS (LNAI), vol. 9728, pp. 168–182. Springer, Cham (2016). https://doi.org/10.1007/978-3-319-41561-1_13
5. Biagioni, J., Gerlich, T., Merrifield, T., Eriksson, J.: EasyTracker: automatic transit tracking, mapping, and arrival time prediction using smartphones. SenSys 2011, 68–81 (2011). https://doi.org/10.1145/2070942.2070950
6. Gong, L., Sato, H., Yamamoto, T., Miwa, T., Morikawa, T.: Identification of activity stop locations in GPS trajectories by density-based clustering method combined with support vector machines. J. Mod. Transp. 23(3), 202–213 (2015). https://doi.org/10.1007/s40534-015-0079-x
7. Holguin-Veras, J., Encarnacion, T., Pérez-Guzmán, S., Yang, X.: Mechanistic identification of freight activity stops from global positioning system data. Transp. Res. Rec. 2674(4), 235–246 (2020). https://doi.org/10.1177/0361198120911922
8. Kinjarapu, A., Demissie, M.G., Kattan, L., Duckworth, R.: Applications of passive GPS data to characterize the movement of freight trucks-A case study in the calgary region of Canada. IEEE Trans. Intell. Transp. Syst. (2021). https://doi.org/10.1109/TITS.2021.3093061
9. Pinelli, F., Calabrese, F., Bouillet, E.P.: Robust bus-stop identification and denoising methodology. In: IEEE Conference on Intelligent Transportation Systems (ITSC), pp. 2298–2303 (2013). https://doi.org/10.1109/ITSC.2013.6728570
10. Pluvinet, P., Gonzalez-Feliu, J., Ambrosini, C.: GPS data analysis for understanding urban goods movement. Procedia Soc. Behav. Sci. 39, 450–462 (2012). https://doi.org/10.1016/j.sbspro.2012.03.121
11. Ribeiro, J., Fontes, T., Soares, C., Borges, J.: Process discovery on geolocation data. Transp. Res. Procedia 47, 139–146 (2020). https://doi.org/10.1016/j.trpro.2020.03.086
12. Taghavi, M., Irannezhad, E., Prato, C.G.: Identifying truck stops from a large stream of GPS data via a hidden Markov chain model. In: 2019 IEEE Intelligent Transportation Systems Conference (ITSC), pp. 2265–2271. IEEE (2019). https://doi.org/10.1109/ITSC.2019.8917156
13. Tavares, J., Ribeiro, J., Fontes, T.: Detection of vehicle-based operations from geolocation data. Transp. Res. Procedia (2021, in press)

14. Van Dijk, J.: Identifying activity-travel points from GPS-data with multiple moving windows. Comput. Environ. Urban Syst. **70**, 84–101 (2018). https://doi.org/10.1016/j.compenvurbsys.2018.02.004
15. Yang, X., Sun, Z., Ban, X.J., Holguín-Veras, J.: Urban freight delivery stop identification with GPS data. Transp. Res. Rec. J. Transp. Res. Board **2411**(1), 55–61 (2014). https://doi.org/10.3141/2411-07

Optimal Strategy
for Autonomous-Vehicle-Dedicated Lane Deployment on Freeway with City Planning and Market as Driving Force

Jun Wang[1]([⊠]), Ilsu Kim[2], and Suleman B. Rana[2]

[1] School of Architecture, Georgia Institute of Technology, Atlanta, GA 30332, USA
jwang3095@gatech.edu
[2] School of Civil and Environmental Engineering, Georgia Institute of Technology,
Atlanta, GA 30332, USA
{ikim302,rsuleman}@gatech.edu

Abstract. This paper proposes a computationally effective mathematical procedure to deploy Autonomous Vehicle (AV)-dedicated lanes considering different AV market penetration rates and the influence of in-advance infrastructure construction behavior offered by the city planning department. With different expected AV market penetration rates, the corresponding limit of the total length of AV-dedicated lanes is put on the network to ensure the infrastructure construction moves ahead of the market performance of AVs, by improving the objective driving conditions to promote people's willingness and enthusiasm about AVs. MSA method is used to solve the UE traffic assignment problem with two types of traffic flows. A new measure to find optimal AV-lanes deployment location is formulated by calculating and comparing the instantaneous total paired-links travel time changes iteratively. The results show that the network can benefit from the newly constructed AV-lanes when the AV market penetration rate is lower than 55% and the total network travel time might increase once the AV market penetration rate is higher than 65%. Suggestions are given for city planners on how to use planning and zoning as tools to navigate the development of AVs to improve the overall living environment.

Keywords: Autonomous vehicles · Transportation modeling · City planning

1 Introduction

Autonomous Vehicles (AVs) have become a major component of future infrastructure planning. Many companies, including Tesla, are actively pursuing tremendous growth for the automation of vehicular transport. Deploying AVs on roads promises exceptional operational benefits. Some of the future advancements, such as V2X communications and platooning, pledge substantial safety and travel time refinement. The potential benefits that AVs will bring are emphasized by numerous studies [3, 4, 8, 10].

© ICST Institute for Computer Sciences, Social Informatics and Telecommunications Engineering 2022
Published by Springer Nature Switzerland AG 2022. All Rights Reserved
A. L. Martins et al. (Eds.): INTSYS 2021, LNICST 426, pp. 206–227, 2022.
https://doi.org/10.1007/978-3-030-97603-3_15

Even though the advent of AVs is fast approaching, it does not mean that Conventional Vehicles (CVs) on roads are going to be changed to AVs in a moment. We will experience heterogeneous traffic flow until CVs can be completely phased out. Considering the purchase cycle of CVs and the expected high price of AVs, the transition period will last for a significant amount of time.

Therefore, governments are required to find ways to maximize the promising outcomes from the emergence of AVs during the transition period in addition to the period after. The behaviors of AVs are different from those of CVs. The characteristics of the mixed traffic flow of AVs and CVs should be considered properly. Taking those characteristics into consideration, governments will be able to plan future transportation infrastructure and weigh against different policy interventions to retrieve the full benefit of AVs.

Some infrastructure adaptations, such as AV-dedicated lanes [2, 5, 7, 10, 12, 14, 15] and AV-only links/zones [3], have been suggested as the ways to promote the adoption of AVs and improve the traffic flows. Accordingly, the impacts of AV-lanes and AV-only links/zones on traffic flow have also been studied. For example, Jordan Ivanchev et al. (2019) investigated how the road network performance of Singapore changes with the increase in the percentage of AVs in the region using AV-lane and no-AV-lane scenarios.

The expected growth of AV users points to the notion that the deployment of AV-dedicated lanes is one of the most optimal solutions to maximize the benefits of such technology. Examples of such benefits are to maximize the efficiency of AV Vehicles and to incentivize the adoption of autonomous vehicles. However, putting AV-dedicated lanes or AV-only links/zones does not always bring positive outcomes. Even when the capacity of a lane increases when the lane is transformed into an AV-dedicated lane, the overall performance of the whole road network could deteriorate [10]. Consequently, the location, total length, and the number of lanes of AV-dedicated lanes should be decided with deliberation. In other words, a network design problem should be defined to optimize the deployment of AV-dedicated lanes. This design problem must be capable of addressing the issue of decreased network performance in the initial stages of AV deployment. In short, the dedicated lanes must be deployed promptly while minimizing their impacts on the existing traffic conditions. The overall goal of the developed algorithm would be to compare the impacts of various AV-dedicated lane deployment scenarios and choose the best deployment locations and the number of lanes for each AV-dedicated lane.

2 Previous Studies

Any major shift in policy calls for many significant changes within the existing networks. Proposing dedicated highway lanes for autonomous vehicles means a significant expenditure, which includes excessive cost and time for the implementation procedure. While the execution of the idea requires much attention, it is pivotal to discuss what are some of the long-term impacts of the dedicated AV lanes. It is a clear prediction that dedicated AV lanes will improve operational capacity, however, a lot of research is underway to investigate its pros and cons.

Adaptive Cruise Control (ACC) and Cooperative Adaptive Cruise Control (CACC) are potential methods of improving traffic flow. However, their interaction with mixed traffic flow hinders their progress. Through a microscopic traffic simulation, the estimated capacity of a given lane was 2050, 2200, and 4550 vehicles per hour for manual, ACC and CACC, respectively [14]. This data can be used to interpret that CACC cars can potentially double the capacity of a highway lane at significant penetration levels. The effects of AVs on Sweden's roadway infrastructure showed that the average delay, average number of stops and average speed could be improved by 56%, 54% and 34%, respectively [4]. However, a significant drawback of this analysis was that mixed traffic flows were neglected. Mixed flow conditions must have been considered to mirror real-world conditions. The idea of platooning promises up to 8500 vehicles per hour per lane only if dedicated lanes are provided and the vehicles can communicate with each other. This phenomenon is known as Automated High Systems [4]. The sole goal of platooning is to enhance existing operational capacity. The highway capacity can be significantly reformed through large platoons of AVs [11]. This concept leads to a reduction in the inter-platooning distance when larger platoons are arranged. On the contrary, if mixed traffic flows are considered, it might pose a negative impact. The negative effect on highway speed that arises after the saturation points must also be considered. The effect of AV dedicated lanes on average travel time can be studied by simulating various AV penetration rates. AV dedicated lanes penalize CV drivers while incentivizing buying AVs. However, the highway capacity will be underutilized during low levels of AV penetration [12]. These results were drawn under macroscopic conditions that ignored microscopic conditions such as lane interactions. A macroscopic analysis of network flows and system level can be utilized to develop a methodology that indicates when and where the AV dedicated lanes must be deployed [5]. It was identified that the time consumption required to produce saturation level AV penetration on highways would be fairly significant. Until those levels can be achieved, Autonomous Vehicle Toll Lanes would prove to be the optimal place holders [10].

Several studies have explored strategies to recognize AV-only Link/Zones on urban road networks. The mixed Routing Equilibrium Model can be used to find the mixed routing behaviors under the scenario of heterogeneous traffic flow and a mixed-integer bi-level programming model to optimize the deployment of AV Zones, in which only AVs can operate and are guided by a central controller. It is believed that the process of optimized locating of AV Zones has a great similarity with the Cordon design problem for Cordon Congestion Pricing, thus such questions could be solved by Simulated Annealing Algorithm (SAA) [3]. To incorporate real-world conditions an optimized time-dependent deployment planning approach of AV lanes on a transportation network with heterogeneous traffic flow, consisting of AVs and CVs must be adopted. This mathematical approach could minimize the social cost to promote the ubiquitous adoption of AVs. A multi-class network equilibrium model can be used to capture the flow distribution of AVs and CVs and a diffusion model must be developed to forecast the evolution of AV market penetration [2]. A unique fundamental diagram approach that reveals the pros and cons of dedicated AV lanes under various Connected Autonomous Vehicle (CAV) penetration rates and demand levels on a three-lane heterogeneous mixed-flow network is capable of deciding the optimal numbers of lanes dedicated to AVs by simulating the dynamic relationship between CAV dedicated lane performance, CAV performance,

CAV penetration rate and density [15]. With a limited number of studies focusing on AV only Zones/Links, the following questions need further discussion:

A) There is a major drawback of AV-only links/zones that the CVs need to take longer detours to finish the trip, which is the main trade-off decision-makers have to make.
B) For AV zones (AVZ), the only one-AVZ scenario is considered and simulated, the effects and efficiency of multiple AVZs on transportation networks with different AV penetration levels are not detailed formulated.
C) The existing major methodologies did not consider enough reality constraints when locating the AV zone/links on the network such as the planning regulation, neighborhood conditions, street vitality levels, etc., and are often simulated on an imaginary network, which is rather simple compared to the real-world transportation network.
D) Only urban expressways and arterial roads are included in the modeling of the AVZ locating process, minor streets are often excluded.

Even though spatial deployment of AV-dedicated lanes or AV-only links/zones matters as much as their deployment strategy, a few studies have investigated the issue. Chen et al. (2016) and Guhathakurta and Kumar (2019) used network-level design approaches to decide where, when, how the dedicated lanes should be located. For AV-only links/zones, Chen et al. (2017) suggested a framework for designing AV-only zones in a network. However, the adoption of AV Links can cause a significant disturbance to the existing transportation networks around the world causing it to be an unwarranted approach, especially until extremely high levels of AV penetration can be achieved.

While some of the literature discussed previously proves its close relevance to the topic of this paper, however, it offers some key limitations. Such as, Chen et al. (2016) fail to consider the variant capacity of link a (ca) that would suffer a disturbance due to the share of AV on the respective link (ra). Furthermore, it limits the deployment of AV dedicated lanes to only a given set of candidate links. Liu and Song (2019) considered the capacity of a link a (ca) as a function of the share of AVs on a link a (ra) using a conversion approach to determine the human-driven vehicle equivalent of the share of AVs on the respective link. The suggested methodology in that paper suggests an optimal deployment model of a generalized semi-infinite min-max program with a solution algorithm using a genetic algorithm approach. This method is computationally costly and negatively affects the efficiency of an algorithm.

This study aims to address this gap in the literature. It will focus on developing a network-level optimization framework dealing with network design problems of the deployment of AV-dedicated lanes on a freeway network system. The developed algorithm will utilize the following inputs and outputs:
Inputs:

1) the road network of a city or metropolitan region
2) O-D demand matrix
3) AV penetration rate
4) limit of total AV-dedicated lane length

Outputs:

1) where to locate the AV-dedicated lanes
2) how many lanes would be AV-dedicated for each link with AV-dedicated lanes

Compared with the previous research, the developed algorithm will have the following benefits:

1) Incorporate relationship between ra and ca
2) Maintain an overall low computational cost
3) The candidate's links for potential dedicated AV lane deployment will not be pre-defined.

The developed algorithm will aim to find the best AV-dedicated lane deployment strategy that minimizes the average travel time cost of road users. After developing the algorithm, the outputs on using different AV market penetration rates will be presented to show how the road network increases its proportion of AV-dedicated lanes gradually as the AV market penetration rate increases.

3 Network Equilibrium Problem and AV Lanes Deployment Problem

3.1 Methodology

This paper offers a bi-level methodological framework to get the most beneficial strategy for the deployment of AV-dedicated lanes in terms of network performance. The first level is understanding the traffic flow characteristics of vehicles on a network when AVs and CVs co-exist, which leads to a mathematical formulation for user equilibrium (UE) traffic assignments of AVs and CVs on a given network with AV-dedicated lanes in some parts of the network. The second step is to develop an algorithm that decides the locations for deploying AV-dedicated lanes to minimize the negative impact of the installation on traffic flows. With a given AV market penetration rate and the limit of the total length of AV-dedicated lanes on the network, the developed algorithm will output where to deploy AV-dedicated lanes, how many lanes for each link will be transformed to AV-dedicated lanes.

Before getting into more detail, notations that will be used throughout the explanation of the proposed methodological framework need to be set. The defined notations are summarized as shown below in Table 1:

Table 1. Basic notations

Notation	Definition
N	Set of node index
A	Set of link index of mixed-flow links = $\{1, 2, 3, ..., n\}$
$\widehat{A}$	Set of link index of AV-dedicated links = $\{n + 1, n + 2, ..., 2n\}$
R	Set of origin nodes; $R \subseteq N$
S	Set of destination nodes; $S \subseteq N$
Krs	Set of paths connecting O-D pair r-s; $r \in R, s \in S$
M	Set of vehicle types = $\{1, 2\}$; CVs = 1 and AVs = 2
y_a	Number of lanes on link $a \in A \cup \widehat{A}$
t_a	Travel time on link $a \in A \cup \widehat{A}$
l_a	Length of link $a \in A \cup \widehat{A}$
c_a	Capacity of link $a \in A \cup \widehat{A}$
r_a	Share of AVs on link $a \in A \cup \widehat{A}$
p_{av}	Market penetration rate of AVs
x_a^m	Flow of vehicles of mode $m \in M$ on link $a \in A \cup \widehat{A}$; $x_a = \Sigma_{m \in M} x_a^m$
$f_k^{rs, m}$	Flow of vehicles of mode m on path k connecting O-D pair r-s; $f_k^{rs} = \Sigma_{m \in M} f_k^{rs, m}$
q_{rs}^m	Trip rate of vehicles of mode m between origin r and destination s $q_{rs} = \Sigma_{m \in M} q_{rs}^m$
$\delta^{rs}_{a, k}$	Indicator variable; 1 if link a is on path k between O-D pair r-s, 0 otherwise
h_{av}	Minimum headway time of AVs (in seconds)
h_{cv}	Minimum headway time of CVs (in seconds)
α_a, β_a	Positive parameters for defining link performance function of link $a \in A \cup \widehat{A}$

One noteworthy point regarding the notations in Table 1 is that the set of link indexes is divided into two: A (set of link index of mixed-flow links) and $\widehat{A}$ (set of link index of AV-dedicated links). When the network has n links, $A = \{1, 2, 3, ..., n\}$ and $\widehat{A} = \{n + 1, n + 2, ..., 2n\}$. The pair of link $a \in A$ and link $(a + n)$ represent a specific link in the real world. Even though both link a and link $(a + n)$ are called 'link', they indicate the part of mixed-flow lanes and the part of AV-dedicated lanes, respectively. Thus, if no AV-dedicated lane exists on a network, y_a (the number of lanes of link a) would be 0 for all $a \in \widehat{A}$. If there are some links with AV-dedicated lanes, y_a (that a $\in \widehat{A}$) for the corresponding links will be positive integers. In this study, deploying an

AV-dedicated lane on the link represented by link a and link (a + n) is decreasing ya by one and increasing ya + n by one.

3.2 Traffic Assignment Problem Under UE Condition

Algorithm Setup. In this study, we assume that vehicles can change lanes at nodes only as other studies about AV-dedicated lane deployment did [3, 10]. Besides, for simplicity, the AV market penetration rate is equally applied to all trip rates.

The link performance function that modified the link performance function from Liu and Song (2019) is given below:

$$t_a = t_a^0 \left(1 + \alpha_a \left(\frac{x_a}{c_a} \right)^{\beta_a} \right)$$

The t_a^0 is the free-flow travel time of link $a \in A \cup \hat{A}$. The α_a and β_a are the constant parameters for the link performance function of link a. The c_a denotes the capacity to link a which is a function of the share of AVs on link a. The c_a below is the modified version of Ivanchev et al. (2019).

$$c_a = \frac{3600}{h_{av} r_a + h_{cv}(1 - r_a)} * y_a$$

Here the h_{av} and h_{cv} are respectively the headway time of AV and CV in seconds, which are constant numbers we concluded from related studies. The r_a is the share of AVs on link a. It is acquired by divide AV flow on link a by the total flow:

$$r_a = \frac{x_a^2}{x_a^1 + x_a^2}$$

Considering that we defined the set of vehicle types $M = \{1, 2\}$, in which 1 represents CVs and 2 represents AVs and separated the set of link index into two sets, A and $\hat{A}$, the UE traffic assignment problem can be defined as shown below:

$$z(x) = \sum_{a \in A \cup \hat{A}} \int_0^{x_a} t(w) dw$$

Subject to:

$$\sum_{k \in K_{rs}} f_k^{rs,m} = q_{rs}^m \qquad \forall r, s, m \tag{1}$$

$$q_{rs}^1 = (1 - p_{av}) * q_{rs} \qquad \forall r, s \tag{2}$$

$$q_{rs}^2 = p_{av} * q_{rs} \qquad \forall r, s \tag{3}$$

$$f_k^{rs} = f_k^{rs,1} + f_k^{rs,2} \qquad \forall r, s, k \tag{4}$$

$$f_k^{rs,m} \geq 0 \qquad \forall r, s, k, m \tag{5}$$

$$x_a^m = \sum_{r \in R} \sum_{s \in S} \sum_{k \in K_{rs}} f_k^{rs,m} \delta_{a,k}^{rs} \qquad \forall a \in A \cup \hat{A} \tag{6}$$

$$x_a^1 \geq 0 \qquad \forall a \in A \tag{7}$$

$$x_a^1 = 0 \qquad \forall a \in \hat{A} \tag{8}$$

$$x_a^2 \geq 0 \qquad \forall a \in A \cup \hat{A} \tag{9}$$

In the above optimization problem, constraint (1) ensures the conservation of flow. Constraints (2) and (3) show that the share of trips of AVs from an origin and a destination is p_{av} for every O-D pair. Constraints (5) holds the path flow non-negative. Constraint (6) defines the relationship between link flow and path flow. $\delta_{a,k}^{rs}$ in the constraint is an element of the node-link incidence matrix; its value equals 1 if link a is on the path k from origin r and destination s while being 0 otherwise. Constraints (7)–(9) describe the vehicles' behaviors on lanes, where AVs are allowed to use any lanes while CVs do not have access to the AV-dedicated lanes.

The UE traffic assignment problem can easily be proven as strictly convex on its feasible region and its equivalence can be established by comparing KKT conditions of UE with the defined network equilibrium conditions (1)–(9).

AV Lanes Deployment Model. After getting the traffic flow assignment result by solving the UE problem, we need to decide where to deploy AV-dedicated lanes and how many lanes to deploy for each link. Thus, we devised a concept named 'the instantaneous total travel time change' of a link (represented as link a and link $(a + n)$ in the model), which indicates the change in the total travel time of vehicles on the link when one lane from the mixed-flow part (link a) is assigned as an AV-dedicated lane. This situation is equivalent to decrease y_a by one and increase y_{a+n} by one. It will change the capacities of link a and link $(a + n)$ so that t_a and t_{a+n} change. Thus, the link flows x_a and x_{a+n} will be adjusted while keeping the sum of them the same. Based on the new traffic flow assignment on link a and link $(a + n)$, the new total travel time of vehicles on both links can be calculated. The instantaneous total travel time change means the new total travel time of vehicles on link a and link $(a + n)$ subtracted by the original value of total travel time before assigning a lane from link a to an AV-dedicated lane.

The process of calculating the instantaneous total travel time change value of one link subject to the AV-dedicated lane installation can be explained in more detail using the graphics and equations below:

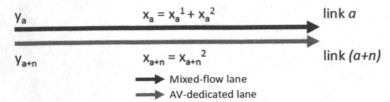

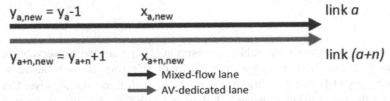

Fig. 1. The original condition of link a and link $(a + n)$ and flows on the links (representing one link in the real world)

Fig. 2. The new condition of link a and link $(a + n)$ and flows on the links (representing one link in the real world)

The functions to calculate the instantaneous link travel time of a link (link a and link $(a + n)$ combined) are:

The original travel time of link a:

$$t_a(x_a) = t_a^0 \left(1 + \alpha_a \left(\frac{x_a}{\frac{3600}{h_{av}r_a + h_{cv}(1-r_a)} * (y_a)} \right)^{\beta_a} \right)$$

The original travel time of link $(a + n)$:

$$t_{a+n}(x_{a+n}) = t_{a+n}^0 \left(1 + \alpha_{a+n} \left(\frac{x_a}{\frac{3600}{h_{av}} * (y_{a+n})} \right)^{\beta_{a+n}} \right)$$

The new travel time of link a:

$$t_{a,new}(x_{a,new}) = t_a^0 \left(1 + \alpha_a \left(\frac{x_{a,new}}{\frac{3600}{h_{av}r_{a,new} + h_{cv}(1-r_{a,new})} * (y_{a,new})} \right)^{\beta_a} \right)$$

The new travel time of link $(a + n)$:

$$t_{a+n,new}(x_{a+n,new}) = t_{a+n}^0 \left(1 + \alpha_{a+n} \left(\frac{x_{a+n,new}}{\frac{3600}{h_{av}} * (y_{a+n,new})} \right)^{\beta_{a+n}} \right)$$

Thus, the original total travel time $= t_a(x_a) * x_a + t_{a+n}(x_{a+n}) * x_{a+n}$
The new total travel time $= t_{a,new}(x_{a,new}) * x_{a,new} + t_{a+n,new}(x_{a+n,new}) * x_{a+n,new}$

$$y_{a,new} = y_a - 1 \text{ and } y_{a+n,new} = y_{a+n} + 1.$$

After $y_{a,new}$ and $y_{a+n,new}$ are decided, $x_{a,new}$ and $x_{a+n,new}$ needs to be decided. We assume that the vehicles will adjust their lane choices such that the UE condition is satisfied. Because of the increased capacity and reduced travel time of link $(a + n)$, the AVs on link a will move to link $(a + n)$. Thus, if the travel time on link a is still larger than that of link $(a + n)$ even after all the AVs on link a move to link $(a+n)$, all the AVs on link a will move to link $(a + n)$ since CVs cannot use link $(a + n)$ even though the travel time is shorter on link $(a + n)$. However, if the travel time on link a is still smaller than that of link $(a + n)$ after all the AVs on link a move to link $(a + n)$, some of AVs are not going to move to link a such that the travel time of link a become identical to that of link $(a + n)$. The way $x_{a,new}$ and $x_{a+n,new}$ are decided is described in the below equation with an '*if*' condition:

$$\text{If } t_{a,new}\left(x_a - x_a^2\right) > t_{a+n,new}\left(x_{a+n} + x_a^2\right),$$

$$x_{a,new} = x_a - x_a^2, x_{a+n,new} = x_{a+n} + x_a^2.$$

Otherwise,

$$x_{a,new} = x_a - \left(x_a^2 - b\right), x_{a+n,new} = x_{a+n} + \left(x_a^2 - b\right),$$

such that $t_{a,new}\left(x_a - \left(x_a^2 - b\right)\right) = t_{a+n,new}\left(x_{a+n} + \left(x_a^2 - b\right)\right)$.
Accordingly,

$$\text{If } t_{a,new}\left(x_a - x_a^2\right) > t_{a+n,new}\left(x_{a+n} + x_a^2\right),$$

$$x_{a,new}^1 = x_a^1, x_{a,new}^2 = 0, x_{a+n,new}^1 = 0, x_{a+n,new}^2 = x_{a+n} + x_a^2,$$

Otherwise,

$$x_{a,new}^1 = x_a^1, x_{a,new}^2 = b, x_{a+n,new}^1 = 0, x_{a+n,new}^2 = x_{a+n} + (x_a^2 - b).$$

With the results, $r_{a,new}$ and $r_{a+n,new}$ can be calculated easily using the new flows of AVs and CVs.

By comparing the instantaneous total travel time change of all the mixed-flow links with more than 1 lane (all the link a that $a \in A$ and $y_a > 1$), the algorithm chooses the one with the minimum change and let one lane from the link be an AV-dedicated lane. The reason for restricting the mixed-flow links of which the instantaneous total travel time changes are examined to the links with more than one lane is that it is necessary to provide at least one lane for CVs to ensure mobility and accessibility of CVs until they vanish entirely.

This process of choosing the link for AV-dedicated lane installation repeats until the total length of AV-dedicated lanes reaches the limit we set before running the algorithm or there is no mixed-flow link with more than one lane. It is possible to easily imagine that the government has an idea about the different levels of AV market penetration rate and the associated limit on the total length of AV-dedicated lanes as shown in Table 2. Before the start of the algorithm, we need to set the p_{av} that also decides the limit.

Table 2. AV market penetration rate (p_{av}) and corresponding AV lanes length cap (L)

Market AV penetration rate (%)	Limit on the total length of AV-dedicated lanes (% of the total length of all the lanes)
$p_{av} < 10\%$	$Q_1\%$
$10\% \leq p_{av} < 20\%$	$Q_2\%$
$20\% \leq p_{av} < 30\%$	$Q_3\%$
$30\% \leq p_{av} < 40\%$	$Q_4\%$
$40\% \leq p_{av} < 50\%$	$Q_5\%$

When we have a predefined limit on the total length of AV-dedicated lanes, we can let the algorithm test two conditions below, after 1) choosing the link of AV-dedicated lane installation, 2) assigning one lane from the link to the AV-dedicated lane, and 3) assigning the entire traffic of all the O-D pairs under UE condition with the updated network. If either one of the conditions (10) and (11) is fulfilled, the algorithm stops to add an AV-dedicated lane. If not, the algorithm compares the instantaneous travel time changes for all the mixed-flow links with more than one lane to find the link to deploy an AV-dedicated lane.

$$y_a = 1 \ \forall a \in A \tag{10}$$

$$l_b + \Sigma_{a \in \hat{A}} l_a y_a > L \ \forall b \in A \tag{11}$$

The flow chart of the algorithm is shown in Fig. 3.

With Table 2, it is possible to simulate how the deployment of AV-dedicated lanes grows as p_{av} increases. For example, we can run the algorithm with a network without any AV-dedicated lanes, after setting $p_{av} = 5\%$, and $L = Q_1\%$. After that, using the output network with AV-dedicated lanes from the algorithm run, we can set $p_{av} = 10\%$ and $L = Q_2\%$ to run the algorithm again. The algorithm run will add more AV-dedicated lanes to the network. Continuing this process again and again by increasing p_{av} value step-by-step will give results that show the growth of AV-dedicated lanes on the network. This will give a vivid idea of how the government can deploy AV-dedicated lanes at the right locations promptly.

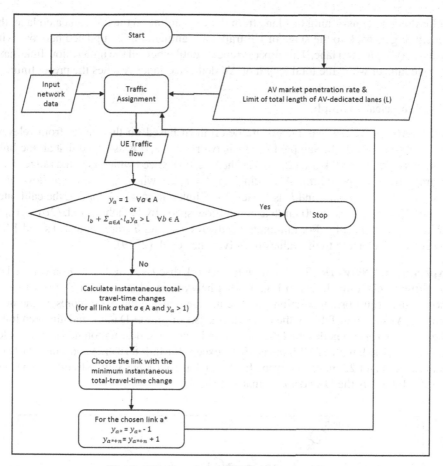

Fig. 3. The flowchart of the bi-level algorithm

4 Solution Framework and Numerical Example

4.1 Solution Framework

The Frank-Wolfe algorithm is used with the Method of Successive Averages (MSA) for user equilibrium (UE) traffic assignments. When the algorithm for AV-dedicated lane deployment starts, the first step is to assign all the O-D demand for AVs and CVs on the network. In the iterative process of the Frank-Wolfe algorithm for UE traffic assignment, the MSA enables finding the solution with relative ease by removing the need for calculating the move size for each iteration.

With the resulting UE solution, the algorithm moves on to the next step for calculating the instantaneous travel time for each mixed-flow link and then chooses the one with the smallest instantaneous travel time change that occurs one lane of the mixed-flow link becomes an AV-dedicated lane. A positive instantaneous travel time change of a link indicates that the installment of an AV-dedicated lane has a negative impact on traffic flow, while a negative instantaneous travel time change implies a positive impact on traffic flow. After assigning one lane from the chosen link to the AV-dedicated lane, the algorithm gets back to the stage of UE traffic assignment on the updated network with the new AV-dedicated lane. This process repeats until when all the mixed-flow links have just one lane or when the total length of AV-dedicated lanes reaches the preset limit.

4.2 Numerical Example

Basic Settings. A few parameters are determined based on the values from relevant previous studies. For the sample freeway network in use, it is assumed that all the links in the network have 90 km/h (25 m/s) as the free-flow speed which is in the range of the common freeway speed limit. Accordingly, $t_a^0 = l_a/25$, where t_a^0 is the free-flow travel time of link a in seconds and l_a is the length of link a in meter. Adopting the calibrated α_a and β_a for roads with 90 km/h as a free-flow speed by Ivanchev et al. (2016), $\alpha_a = 1.2$ and $\beta_a = 5$ for all a. For minimum headways, h_{av} and h_{cv} are set to 1.0 s and 1.8 s, respectively, referring to the values from Ivanchev et al. (2019).

Experimental Network. The solution framework discussed in this section is based on the network diagram shown in Fig. 4. This network is adopted from Zheng Li's post about a user-equilibrium solution [9]. The numbers inside the node represent the node number. As shown in Table 3, the network consists of four O-D pairs and nineteen links. There are two origin nodes are labeled as 1 and 2 and two destination nodes are labeled as 3 and 4. The length of all links is 10 m, except for link 8 (8–12) and link 10 (9–16) that are 14 m and 22 m, respectively. Each link has four lanes with a free-flow speed of 25 m/s. Table 4 is the O-D demand matrix (Fig. 4).

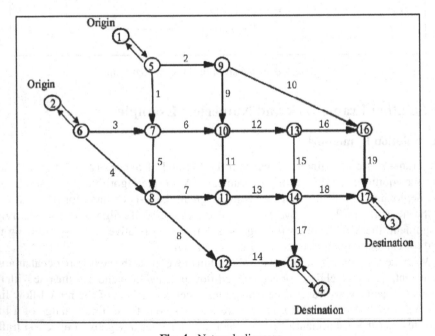

Fig. 4. Network diagram

Table 3. Link information

Link label	Origin	Destination	Length (m)	No. of lanes	Free flow speed (m/s)	t_a^0(sec)
1	5	7	10	4	25	0.40
2	5	9	10	4	25	0.40
3	6	7	10	4	25	0.40
4	6	8	14	4	25	0.56
5	7	8	10	4	25	0.40
6	7	10	10	4	25	0.40
7	8	11	10	4	25	0.40
8	8	12	14	4	25	0.56
9	9	10	10	4	25	0.40
10	9	16	22	4	25	0.90
11	10	11	10	4	25	0.40
12	10	13	10	4	25	0.40
13	11	14	10	4	25	0.40
14	12	15	10	4	25	0.40
15	13	14	10	4	25	0.40
16	13	16	10	4	25	0.40
17	14	15	10	4	25	0.40
18	14	17	10	4	25	0.40
19	16	17	10	4	25	0.40

Table 4. O-D demand matrix

		Destinations	
		15	17
Origins	5	6000	6750
	6	7500	5250

The whole process of AV-dedicated lane deployment is separated into 10 stages, each one has its corresponding experimental market AV penetration rate and limit of the total length of AV-dedicated lanes. As shown in Table 5, Stage 0 is a special case where the market AV penetration rate is 5% while the percent of the total length allowed to be converted to AV-dedicated lanes is 0%. Stage 0 is utilized as a comparison to Stage 1 to illustrate the effectiveness of the added AV lanes in terms of improving the total network travel time. Theoretically, the limit of AV-dedicated lanes when $p_{av} = 85\%$ is 90%.

However, the action of converting a mixed-flow lane of a link to an AV-dedicated lane stops once all mixed-flow links have only one lane, which aims to ensure a minimum level of connectivity of the network to CV users.

Table 5. Market penetration rate and the limit on the length of AV-dedicated lanes for each deployment stage

Deployment stage	Market AV penetration rate (%)	Limit on the total length of AV-dedicated lanes (% of the total length of all the lanes)
0	$p_{av} = 5\%$	0%
1	$p_{av} = 5\%$	10%
2	$p_{av} = 15\%$	20%
3	$p_{av} = 25\%$	30%
4	$p_{av} = 35\%$	40%
5	$p_{av} = 45\%$	50%
6	$p_{av} = 55\%$	60%
7	$p_{av} = 65\%$	70%
8	$p_{av} = 75\%$	80%
9	$p_{av} = 85\%$	90%

Results Analysis. This numerical experiment is based on the network condition illustrated above and this study uses a forced-increasing limit of the total length of AV-dedicated lanes based on the assumption that the market penetration rate of AV will keep growing. Thus, the results show how a freeway network should react to the developing AV market and what can be done to help to promote the increase of the share of AVs on the whole market.

Figure 5 shows that the total network travel time decreases fast between deployment stage 1–4 which indicates that converting the specified length of mixed-flow lanes to AV-dedicated lanes can effectively improve the performance of the overall network, shown here as the dramatically decreased network total travel time. As aforementioned, stage 0 is used as a comparison to stage 1, indicating that when p_{av} is low, for example, 5%, the impact of newly converted AV-dedicated lanes won't have much influence on the network, causing a 0.002% decrease.

However, when the market AV penetration rate is greater than 45%, the network can no longer benefit as much as when p_{av} is relatively smaller from the forced-increasing AV-dedicated lanes. When at stage 7, 7 links have only 1 mixed-flow lane, meaning that they are not available for adding new AV-dedicated lanes. This shows that when $p_{av} > 65\%$, the network can no longer continue to benefit from the newly converted AV-dedicated lanes. Stage 9 is special because there were only 6 lanes left in stage 8 that can be converted to AV-dedicated lanes, thus stage 9 does not have any new AV-dedicated lane.

The travel times decrease after stage 7. This is the result of decreased human-driven vehicle demands. This decrease slows down when no new AV-dedicated lane can be added to the network (stage 8) while the AV-market penetration rate is still increasing resulting in more AV demands between O-D pairs.

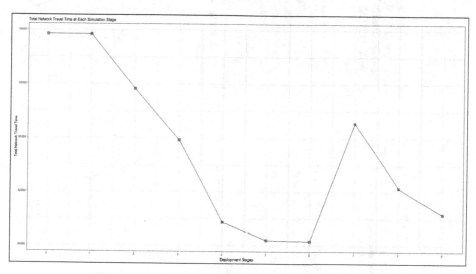

Fig. 5. Total network travel time at each deployment stage

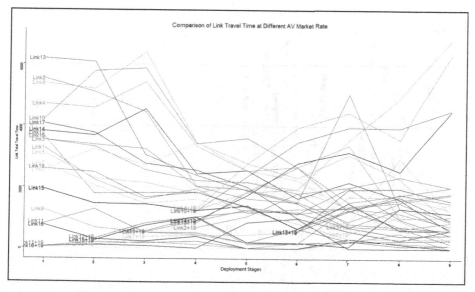

Fig. 6. Link travel time changes at the different deployment stage

As shown in Fig. 6, the link travel time of link 8, link 19, and link 4 + 19 increase significantly at stage 7, which certifies the previously discussed phenomenon of the sudden

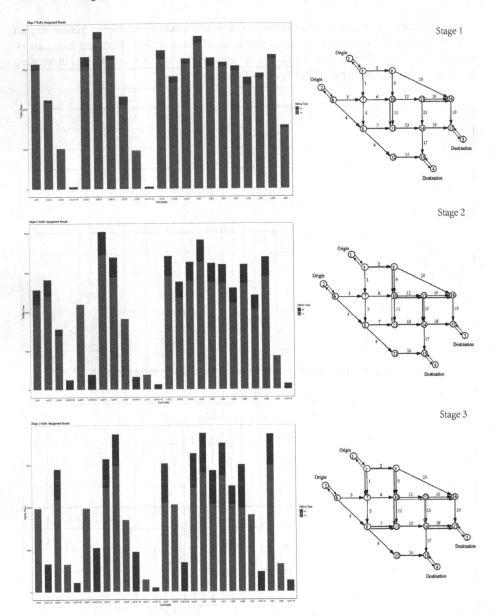

Fig. 7. AV-lanes deployment and traffic assignment results of Stage 1–9

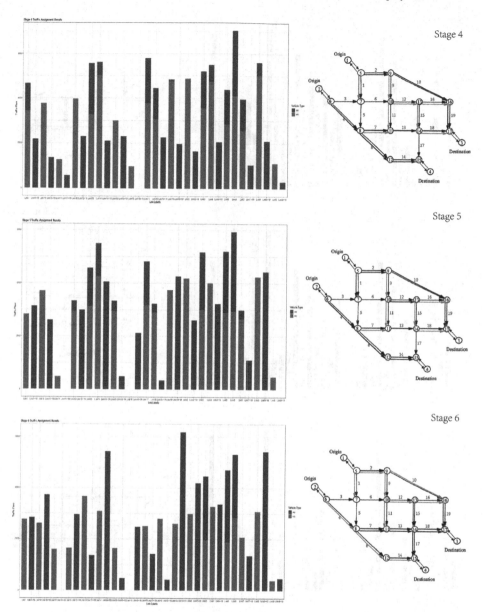

Fig. 7. continued

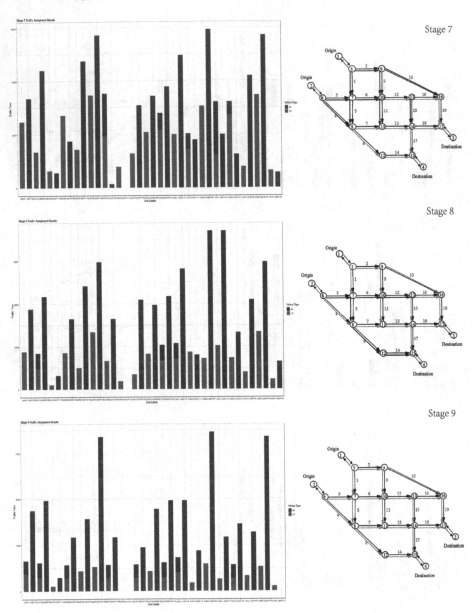

Fig. 7. continued

increase of total network travel time at stage 7, that limited available AV-dedicated lanes candidates and obligated AV-dedicated lane total length weaken the benefits produced by adding the AV dedicated lanes to the network. The travel time of Link 8 + 19 and link 14 + 19 initially decreases in stage 8 but later increases at stage 9. This occurs because the links with newly added AV-lanes at stage 8 are assigned with more AV flows, however, no new AV lane is added at stage 9 but the demand for AV keeps increasing by 10%, link 8 + 19 and link 14 + 19 carries a large portion of the 10% growth of AV demands at stage 9 resulting in its sudden increase of link travel times.

Figure 7 displays the AV-dedicated lanes deployment and UE traffic assignment results at every stage. There exists a concept that the AV-lanes are first allocated to the links in the middle of the network that is being shared by many paths and several O-D pairs, then to the links at two ends (near O-D pairs) and the links on the edges. This shows an underlying sequence of the deployment of the AV-lanes that the links that are being used by more paths are more likely to be first chosen as the candidate of new AV-lanes. Contrary, the links on the edge of the network are assigned with more traffic flows, both CVs and AVs.

Link 16 and its paired link Link16 + 19 are not being utilized as much as other links after stage 7 given the fact that link 16 is one of the links being assigned with AV-lanes within the first 3 stages. While the added AV-lanes have positive effects on the network during stage 1–4. This might be a result of the surrogate measure, instantaneous travel time changes. At stage 1–3 all the instantaneous travel time change measures are positive. The chosen links as candidates for new AV-lanes are those with comparatively smaller traffic flows. that the ones chosen to be added AV-lanes on at first might be the ones are affected negatively the least among all links. This might cause other problems when the model is used on more complex networks. However, this could also be a sign of potential urban design changes. The experimental network is under a high-speed highway scenario where the link free flow speed is homogenous. The links that are being chosen first as the AV-lanes candidates while being utilized the least when AV market penetration rate is high suggest possibilities to convert some of the regions of these links locate in to new zones with different facilities and functions rather than highway surrounded places and possibilities of a less vehicle-oriented, more walkable area. These areas could be utilized as the flag bearers of urban design changes.

5 Conclusion

This paper proposes a computationally effective mathematical procedure to deploy AV-dedicated lanes considering different AV market penetration rates. The idea of the corresponding limit of the total length of AV-dedicated lanes ensures the infrastructure construction moves ahead of the market performance of AVs, by improving the objective driving conditions to promote people's willingness and enthusiasm about AVs. The deployment results at different stages show where, when, and how many mix-flow lanes should be converted to AV-dedicated lanes at its corresponding AV market penetration rate. MSA is used to solve the UE traffic assignment problem with two variables, the CV flow and AV flow. A new measure to find optimal AV-lanes deployment location is formulated by calculating and comparing the instantaneous total paired-links travel time changes, iteratively. The analysis of the deployment results shows that the network can benefit from the new AV-lanes when the AV market penetration rate is lower than 55% and the total network travel time might increase once the AV market penetration rate is higher than 65%. Which indicates that 1) the construction of AV lanes at the early stage of the AV market development can benefit not only the market itself but the overall performance of the network; 2) policy makers should be more cautious about the deployment location of AV-lanes when AV market penetration is relatively high; 3) the "ahead construction" of AV-lanes and its related infrastructures might bring new opportunities for city planning and urban design.

The model proposed in this study presents some limitations that require further investigation. Firstly, the network uses homogenous free flow speed and lacks variation in link length, and no intersection behavior is included in the model. The network has a limited number of O-D pairs. It can only represent a highway scenario and its realness is not sufficient. Further investigations must be performed to understand intersection behavior and complex link interactions. To evaluate such characteristics of the algorithm, a dynamic network must be adopted, such as a core urban network that offers additional O-D pairs and link interactions. Secondly, the instantaneous total travel time change measure is a surrogate measure on which the tradeoff of computational effectiveness and realness is achieved. Higher accuracy can be obtained if more link interactions are captured. Thirdly, MSA is used to solve the UE traffic assignment problem which can only provide an approximate-optimal solution. Although the results are acceptable, the differences between the approximate-optimal solution and the real solution might result in problems in more complex assignment works.

References

1. Bohm, F., Häger, K.: Introduction of autonomous vehicles in the Swedish traffic system: effects and changes due to the new self-driving car technology. Digitala Vetenskapliga Arkivet (2015)
2. Chen, Z., He, F., Zhang, L., Yin, Y.: Optimal deployment of autonomous vehicle lanes with endogenous market penetration. Transp. Res. Part C Emerg. Technol. 72, 143–156 (2016)
3. Zhibin, C., He, F., Yafeng, Y., Yuchuan, D.: Optimal design of autonomous vehicle zones in transportation networks. Transp. Res. Part B Methodol. 99, 44–61 (2017)
4. Fagnant, D.J., Kara, K.: Preparing a nation for autonomous vehicles: opportunities, barriers and policy recommendations. Transp. Res. Part A Policy Pract. 77, 167–181 (2015)
5. Guhathakurta, S., Kumar, A.: When and Where are Dedicated Lanes Needed under Mixed Traffic of Automated and Non-Automated Vehicles for Optimal System Level Benefits? No. CTEDD: 017-04 (2019)
6. Ivanchev, J., Litescu, S., Zehe, D., Lees, M., Aydt, H., Knoll, A.: Determining the most harmful roads in search for system optimal routing (2016)
7. Ivanchev, J., Knoll, A., Zehe, D., Nair, S., Eckhoff, D.: A macroscopic study on dedicated highway lanes for autonomous vehicles. In: Rodrigues, J.M.F., et al. (eds.) ICCS 2019. LNCS, vol. 11536, pp. 520–533. Springer, Cham (2019). https://doi.org/10.1007/978-3-030-22734-0_38
8. Levin, M.W., Boyles, S.D.: A multiclass cell transmission model for shared human and autonomous vehicle roads. Transp. Res. Part C Emerg. Technol. 62, 103–116 (2016)

9. Li, Z.: ZhengLi95/User-Equilibrium-Solution. GitHub (2019). https://github.com/ZhengL i95/User-Equilibrium-Solution

10. Liu, Z., Song, Z.: Strategic planning of dedicated autonomous vehicle lanes and autonomous vehicle/toll lanes in transportation networks. Transp. Res. Part C Emerg. Technol. **106**, 381–403 (2019)

11. Michael, J.B., Godbole, D.N., Lygeros, J., Sengupta, R.: Capacity analysis of traffic flow over a single-lane automated highway system. J. Intell. Transp. Syst. **4**(1–2), 49–80 (1998)

12. Cohen, S.: Impact of a dedicated lane on the capacity and the level of service of an urban motorway. Procedia Soc. Behav. Sci. **16**, 196–206 (2011)

13. Sheffi, Y.: Urban Transportation Networks, vol. 6. Prentice-Hall, Englewood Cliffs (1985)

14. Van Arem, B., Van Driel, C.J., Visser, R.: The impact of cooperative adaptive cruise control on traffic-flow characteristics. IEEE Trans. Intell. Transp. Syst. **7**(4), 429–436 (2006)

15. Ye, L., Yamamoto, T.: Impact of dedicated lanes for connected and autonomous vehicle on traffic flow throughput. Physica A **512**, 588–597 (2018)

Author Index

Printed in the United States
by Baker & Taylor Publisher Services